# And I Will Dwell in Their Midst

# And I Will Dwell in Their Midst

Orthodox Jews in Suburbia

by ETAN DIAMOND

The University of North Carolina Press

Chapel Hill and London

The University of North Carolina Press

Set in Minion types by G&S Typesetters

Manufactured in the United States of America

The paper in this book meets the guidelines for permanence and durability of
the Committee on Production Guidelines for Book Longevity of the Council
on Library Resources.

Library of Congress Cataloging-in-Publication Data

Diamond, Etan.

    And I will dwell in their midst : Orthodox Jews in suburbia /
by Etan Diamond.

      p. cm.

    Includes bibliographical references and index.

    ISBN 0-8078-2576-x (cloth : alk. paper)—

    ISBN 0-8078-4889-1 (pbk. alk. paper)

    1. Orthodox Judaism—Ontario—Toronto Suburban Area. 2. Jews—
Ontario—Toronto Suburban Area—Social life and customs. 3. Toronto
Suburban Area (Ont.)—Religious life and customs. I. Title.

    BM229.T67 D53 2000

    296.8'32'0971354091733—dc21      00-029880

Chapter 2 appeared earlier, in somewhat different form, as "Sanctifying Suburban
Space: Creating a 'Jewish' Bathurst Street in Post-War Toronto," in Land and
Community: Geography in Jewish Studies, ed. Harold Brodsky (Bethesda:
University Press of Maryland, 1997), 257–86, and is reprinted here with permission
of the publisher.

04  03  02  01  00    5  4  3  2  1

FOR JUDY

*She opens her mouth with wisdom, and kindly counsel is on her tongue.*

*She looks after her household; she never eats the bread of idleness.*

*Her children rise and bless her; her husband praises her, saying,*

*"Many women do worthily, but you excel over them all."*

*—Proverbs 32:26–29*

# CONTENTS

Preface *xiii*

1 Religion and Suburbia: To Choose or Not To Choose *3*

2 Sanctifying Suburban Space *26*

3 Religious Pioneering on the Suburban Frontier *55*

4 Day Schools and the Socialization of Orthodox Jewish Youth *87*

5 Fake Bacon: Orthodox Jewish Religious Consumerism *111*

6 Continental Connections *131*

7 Square Pegs into Round Holes: Religion, Place, and

   Community in the Late Twentieth Century *146*

Glossary *161*

Notes *165*

Bibliography *189*

Index *209*

# TABLES, MAPS, & FIGURE

*Tables*

1. Jewish Population of Greater Toronto, 1901–1991  29
2. Religious Affiliation, North York, 1941–1991  34
3. Occupations of Congregation Members, Clanton Park Synagogue, 1957  62
4. Occupation of New Homeowners, Bathurst Village Subdivision, North York, 1963  76

*Maps*

1. Greater Toronto Area and North America  2
2. City of North York, Ontario  2
3. Orthodox Jewish Synagogues, Toronto, 1954  31
4. Stages of Jewish Settlement and Suburbanization, Toronto, 1900–2000  33
5. Shaarei Tefillah Synagogue Membership, 1957  58
6. Orthodox Jewish Synagogues, Toronto, 1995  59
7. Orthodox Jewish Schools, Toronto, 1995  93
8. Kosher Facilities by Metropolitan Area, 1999  143
9. Orthodox Jewish Synagogues by Metropolitan Area, 1999  144

*Figure*

1. Kosher Food Establishments in Toronto, 1961–1989  121

# ILLUSTRATIONS

Spadina Avenue, looking north from Queen Street, 1910  *30*
Aerial photograph of the Bathurst-Lawrence intersection, 1969  *36*
Looking north on Bathurst Street at the intersection of
    Drewry Avenue, May 1958  *37*
Looking north on Bathurst Street at the intersection of
    Drewry Avenue, June 1999  *38*
Groundbreaking ceremony, Shaarei Shomayim Synagogue,
    13 September 1964  *48*
Interior of the B'nai Torah Congregation  *80*
Associated Hebrew Day School classroom, 1950s  *94*
"Hanging out" on Roberta Lane in North York, September 1957  *99*
Millbrook Marketeria, 3101 Bathurst Street, 1950s  *120*

# PREFACE

Early in my graduate school experience, I was taught that to understand a book, one must first understand the author. Now, sitting on the other side of the page, so to speak, I have a duty to help the reader in that process. Let me state for the record that I consider myself a suburban Orthodox Jew and a part of the community I have written about. There is more to this story, however, and I hope here to give the reader a bit of insight into who I am and why I have written this book.

First, I should explain the suburban part of me. Except for a few years as an undergraduate at the University of Pennsylvania in Philadelphia and ten months in Manhattan, I have lived my life in suburbia. (For those who know me and might quibble, I am including my graduate school years living in Squirrel Hill, a neighborhood in Pittsburgh that is technically within the city limits but was once a suburban neighborhood.) When I was four years old, my family moved to a neighborhood at the eastern end of University City, a quiet, tree-filled suburb of St. Louis, Missouri. Although a public school was located about two hundred yards from my house, my sisters and I attended the Epstein Hebrew Academy, a private Jewish day school in Olivette, the next suburban municipality to the west. With the exception of a pharmacy, a Baskin-Robbins ice cream store, and a bookstore a couple of blocks away, there was little else within walking distance of our home. As a result, we had to drive (or, more accurately, be driven) anywhere else—to a friend's house, to the movies, to the mall. Sometimes I went downtown to Busch Stadium to see a Cardinals baseball game or to the Arch, but apart from these occasional forays into a denser urban setting, my childhood in St. Louis was entirely suburban.

Although my formal exposure to urban and suburban history came later, I remember even as a teenager being interested in cities and suburbs. More important, I remember being bothered by critiques of suburbs as bland, boring landscapes with little culture or diversity. Such comments bothered me because I had grown up in suburbia and *I* seemed to be turning out all right. My friends had grown up in suburbia and *they* seemed to be turning out all right. All around me, in my neighborhood and in my school, were seemingly good, well-adjusted people who were happily living their lives in suburbia. Were we all fooling ourselves, or was the standard story about suburban vacuousness more complex? Later, as I embarked on my academic career, I came to realize that the analyses of suburbia were in fact more varied than I had originally thought. But unbeknownst to me then, the seed of an academic inquiry into suburban society had already been planted.

That that seed would be combined with a study of Orthodox Jews was much less clear. In fact, as a child I did not even think of myself as an "Orthodox" Jew. Actually, I did not think of myself in any denominational terms, Orthodox, Conservative, or other. One might have assumed that because my father had received his rabbinical ordination from the Conservative-affiliated Jewish Theological Seminary in New York, I would have thought of myself as Conservative. But my parents never placed labels on us. I think we were spared the denominational labeling because unlike most families involved in active Jewish life, ours did not belong to any synagogue. Instead, we attended services at the Washington University Hillel House, the center of campus Jewish life, of which my father was the director. Not Orthodox, not Conservative, we were just a Jewish family that observed the Shabbat (Sabbath) and holidays and kept a kosher home.

By my early teens, however, other factors in my life pushed me toward a more self-conscious identification with Orthodoxy and the Orthodox Jewish subculture. I was being educated in an Orthodox Jewish environment, at the Epstein Hebrew Academy. All of my friends also attended Epstein, and most belonged to an Orthodox Jewish synagogue, some at Bais Abraham (House of Abraham) Congregation in my neighborhood and others at the Young Israel of St. Louis at the western end of University City. For one summer, after my seventh grade, I went to Camp Moshava, a religious Zionist camp in Wisconsin. When I graduated from Epstein, most of my friends and I continued at the Block Yeshiva High School of St. Louis, where we studied an intensive dual curriculum of Judaic and secular studies. I became further enmeshed in the Orthodox Jewish subculture in high school through basketball tournaments and *shabbatons* (weekend retreats held over the Sabbath) with other Yeshiva high schools in other cities, where we would spend time with other teenagers of generally the same backgrounds.

By the time I left St. Louis to attend the University of Pennsylvania, I had come to think of myself fully as an Orthodox Jew. At Penn, I developed a close circle of friends at that campus's Hillel House. There, I found that most of my friends had grown up in suburban middle-class Orthodox Jewish homes, had worshiped at suburban Orthodox Jewish synagogues, and had attended suburban Orthodox Jewish day schools and high schools. Like me, they had participated in youth groups in their communities, and some even attended the same summer camps and played in the same basketball tournaments I had. When, on occasional weekends or Jewish holidays, I visited their homes, I was struck by a strong sense of familiarity. Although I had never set foot in their home or synagogue, I could anticipate not only the way synagogue services would be, but what kinds of people would be in the synagogue, what melodies would be used, and even what foods would be served during the Sabbath meals. Over the years, this sense of familiarity repeated itself during the time I lived in New York, Pittsburgh, Toronto, and Indianapolis and during the weekends and holidays spent in suburban Orthodox Jewish neighborhoods in Baltimore, Atlanta, Great Neck, Montreal, Los Angeles, Cincinnati, Phoenix, Boston, Teaneck, Washington, D.C., North Miami Beach, Seattle, and West Orange, among other places.

As I developed my academic interest in suburban history and the history of religion, I began to think about my own experiences in more formal terms. Why did all these Orthodox Jewish communities seem so similar? Why could complete strangers meet and within a few minutes invariably find common links among them? (This "game" of "Jewish geography" follows a simple pattern. One person asks, "You're from [insert city name here]? Do you know [insert person's name here]?" The other one usually responds something like, "Sure, he sits behind my uncle in synagogue," or "I met her once at a youth group convention," or "She is really good friends with my sister's college roommate." Non-Jews often find it astounding that such links are made so easily, but given both the relative smallness of the Jewish community—and the even smaller size of the Orthodox Jewish community—and the extensive overlapping social networks within these communities, it should not surprise too much.) The more I thought about it, the more I realized that shared religion and religious networks were only one piece of the puzzle. Socioeconomic factors, and suburban factors specifically, were also essential to creating these bonds, I was convinced.

Wanting to root my inquiry in some academic form, I tried to track down what had been written about religion and suburbanization in general and about Orthodox Jews and suburbia specifically. I found almost nothing on these subjects, and what I did find seemed rooted in a 1950s conception of Orthodox Jewish communities as anachronistic and destined to disappear in modern society. Suburban Orthodox Jewish communities were nowhere to be found in the academic writings. In the religious studies literature, the Jewish studies literature, and the suburban studies literature, almost no one recognized the possibility of an upwardly mobile, consumerist-oriented group that would remain religiously traditional and even religiously strict. No one placed issues of secular mobility and the continental homogenization of consumer culture adjacent to the mobility and continental homogenization of Orthodox Jewish culture. No one, in short, had examined the historical development of this small but thriving religious community—*my* small but thriving religious community—in the late twentieth century. I set out to research and write this book, then, to fill an important gap in the academic literature. But I also saw this project in personal terms, as a way to understand the connections between the suburban society in which I grew up and the Orthodox Jewish subculture of which I had become a part.

Before embarking on that journey, however, a few words of acknowledgment are in order, particularly because one of the most important values in Jewish tradition is the concept of *hakarath hatov* (acknowledgment of good, appreciation). Although ideally, I would personally thank everyone who assisted my task of researching and writing this book, I can use this space only to list their names and to state publicly my appreciation for their help.

The initial supervision and guidance for this project came from Professors Joel Tarr, David Miller, and John Modell at Carnegie Mellon University. Although none of the three worked directly in my field, they all provided excellent direction by consistently challenging me to broaden my perspectives and to deepen my conclusions. Fortunately, their advice and friendship did not end with my graduation, and I have appreciated their mentoring during my first few years in the historical profession.

My research took me to several archives and libraries, and my work was made easier with the help of many individuals. Stephen Speisman, director of the Ontario Jewish Archives, merits special mention. In the early stages of this work, he was a valuable resource for locating primary source material on Toronto's Orthodox Jewish community. In the later stages, he helped locate some of the photographs included in this book. Speisman's work on the Toronto Jewish community of the early twentieth century was especially helpful for providing a historical context to my story.

Other archivists and librarians who graciously assisted my work over the years included Gail Ferguson, North York Public Library; Sue Collins, Hunt Library, Carnegie Mellon University; Hava Aharoni, Scott Library, York University; Peggy MacKenzie, Metro Toronto Archives; Sarah Funston-Mills, Department of Corporate Access and Privacy, Municipality of Metropolitan Toronto; Lalitha Flach, City of North York City Clerk's Department; David Douglas, City of North York Planning Department; and the staffs of the Archives of Ontario, the Multicultural Historical Society of Toronto, the Presbyterian Church of Canada Archives (Toronto), the United Church of Canada/Victoria University Archives (Toronto), University of Toronto John Robarts Library, Metropolitan Toronto Reference Library, Albert J. Latner Jewish Public Library (Toronto), Yeshiva University Library and Archives (New York), St. Louis Jewish Community Archives, University City (Missouri) Public Library, and Indiana Historical Society (Indianapolis).

My research included oral interviews. I appreciate having had the opportunity to speak with the following individuals: Rabbi Jeffrey Bienenfeld; Sol Edell; Cynthia Gasner; Joe Godfrey; Shaya Izenberg; Rabbi Shlomo Jakobovits; Mark, Ruth, and David Lane; Max Neuberger; Bill and Judith Rubinstein; Lillian Silverberg; Aaron Weisblatt; Marvin Wenner; and Bernie and Hedda Zaionz.

Other individuals who took the time to meet with me and offer their ideas and feedback, whether in person, by mail, or over the Internet, included Trent Alexander, Jonathan Ament, Randall Balmer, Harold Brodsky, Seth Farber, Paul Forman, Jeffrey Gurock, Samuel Heilman, Paula Kane, Rabbi Joseph Kelman, Peter Knights, Zane Miller, Michael Neiberg, Anne Orum, Rabbi Marvin B. Pachino, Anthony Richmond, Fern Sanders, Roger Selya, Arthur Tannenbaum, and William Westfall. I particularly thank Michael Ebner and Jonathan Sarna for reading the entire manuscript and for providing insightful critiques of the argument and the content. I appreciate their diligence and persistence in pushing me to develop my ideas.

While I was living in Toronto, I received "Graduate Fellow" status from the York University Center for Jewish Studies, enabling me to use the library and computing facilities. I appreciated the efforts of Professors Sydney Eisen and Michael Brown in obtaining this status for me. Other members of the center who assisted my project were Martin Lockshin, Stuart Schoenfeld, Leo Davids, Sol Tanenzapf, and Aaron Nussbaum.

The funding by philanthropic institutions for scholars to pursue their academic interests is a wonderful by-product of a modern affluent society. The gifts of the following institutions were greatly appreciated: Pew Program in Religion and American History, Yale University, Dissertation Fellowship (July 1995–June 1996); Canadian Embassy, Washington, D.C., Canadian Studies Graduate Student Fellowship (September 1994–August 1995); Center for Jewish Studies, Temple University, Graduate Summer Fellowship, (May 1994–September 1994); and Carnegie Mellon University, Graduate Student Fellowship (September 1992–December 1994).

The photographs in this book were obtained from a variety of sources in the Toronto area. Again, Stephen Speisman of the Ontario Jewish Archives proved invaluable in helping me to track down pictures of various synagogues. I also appreciate the efforts of Carole Kravetsky of the Shaarei Shomayim Synagogue in allowing me to use pictures of the synagogue's groundbreaking. Ted Chirnside spent many hours photographing North York during its initial development in the postwar years, and I am grateful that he allowed me to use one of those historical prints. Special thanks go to the staff of the Canadiana Room of the Toronto Public Library's North York branch for allowing me use of its photographic stand and to my uncle-in-law Leo Snowbell for taking contemporary shots of Bathurst Street and for photographing several historical photos at the Canadiana Room. Finally, I especially appreciate Aaron Weisblatt's generosity in letting me peruse his albums to select several pictures for inclusion in this book.

Several of the maps in this book were generated using street data purchased from Digimap Data Sources in Toronto, with funds generously provided by the Center for Business, Technology, and the Environment at Carnegie Mellon University. I appreciate the efforts of Steven Schlossman and Joel Tarr in securing these funds for me. On the technical side, Kevin Mickey of the Polis Center offered several helpful mapmaking tips.

Kevin is just one of many colleagues with whom I have worked over the past few years at the Polis Center, an innovative urban research center located on the campus of Indiana University–Purdue University at Indianapolis. Although my work with the Project on Religion and Urban Culture has taken me far afield from the present work, I have been enriched by the friendship and support I have received from David Bodenhamer, Arthur E. Farnsley II, Elfriede Wedam, David Vanderstel, Jan Shipps, Mary Mapes, and Robert Barrows. Thank you also to Kathleen Cahalan of the Lilly Endowment for providing me with a copy of the National Council of Synagogue Youth study.

As mentioned earlier, I have lived in several Orthodox Jewish communities. Although I never considered myself a formal participant-observer, I benefited from the interactions with a wide range of people and many close friends. Among the people who, intentionally or not, provided the kernels of ideas for this book are Mickey and Rose Ann Ariel; Rabbi Moshe and Rivy Kletenik; Harold and Ronit Weisenfeld; Steve and Roni Kurtz; David Zimbalist; Andrew Borodach; David and Amy Lasko; Jon Sadinoff; Malka Davis; Steven Schneider, Elisha Sacks and Jennifer Berday; Rabbi Zev and Judy Silber; and Rabbi Shlomo and Yaffa Crandall.

Unless one is independently wealthy, an author usually needs a publisher that is willing to publish his or her manuscript. I have been fortunate to work with the University of North Carolina Press and a wonderful editor, Elaine Maisner. From my initial e-mail contact to the final stages of copy editing, Elaine navigated the publishing waters for this first-time author. All authors should be as lucky as I have been in having as wonderful and supportive an editor as I have had in this long process. I must also state my appreciation to Managing Editor Ron Maner for patiently answering my many editorial questions and to Trudie Calvert for strengthening the manuscript with a critical editorial eye.

My family has been a wonderful source of support and a welcome diversion from this project. My deepest appreciation goes to Shifra Diamond; Gila, Alan, Jordan, and Rebecca Shusterman; Miriam, Robert, Benjamin, Rebecca, and Daniel Buckler; Michael, Tova, Ariella, and Natan Snowbell; and Jonathan Snowbell. Special thanks also go to my uncle and aunt, Gary and Ella Diamond, who hosted me during my early trips to Toronto and who first opened my eyes to Toronto's Orthodox Jewish community.

My parents-in-law, Harvey and Elaine Snowbell, opened their home and their lives to me and I thank them deeply for their hospitality and love. My parents, Jim and Judy Diamond, have never ceased to be the perfect role models, intellectually, religiously, and personally. They instilled in me a love of learning and a passion for ideas. I thank them for that wonderful legacy.

My son Eli and daughter Shira joined our family when this book was well under way. Although they need not feel that they have to become historians (their mother would prefer not!), I hope this book begins to show them the importance of history and the value of knowing where one has come from and where one is going. Finally, the greatest debt I have accumulated is to my best friend and wife, Judith Snowbell Diamond. Over the several years of our marriage, Judy has provided the emotional, intellectual, and financial support necessary to complete this project. She also has been the primary caregiver to Eli and Shira during this drawn-out period. Judy's love for life and her life of love have made her an *esheth ḥayil*, a woman of valor. This book is for her.

# And I Will Dwell in Their Midst

MAP 1. *Greater Toronto Area and North America*

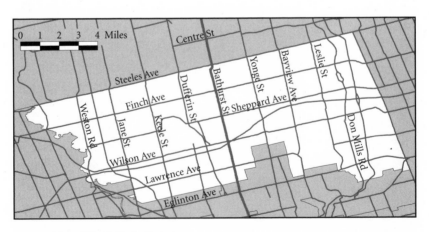

MAP 2. *City of North York, Ontario*

# One

---

## RELIGION AND SUBURBIA: TO CHOOSE OR NOT TO CHOOSE

Like many of his contemporaries in 1952, Sol Edell was looking for a place to live in Toronto. And like many of his fellow Orthodox Jews, he was looking in the "better neighborhoods downtown," where most of the city's traditionalist Jews lived. He quickly changed his mind, however, when one of his friends asked, "'What do you mean you're going to look downtown? Everyone is moving out of downtown. Where are you going to go? You're a young man. Why do you want to go with the old people? Old people are down there. Young man, you want to get out. Out there. Everybody's going up north, north of Eglinton and Lawrence.' So I said, okay." Responding to a newspaper advertisement for a house at Bidewell Avenue, just east of Bathurst Street and north of Wilson Avenue, Edell agreed to meet a real estate agent on Avenue Road, just north of Wilson Avenue. "I drove and I drove and I drove, and I thought I'd never reach it or find this place, it seemed like a hundred miles away. Anyway, I finally got to this place, and went around the corner, and he showed me this house. The first house I saw had picture windows, a gorgeous garden, open. Where we used to live was closed in. This was all open."

Standing outside the house with the agent, Edell heard a car horn. "I take a look and it's Joe Silverberg. I knew him since I was a kid, and his father and my father were in business together. He said, 'What are you doing up here?' He was already up here. I said I was looking at a house and he said, 'Buy it!' 'What do you mean, buy it?' 'We need you for a minyan [quorum of ten men necessary for Orthodox Jewish worship services]. We're looking for people.' So I said, 'Is there any place around?' He said 'Yes, we're *davening* [praying] together already, but every person counts.' So I thought about it. I went back, I eventually negotiated a deal that I could handle and I bought it. But if it wasn't for him going by saying that there was a minyan, that they were already starting to *daven* together, it wouldn't have been. So I say the *Ribono Shel Olam* [Master of the Universe] works in weird and wonderful ways. I hadn't seen Joe maybe in months, but all of a sudden he passed right there and spots me on the street. You never know, but that's the way community is built."[1]

The early 1950s were a time for relocation for Lillian Silverberg as well. She and her husband were living in a house on Rusholme Street, in downtown Toronto, but were looking for a newer and bigger home. She recalled that Bathurst Street north of Wilson Avenue was "just being developed. It was all farm at that time." Still, her younger brother decided to relocate to those newly built neighborhoods of north Bathurst Street. "He's the one that made the move up here. He moved up here on Raeburn east of Bathurst. We were very close and this was our incentive to move along. Sol [Edell] was living in this area. My brother-in-law, Joe Silverberg, he lived in this area. We knew quite a number of people living up this way." So Silverberg and her husband moved too, although their home was just "partially built, the streets weren't paved, [and] we didn't have phones for quite a while." Despite these hardships, one essential institution was already in place: the synagogue. After all, she explained, "If you're Orthodox you have to be close to [a synagogue] to attend your services." When we first moved up we *davened* in a tent. Then they built a hall where we used to *daven*."[2]

Aaron Weisblatt is a generation younger than Edell and Silverberg. Right before his thirteenth birthday in 1956, his parents moved from downtown Toronto to an apartment along Bathurst Street. After living downtown for a year following his wedding in 1969, he and his wife, Anne, hoped to settle down. Rather than stay downtown or in the neighborhoods of his childhood, he looked further north and bought a semidetached house in the Greenwin

Village subdivision within walking distance of B'nai Torah Congregation. Weisblatt chose that neighborhood and that synagogue because "a lot of the young community was moving up here. I was a young grad, just starting out, trying to attract new business. This was where the action was." Besides, "it was fun, getting involved" in a new synagogue and a new community.[3]

Religion. Prayer services. God. Community. Not terms that one might typically associate with postwar suburbia. But then, one does not typically associate Orthodox Jews with postwar suburbia either. Yet in almost every major city in the United States and Canada, Orthodox Jews live lives that are far removed from the stereotypes of lower-class, urban immigrants of the early twentieth century or of modern suburbanites with few religious ties or community relationships. Instead, the late twentieth-century Orthodox Jewish suburbanite has blended into the upwardly mobile, consumerist world of North American suburban culture, all the while retaining a strong sense of religious traditionalism and community cohesion. This amalgamation did not evolve smoothly or free of conflict, but its sheer existence offers a strong counterpoint to the dominant assumptions about suburban society and religious culture in the twentieth century. How this blend of traditionalist religion and consumerist middle-class suburban secularism developed— what the historian Jack Wertheimer has described as a "law- and community-bound movement in the midst of freewheeling, individualist, late-20th-century America"—is the story told in the pages that follow.[4]

That an Orthodox Jewish community evolved in twentieth-century suburbia might strike many readers as odd, considering the fundamental clash between the nature of traditionalist religion, as manifested by Orthodox Judaism, and that of postwar society, as found in metropolitan suburbs. One can understand this clash in two ways. The first posits the restrictiveness of traditionalist religion against suburban society's emphasis on lifestyle choices. At its core, a traditionalist religion such as that practiced by Orthodox Jews mediates, structures, and, most important, limits one's life experiences. Orthodox Judaism contains rules and restrictions that demand that a religiously observant individual practice certain rituals and believe certain doctrines to the specific exclusion of others. These rules, regulations, beliefs, and practices are not random or man-made but have divine roots; in the case of Orthodox Jews, God transmitted to Moses a written text (the Torah) and an oral tradition (the Talmud). The divinity of these texts means that they are inflexible and beyond reinterpretation; one accepts the authority of halakhah (Jewish religious law) and observes its dictums, even if that halakhah is not "modern," "relevant," or "in touch with contemporary ideas."

In a society where religious observance has been transformed into a matter of personal choice, choosing a lifestyle rooted in a traditionalist religion such as Orthodox Judaism means choosing for oneself a lifestyle of limitations. Such a choice directly opposes a modern metropolitan mentality that encourages and even demands individual choice and multiple options. As early as the 1930s, the pioneering urban sociologist Louis Wirth characterized the city as an environment in which a person faces an array of social and cultural choices far more extensive than found in rural communities.[5] More recently, the historian Robert Fishman described the modern metropolis as a "city à la carte," where individuals construct their own networks in which they live, work, shop, and play.[6] Other trends confirm these observations. A cycle of material acquisition, consumption, and discarding drives the daily activities of metropolitan society, with advertisers tantalizing metropolitan residents to choose "new and improved" products to replace those "old and obsolete" ones bought only a year before. As metropolitan regions have increased in size and decreased in density, individuals have gained the ability to experience a wider range of environments.[7] The automobile and a comprehensive highway system have facilitated this access, resulting in highly personalized patterns of metropolitan movement. In short, post–World War II metropolitan suburbia—identified here by the socioeconomic and cultural expansion of a middle-class, consumerist society and the spatial expansion of the urban periphery—can be characterized as an experience of unlimited choice.

Traditionalist religion and secular suburbia also clash over the issue of "community." Religion fosters community as few other social institutions do. Members of a single congregation typically share a wide range of beliefs and behaviors, as well as similar socioeconomic characteristics. Such shared backgrounds, attitudes, and lifestyles create a sense of community among congregational members, who look out for one another, offering help in times of need and a smile in times of happiness. These faith-based "caring communities" contrast with a twentieth-century suburban culture that fosters isolation and unconnectedness. Suburbia is often criticized for impeding the development of close social bonds with one's neighbors or anyone else for that matter. In classical postwar analyses, suburbia is a place inhabited by the "lonely crowd," individuals and families unconnected to one another in any meaningful way.[8] Contrasted with those who live in tight-knit small towns or ethnically connected urban neighborhoods, suburban residents are described as being connected only to communities of "limited liability," where neighbors have a minimal and pragmatic interest in fostering community bonds.[9]

If traditionalist religion is "choice-limiting" and "community-promoting" and secular metropolitan society is "choice-enhancing" and "community-limiting," then one can clearly see the potential for problems when the two intersect. Furthermore, if one examines specifically Orthodox Judaism in the context of contemporary suburban society, even more tensions appear. Two of the most basic elements that structure any society are time and space. Regarding time, North American metropolitan society follows a distinctly secular rhythm. The daily routines of suburban family life require adherence to a strict schedule: beating the morning rush hour, driving the children's school carpool, delivering children to after-school sports practices or music lessons. On a weekly basis, suburban life alternates between the five-day workweek and the two-day weekend, with the latter having particularly suburban qualities. The suburban weekend is a time for engaging in various projects around the house, recreational sports, or other hobbies, often with as much seriousness and diligence as the occupational activities of the workweek. As Witold Rybczynski has explained, on the weekend, "people used to 'play' tennis; now they 'work' on their backhand."[10] Other civic and religious holidays, and even the seasons of the year, have been reformulated into economic events when stores and shopping malls mark the calendar with sales and promotions. These daily, weekly, and annual rhythms organize suburban life throughout the year, with occasional breaks for children during the summer and for adults during their standard two-week paid vacation.[11]

Time in Orthodox Judaism follows a very different structure. One must pray specific prayers during specific periods during the day, which, unlike secular time that is marked from sunrise to sunset, begins at sundown and ends at sundown. The clearest distinctions between secular and religious time occur on the Sabbath, when Orthodox Jews hew "a day of sacred respite out of the rock-hard secularity" surrounding them.[12] On the Sabbath, Orthodox Jews must abstain from any secular activities from sundown on Friday to sundown on Saturday. Also forbidden within that sacred time are many types of "work," which through rabbinical interpretation include such common activities as writing, cooking, using electricity, and driving or riding in vehicles. The Jewish calendar also creates conflicts with the secular calendar. The former follows a lunar cycle, meaning that holidays occur on different secular days in different years. For an Orthodox Jew, this sacred temporal structure means that one often has to be absent from work or school when a holiday falls on a weekday; unlike the weekly Sabbath, Jewish holidays are not fixed to specific days of the week as secular civic holidays often are.

The temporally based structure of the Orthodox Jewish Sabbath and other holidays also leads to spatially based structures in the Orthodox Jewish community. Because the many prohibited activities on the Sabbath and holidays include a restriction against driving or riding in vehicles, to fully observe the Sabbath, a *shomer shabbos* (Sabbath-observant) family must live within walking distance of a synagogue or else forgo attending synagogue services.[13] Although this religious law matters to an Orthodox Jew only every seventh day, it nevertheless structures one's life by limiting residential choice to areas close enough to walk to a synagogue. At the same time that Sabbath laws constrain individual choice, they also structure the entire community, since the situation of many Sabbath-observant families living within walking distance of the same synagogue necessarily creates a religious community with clear spatial and social boundaries. It is, as well, a caring community to a high degree. Jews routinely share meals on the Sabbath and on holidays, provide meals for one another when a baby is born, celebrate one another's family *simḥas* (lit., happinesses, refers to celebrations such as weddings and bar mitzvahs), and comfort one another during the shiva period (lit., seven, refers to the seven-day period following the death of a relative when friends and family members comfort mourners). Although these other aspects of the caring nature of Orthodox Judaism are not explicitly linked to the Sabbath, the spatial proximity engendered by Sabbath observance facilitates these other shared experiences. The sociologist Chaim Waxman articulated this centrality of the Sabbath, writing that "the fact that Orthodoxy proscribes driving a car on the Sabbath even for the purpose of attending services at synagogue, thus, has a very deep sociological significance. It lays the foundation for the 'omnipresent sense of community' which is unequaled in other branches of Jewry."[14]

It is also unequaled in other religions. To be sure, other religious groups have lifestyle regulations. The Church of Jesus Christ of Latter-day Saints, for example, demands many lifestyle modifications from its adherents, including financial tithing and abstention from drinking and gambling. Certain evangelical Christian denominations also discourage consumption of alcohol and such aspects of popular culture as movies and rock music. A Muslim's life is regimented by requirements to pray at specific times during the day and to fast in specific months.[15] But none of these groups face the same spatial restraints that Orthodox Jews face because of the Sabbath. Therefore, they can much more easily fit into the flow of suburban life. Perhaps the one group that does confront spatial constraints is the Amish, whose religion prohibits technology such as automobiles. These groups generally isolate themselves in rural communities, however, and thus avoid the problems that such spatial constraints would impose if they were to live in a metropolitan environment. In contrast to all these groups, Orthodox Jews live fully within suburban society, despite the once-a-week hardship of the Sabbath and the daily structure of the Orthodox Jewish lifestyle.

To most people in the metropolis, religious or not, choosing a place to live involves finding a place that balances attractions of the immediate surroundings (nice neighborhood, house, neighbors) with metropolitan needs (convenience to work, school, shopping). The location that best meets all of these needs and also fits into a household budget is usually the one that is chosen. This holds true even for members of faiths that are religiously restrictive. Fundamentalist Protestant families might desire to live near a church or near other fundamentalist Protestant families, but they are not religiously mandated to do so. Residential choice for Orthodox Jews involves a very different, and far simpler, process. For members of this group, one question usually supersedes all others when moving households: is it near an Orthodox Jewish synagogue? If not, then that particular place will get crossed off the list, no matter how nice, affordable, or convenient it might be.

The many disjunctures between Orthodox Judaism and suburban society should not obscure the fact that the two cultures share other characteristics. For example, both Orthodox Judaism and middle-class suburban society emphasize the family and the education and socialization of children. The family and the home are central to the religious schema of Orthodox Judaism. In the home, religion involves the entire family, from dietary practices to Sabbath and holiday observances to life cycle rituals. For generations, traditions and observances were transmitted informally from parents to children in the home. Together with this informal education, formal education of Jewish texts has also long been central to Orthodox Jewish life. Though focused on an entirely different set of values, these emphases parallel the values typically associated with middle-class suburbia: the nuclear family, the transmission of middle-class values to children, and the role of education in providing opportunities for upward mobility. Orthodox Judaism and suburban society share similar emphases regarding issues of material culture as well. Perhaps more than any other religion, Orthodox Judaism is a religion of "doing" (or not doing in many cases). Most religious commandments, or mitzvoth, involve some action: reciting blessings, eating ritual foods, giving charity. Many of these mitzvoth require the use of material objects such as wine goblets and candelabras. A long-standing tradition of *hiddur mitzvah*, or the enhancement of the mitzvah, encouraged people to use objects that were not only functional but also materially attractive. This emphasis on material culture and the enhancement of ritual objects stands as a religious version of suburban materialism, in which houses are filled with an array of objects that "enhance" one's lifestyle. Again, though derived from entirely different value systems, this shared emphasis on material culture helped to bridge the gap between Orthodox Judaism and twentieth-century suburban culture.

Given the many social, cultural, spatial, and temporal tensions with suburban society on one hand and the many characteristics shared with that society on the other, the development of a suburban-based Orthodox Jewish community in the twentieth century would seem to have been a complex and even counterintuitive process. Something had to happen for the "square peg" of Orthodox Judaism to fit into the "round hole" of suburban society. This book explores that "something." What were the processes through which Orthodox Jews religiously integrated into the suburban environment? Were compromises or modifications made in Orthodox Jewish religious observance to make it more compatible with the suburban way of life? How did Orthodox Jewish institutions—the synagogue, the school, the religious home—adapt to suburban styles and attitudes? More broadly, what did it mean to have a suburbanized Orthodox Jewish community in the postwar period? As the rest of this book explains, Orthodox Judaism proved flexible enough in its structure and adaptable enough in its culture to allow the Orthodox Jewish community to overcome the many tensions and clashes noted above and to find its place in the culture of postwar suburban society.

For readers not familiar with the world of Orthodox Jewry, the discussion thus far might have seemed somewhat abstract and vague. One might ask, Who are the Orthodox Jews of North America? This question is a good one, considering that most people's image of Orthodox Jews is probably a Hollywood-filtered stereotype of bearded men with curled earlocks, wearing black hats and black coats, mumbling in Yiddish, and accompanied by stern-looking, kerchief-wearing women and several small children. One might call this the *Fiddler on the Roof* stereotype, and it has been perpetuated in movies, television shows, and books. But while such an image might have been true for nineteenth-century Eastern Europe or early twentieth-century North American urban neighborhoods (and it is not entirely accurate for those times either), this stereotype clearly fails to describe Orthodox Jews in late twentieth-century suburbia. At least since mid-century, the Orthodox Jewish community has moved far beyond these aforementioned stereotypes. Though it sounds like the statement of an anti-Jewish conspiracist, the fact is that suburban Orthodox Jews generally look like everyone else in suburbia—with the exception of their religious observances. Suburban Orthodox Jews of the late twentieth century "choose the corset of Orthodoxy" but "wear it in their own way." Today, most Orthodox Jews shop at the same trendy stores that other middle-class suburbanites shop at, live in the same kind of ranch and split-level houses as other suburbanites, and drive the same models of cars as other suburbanites. Orthodox Jewish men have clean-shaven faces, work in typical white-collar and professional occupations, and speak English. Orthodox Jewish children are no less fluent in the world of Pokemon and basketball superstars than are their less religious peers. Suburban Orthodox Jewish communities include "men who both pray and pump iron before work, women with a cell phone at their ear and a baby at their breast, youngsters in Rollerblades and yarmulkes." Together they have created "a style of Jewish life that blends the rituals of Orthodoxy with the rituals of the mall, the gym, and the Long Island Rail Road."[16]

To understand the roughly three to five hundred thousand people living in North America who identify themselves as Orthodox Jews, then, one must begin with those "rituals of Orthodoxy."[17] Orthodox Jews adhere to the halakhah to a greater degree than do Jews affiliating with the more liberal Reform, Reconstructionist, and Conservative denominations. As the sociologist Charles Liebman has explained, "Jews who define themselves as Orthodox score higher on measures of religious observance and devotion than do Jews who define themselves as Conservatives, and Conservatives higher than Reform."[18] Despite this "standard" of practice, there is in fact a great range of individual levels of observance and adherence, and the levels of observance of those claiming adherence to Orthodox Judaism range from very strict to very nominal.[19] Even within a single synagogue, people with many degrees of practice claim the same Orthodox Jewish affiliation. In this way, Orthodox Jews are similar to the religious community of Catholics, where certain basic ideas and rituals underlie a great variety of actual practices by adherents.

One can identify two general groups within the Orthodox Jewish community, "ultra-Orthodox" Jews and "Modern Orthodox" Jews.[20] Although both fall at the strict end of the religious spectrum described by Liebman, the two groups can be differentiated on a number of issues. For example, Modern Orthodox Jews accept and value the State of Israel as a political entity, while ultra-Orthodox Jews tend to reject the legitimacy of a Jewish state, emphasizing instead that only the messianic age can herald in an independent Jewish country. In social issues, Modern Orthodox Jews tend to be somewhat more liberal on women's issues and women's education, while ultra-Orthodox Jews are not (although even in Modern Orthodox Jewry, women are not formally obligated to participate in most religious activities). Perhaps the most important differences between ultra-Orthodox and Modern Orthodox Jews, however, are their attitudes toward secular society.

"Centrist" Modern Orthodox Judaism emerged in nineteenth-century Germany as a response to religious reforms introduced by liberal factions in the Jewish community. But even as rabbinical leaders such as Samson Raphael Hirsch and Esriel Hildesheimer sought to uphold the tradition in the face of liberalizing pressures, they also understood that modernity was not entirely evil. At the very least, halakhic Judaism did not reject secular knowledge or modernity. The study of science, mathematics, even literature, had value if it could help a student to understand his own religious tradition better. As termed by Hirsch, this synthesis represented "*Torah Im Derekh Erets*" (Torah with the ways of the world).[21] Beyond the specific issue of secular education, Modern Orthodoxy argued that one could "accept the authority of the past, while still maintaining some modicum of personal autonomy in an age that increasingly emphasized individual freedom."[22] To do so, one had to separate the halakhah, which was unchangeable, from communal custom, which had been socially constructed. As Steven Cohen has argued, "Where Modern Orthodox leaders [saw] the *halacha* as silent, they allowed modernity to fill the normative void created by the retreat of traditional law and custom. Modern Orthodoxy facilitated integration by relaxing controls over many areas of life that were formerly regulated by custom and social sanction."[23] Historically, most of the Orthodox Jews who emigrated from Europe came from this centrist Orthodox Jewish background. But most immigrants, however "traditional" they might have been when they arrived, quickly shed both the external trappings of Orthodox Judaism and the specific practices. Only a smaller population maintained this religious-secular balance. These rabbis and lay leaders were among the founders of the early Orthodox Jewish organizations such as Yeshiva University and the Union of Orthodox Jewish Congregations of America. In the postwar period, Modern Orthodox Jews continued this negotiation between halakhic needs and secular wants in several ways. Centrist Orthodox Jewish women will enjoy the latest clothing fashions, provided they are not too immodestly cut. They also watch movies and television shows, as long as they too do not cross boundaries of religious modesty. Furthermore, the hallmark of Modern Orthodox synthesis, Yeshiva University in New York, offers an intense Jewish religious education *and* a full secular university program under one institutional roof.[24]

Although sharing centrist Orthodoxy's historical roots as a reaction to nineteenth-century German Jewish reforms, ultra-Orthodox Jews rejected any hint of accommodation with secular society. Instead, ultra-Orthodox Jewish leaders turned inward, believing that all that an observant Jew would need can be found in the world of Torah and halakhah.[25] These *haredi* (lit., fearful) Orthodox Jews emphasized the distinctiveness of observant Judaism and downplayed or even banned external manifestations of modernity, including secular modes of dress, education, and culture.[26] As part of their rejection of modernity, most nineteenth-century *haredi* Orthodox Jewish leaders strongly discouraged immigration to North America; the United States was a *treyf* (unkosher) land, they said. Immigration across the Atlantic increased only with the rise of Nazism and the onset of World War II. But because of their previous insularity in Europe, those who came to the United States and Canada in the 1930s and 1940s arrived with their religious identities intact. To the extent that they could, these immigrants recreated insulated communities such as they had in Europe. In some cases, whole communities moved far from the urban centers. Rabbi Aaron Kotler, for example, settled in Lakewood, New Jersey, to avoid the corrupting influence of New York City. More common were communities of *haredi* Jews that were mixed in with the larger Jewish community but operated outside and independent of the broader Jewish infrastructure. Here, a classic case is the *haredi* community that developed around the Reichmann family in suburban Toronto, where synagogues and schools serve a tight-knit network of families that have little interaction with other Jewish institutions.[27]

On a superficial level, such an isolationist attitude toward secular society might seem to put the ultra-Orthodox Jewish community in a category similar to other traditionalist religious communities such as the Amish. In reality, this community is far from isolationist. Although they shun the products of popular culture, *haredi* Jews do not shun the technologies of that culture. Network television shows might be frowned on while international cable broadcasts of *Hasidic* (lit., pious Jews, refers to Orthodox Jews who follow the traditions of specific rabbis or communities) Orthodox Jewish gatherings are not.[28] Similar attitudes prevail regarding political involvement. While many *haredi* communities desire a political autonomy to maintain religious standards without outside secular interference, their efforts to obtain this autonomy have forced *ḥaredi* Jews to become politically sophisticated and involved. In several cases in the postwar period, *ḥaredi* Orthodox Jewish communities have attempted to gain a measure of political control over local jurisdictions to enforce religious standards. Perhaps the most famous cases occurred in the 1980s and 1990s, when *ḥaredi* communities in Kiryas Joel and New Square, suburban communities in Rockland County, New York, battled the state of New York over public funding for local schools that were entirely Jewish and religious.[29] In short, the North American *ḥaredi* community is one that works hard to control and limit the points of intersection between its religious values and behaviors and the outside secular society.

Notwithstanding these historical differences between centrist and *ḥaredi* Orthodox Jews, the last two or three decades of the twentieth century have seen a reconvergence between the two groups.[30] More precisely, there has been a distinct and decided shift of the centrist Orthodox Jewish community rightward. (That is, the movement was from the center to the right, not the other way around.) Standards of religious adherence have increased among centrist Orthodox Jews, replacing what were previously acceptable practices. The historian Haym Soloveitchik, one of the leading authorities on the history of Orthodox Judaism, has argued that this elevation of "religious stringency," or *ḥumra*, was caused by a loss of "mimetic culture" among traditionalist Jews. Whereas in the European shtetl (self-contained, often rural Jewish village in Eastern Europe) and to a degree in immigrant urban neighborhoods, traditions were learned from one generation to another mimetically, or by copying, contemporary Orthodox Jews learn rituals "by the book." And because there are many books that quote many opinions on specific practices, a person must adhere to the strictest ones to ensure that he or she does not violate the "right one" (whichever it might be). The result is a tendency toward maximum strictness in interpretation and observance. The tendency toward *ḥumra* first occurred in the *ḥaredi* world, but it has spilled over into the centrist Orthodox Jewish world.[31]

The rightward drift has occurred not only in ritual observance but in intergroup relations as well. Deriving as they do from anti-Reform movements of the nineteenth century, *ḥaredi* Orthodox Jews have never advocated relationships with non-Orthodox Jewish institutions. In contrast, centrist Orthodox historically maintained more open lines of communication with Reform and Conservative organizations and institutions. Over the past few decades, however, such communication became less and less frequent, as centrist Orthodox Jewish leaders felt the pressure of *ḥaredi* Orthodox Jewish rabbis to limit interdenominational contacts. Consider the example of the Synagogue Council of America (SCA). Formed as a cross-denominational rabbinical board in New York, the SCA faced a major challenge from the *ḥaredi* and *Ḥasidic* Orthodox Jewish communities in the mid-1950s. In 1956, a group of eleven rabbis issued a religious ruling against Orthodox Jewish representatives participating in any organization that included non-Orthodox rabbis.[32] The declaration put much pressure on the SCA's centrist Orthodox Jewish representatives to withdraw. The SCA was saved, for the moment, by the refusal of Rabbi Joseph B. Soloveitchik, the dominant figure in centrist Orthodoxy during much of the twentieth century, to sign the decree. Nevertheless, the centrist Orthodox Jewish world got the message: such participation by centrist Orthodox Jewish rabbis diminished their credibility with their *ḥaredi* colleagues. The result was a gradual withdrawal of the centrist Orthodox Jewish community away from interdenominational activities and an increase in isolation and insulation from the broader Jewish community.

This insulation has continued through to the end of the twentieth century, with national and local Orthodox Jewish groups shying away from any activity that might seem to legitimize non-Orthodox Jewish organizations. At the national level, there are few formal intergroup relationships between Orthodox organizations and Conservative and Reform organizations. Locally, Orthodox Jewish synagogues will often not participate in communal activities, even supposedly "neutral" community activities such as a Holocaust memorial service or an Israel Independence Day celebration, when such events are held at Conservative or Reform synagogues because some Orthodox Jews interpret the halakhah as forbidding one to enter non-Orthodox Jewish synagogues (even for a nonreligious activity). This stance toward non-Orthodox Jewish institutions is so hostile that the few Orthodox Jewish groups willing to have dialogue with other Jewish organizations have been marginalized within the Orthodox Jewish world. In the 1970s and 1980s, Yitzchak Greenberg, an Orthodox Jewish rabbi, headed CLAL (the National Jewish Center for Learning and Leadership) to promote dialogue among Jewish denominations and received much criticism and even ostracism from Orthodox Jewish organizations and rabbis. In February 1999, a new organization named Edah held its first international conference on Orthodoxy and modernity. Promoting the "courage to be modern and Orthodox," Edah's participants included several prominent centrist Orthodox rabbis, including Saul Berman, a longtime Orthodox Jewish rabbi and teacher at Yeshiva University; Shlomo Riskin, the for-

mer rabbi of New York's Lincoln Square Synagogue and chief rabbi of the Israeli community of Efrat; and Walter Wurzburger and Marc Angel, both past
presidents of the Rabbinical Council of America. But despite (or because of?)
the presence of these individuals, Edah received criticism from the Orthodox
Jewish right and even from other centrist Orthodox rabbis. In the words of
Rabbi Moshe Tendler, the *Rosh Yeshiva* (head of the academy) at Yeshiva University, Edah latched "onto pluralism as a salable item, when we look at pluralism as the death kiss of Judaism."[33]

Despite the official rhetoric against and isolation from non-Orthodox Jewish institutions, Orthodox Jews do have relationships with individual non-
Orthodox Jews. The distinction might seem hairsplitting to an outsider, but it
is crucial to the worldview of Orthodox Jews. The halakhah might be interpreted as rejecting any alternative forms of Judaism, but nowhere does it reject individual Jews. To the contrary, the goal is to have non-Orthodox Jews
"come closer" to observance—the Hebrew term *kiruv* is popularly used to describe such outreach activity—through learning and participating in religious rituals. Thus activities such as the National Jewish Outreach Program's
"Turn Friday Night into *Shabbos*" and the Discovery Seminars run by Aish
Hatorah (lit., Fire of Torah, refers to an international organization dedicated
to outreach into the unaffiliated Jewish community) are two examples of programs designed to introduce Orthodox Jewish practices and beliefs to nonobservant Jews.

In many ways, this rightward drift of the centrist Orthodox Jewish community has paralleled the broader shift to conservatism among other religious
groups. As Robert Wuthnow had amply documented, the postwar period has
seen a decline in denominationalism and a rise in a liberal-conservative split.[34]
A variety of conservative Christian denominations have grown rapidly in the
past fifty years, while liberal mainline Protestant groups have declined. Catholicism too has seen a split between post–Vatican II liberals and those seeking
to return the church to its more traditional roots. Some scholars have explicitly linked the Orthodox Jewish movement rightward with this wider religious
trend.[35] One has to be careful, however, of labeling Orthodox Jewish behavior
as "fundamentalist," both because of the obvious Protestant Christian origin
of the term and because, unlike fundamentalist Protestants and Moslems,
the Orthodox Jewish movement rightward does not involve debates over
doctrine or belief. Doctrine and belief rarely enter into the conversation of
Orthodox Jews, and the story told in this book will rarely touch on such

issues. Rather, what is fundamental to Orthodox Jews—what has become the "battleground"—is religious practice and the need for maximum application of ritual and practice.

Although this discussion has focused on the differences between the centrist and right wings of Orthodox Judaism, that split (and possible reconciliation) will *not* be the primary focus of this book. It is not my intention to detail the ongoing tensions between the right and the left or the right and the center. Such a discussion is better left to those with more grounding in theology (or, perhaps, to those with a particular theological ax to grind).[36] But explaining the differences between the right-wing *ḥaredi* Orthodox Jewish community and the more centrist and modern Orthodox Jewish community is important to explaining why the book will concentrate primarily on the centrist group and not the right. Because my intention is to document and to explain how the Orthodox Jewish community was transformed into a suburban and consumerist-oriented subculture, I focus on the group in which the religious-secular balance is in its sharpest relief, namely the centrist Orthodox Jewish community. Although the rightward drift of the centrist Orthodox Jewish community has occurred largely in the realm of stricter observance and increased isolation from the broader Jewish community, it has not meant increased withdrawal from certain key aspects of secular suburban society. Rather, this rightward drift has occurred at the exact time that Orthodox Jews have become more affluent, more entrenched in consumerist society, and more tied to the suburban landscape than at any point in their history of settlement in North America—precisely when one would not expect an increase in religious traditionalism. The centrist Orthodox Jewish community, then, serves as an ideal case for examining the relationship between the suburban experience and religious traditionalism.[37]

Relative to non-Jewish and non-Orthodox Jewish communities, the lives of centrist Orthodox Jews are structured by religion on a more comprehensive and constant basis. Yet relative to *ḥaredi* Orthodox Jews, centrist Orthodox Jews have neither shunned the secular suburban environment nor isolated themselves in religious enclaves. Centrist Orthodox Jewish communities have developed within heterogeneous suburban environments. Although there might be specific Orthodox-Jewish-dominated neighborhoods, centrist Orthodox Jews have never sought to cut themselves off from the larger suburban society. The Orthodox Jewish community of post–World War II suburbia has partaken of the secular suburban culture yet has done so within an increasingly traditionalist religious framework. They provide, then, a point of maximum intensity where religion and secular issues are in closer contact than in any other religious group.

Surprisingly, despite the flourishing of Orthodox Jewish communities over the past few decades and the flourishing of literature about these Orthodox Jews, there has been little critical analysis of Orthodox Jewish suburbanization. Following Charles Liebman's declaration in 1965 that Orthodoxy was "on the upsurge" and "experiencing a greater sense of confidence and purpose" than it ever had, a generation of social scientists began to explore the diverse world of North American Orthodox Jewry.[38] Their works documented who Orthodox Jews were, what rituals they practiced, how they behaved in synagogue, and how they studied and transmitted their religious heritage.[39] But even as these many works proved that Orthodox Jews could no longer be described accurately as stereotypical lower-class urban immigrants, they rarely linked this transformation to the question of suburbanization. Instead, they "talked around" the topic of suburbia without ever directly addressing it. For example, an analysis of the changing Orthodox Jewish community by Haym Soloveitchik explored how postwar Orthodox Jews "increasingly adopted the consumer culture and its implicit values, above all the legitimacy of pursuing material gratification." That women adopted fancier though still modest clothing styles and that upscale kosher restaurants served an international cuisine beyond the traditional Eastern European fare indicated the "smooth incorporation of religious practice into a middle-class lifestyle." To Soloveitchik, this was a "tribute to the adaptability of the religious and to the [Orthodox Jews'] new mastery of their environment."[40]

The relevant, and ironic, phrase here is "mastery of their environment," because Soloveitchik's work lacks any discussion of the spatial or social environment in which the Orthodox Jewish community exists. By portraying only the socioeconomic mobility of postwar Orthodox Jews, his and others' analyses tell only half the story. Orthodox Jewish movement up the socioeconomic scale could have occurred within the physical confines of the urban neighborhood with its established religious infrastructure. But in moving from city to suburb, Orthodox Jews literally broke new ground by spatially separating themselves from the old neighborhoods and choosing to become religious pioneers on the suburban periphery. Their adaptation to a new middle-class, suburban way of life occurred in concert with the creation of new suburban synagogues, schools, and a variety of other religious institutions necessary to support their community. By characterizing the postwar Orthodox Jewish experience in terms of religious suburbanization, with both socioeconomic and spatial components, this book seeks to understand even more accurately the processes involved in this religious community's "mastery" of its "environment." Extending the environment metaphor beyond the realm of Orthodox Jews specifically, this book also helps to broaden the general understanding of how religion fits into the metropolitan environment. A small but rapidly growing body of work by historians and other observers of urban religion has begun to make clear that the twentieth-century metropolitan landscape is not a "bland and homogeneous mass" but a rich source of religious and social diversity.[41] Orthodox Jews, as this book explains, are one more piece in that diverse metropolitan landscape.

A final point is the geographic focus of this book, the Orthodox Jewish community of suburban Toronto. Why Canada, a reader might ask. Why not study the more prominent Jewish communities of New York or Miami? Or perhaps a study situated in the more commonly studied suburban landscapes of Los Angeles or Chicago would be more appropriate. Although some have argued that the border between the United States and Canada marks important distinctions between the metropolitan cultures of the United States and Canada, there are several compelling reasons to believe that suburban Toronto and its Orthodox Jewish community is in fact representative of North America.[42]

From the Jewish perspective, much evidence points to a convergence between the American and Canadian Jewish communities in the decades following World War II.[43] For example, Canadian Jewish rates of intermarriage have risen steadily since the 1950s.[44] Institutionally, cross-national relationships have increased, with synagogue and rabbinical organizations composed of members from both sides of the border. Youth groups and summer camps put American and Canadian Jewish teenagers into a common setting. American kosher food products can be found in Canada in abundance. This convergence has resulted in homogeneous religious experiences that have reduced national and cultural differences and have created a continental religious community. Religious practices, after all, are not constrained by political borders; the religious halakhah applies equally to Canadian and American Orthodox Jews. Having these shared religious practices, which are immutable regardless of where in the continent (or world) one lives means that Orthodox Jews can "plug in" to any community with little difficulty. To be sure, individual communities have individual histories and idiosyncrasies, but this has not stopped the process of continentalization that has occurred over the past half-century, a topic discussed further in Chapter 6. Thus even while taking into account cultural differences between Canada and the United States, this book argues that increasing continental similarities make Toronto a viable and valuable case study of North American Orthodox Jewry.

That shared religious practice can transcend national borders is clear, but can one say the same for suburban culture? How continentally representative, or interchangeable, are Toronto's suburbs? Since the conclusion of World War II, the suburban city of North York and the Greater Toronto Area has become increasingly plugged into a broader network of North American metropolitan regions and increasingly representative of the North American suburb. In his now classic analysis of American suburbanization, Kenneth Jackson lists five characteristics of the postwar suburb: peripheral location, low density, architectural homogeneity, low cost, and demographic homogeneity.[45] Upon examining Toronto's suburban fringe and the development of North York in particular, one sees that Jackson's description equally applies north of the border. In Toronto, suburban development occurred at the fringe of urban settlement, where farm after farm was bought by developers, subdivided, and reconstructed into tract housing. Moreover, these subdivisions contained single-family homes on lots that were bigger than could be found in the inner city. Architecturally, Toronto's suburbs reflected a stark homogeneity. In the years after World War II, for example, the Canadian Mortgage and Housing Corporation sponsored periodic house design competitions, the winners of which were usually three-bedroom split-levels, with an L-shaped living room–dining room and a basement.[46] Today, few suburban subdivisions in Toronto reflect any local style or tradition; split-level houses with two-car garages jutting out of the front stretch endlessly along winding streets with typically suburban names such as Goldenwood Road, Brookview Drive, Laurelcrest Avenue. In the several suburban "edge city" corporate-retail complexes that emerged in the 1970s and 1980s, only the logos of Canadian corporations on the facades of office buildings betray the landscape's national setting. As for social homogeneity, few parts of Toronto are truly integrated, and even where ethnic immigrants have succeeded in moving to suburban neighborhoods, they have tended to do so in concentrated sectoral form rather than in any real dispersed patterns. The result is that, like the Jewish density along Bathurst Street, one finds a concentration of Italians along Keele and Dufferin Streets in North York, Portuguese to the west in Mississauga, and Asians to the northeast in Scarborough.[47]

Beyond the specific characteristics of North York's suburban landscape, other factors have conspired to bring metropolitan Toronto into close contact with the network of American metropolitan regions. Changes in transportation and communication technologies rendered political boundaries less meaningful. Toronto's financial industry developed as strong connections to New York's Wall Street as it had to commodities exchanges in western Canada. For example, business pages of the daily newspapers constantly discuss the Toronto Stock Exchange (TSE) in relation to the New York Stock Exchange and describe the market activity in continental terms. "*North American* Stock and Bond Markets [in] a Temporary but Traumatic Tailspin," a typical headline might read, while another might note that "Three Key Indexes Post New Highs as Tech Stocks Soar, but TSE Loses Some Momentum."[48] In professional sports, a Toronto-based baseball team joined the major leagues in 1977 and subsequently twice won the championship of America's "national" pastime. In 1995, a professional basketball team began to play in Toronto, and many in the city continue to hope for a team in the National Football League. Even in other intangible areas, Toronto has become indistinguishable from other North American cities. A nascent television and movie industry had developed in Toronto, with Hollywood productions using the generic-looking cityscape to represent the "typical" North American metropolitan environment. It is clear that although a distinctive Canadian culture remains, in the postwar North American metropolitan network these peculiarities have become no different from the American southern style of Atlanta or the New England nature of Boston. While not ignoring the idiosyncrasies of the local environment of suburban Toronto, then, this book concentrates instead on the continental representativeness of North York and the Toronto region.

There is an additional and quite practical purpose for choosing a Canadian rather than an American setting for this study. Because of public recognition of religion in Canada, governments may inquire about the religious backgrounds of its citizens. As a result, unlike in the United States, Canadian census data contain tabulations of Jewish populations. At the local level as well, records such as property assessments list the religious affiliation of homeowners and tenants. Having access to this information enables researchers of Canadian subjects to make far more accurate descriptions of religion in society than can researchers of the same subjects in the United States, who must rely on secondary data on mother tongue or ethnic background to determine religious affiliation. Although the Canadian data are not broken down according to Orthodox, Conservative, or Reform Jews, the sheer availability of Jewish population figures makes the choice of Toronto, rather than an American city with a comparable suburban Orthodox Jewish population, a wise decision.

Given this entire discussion, then, how exactly does this book go about studying the points of intersection between the religiously traditional Orthodox Jewish community and the secular suburban environment? It begins by taking a cue from the geographer Lily Kong, who has suggested that an inquiry into religious geography should try to "understand the processes through which specific environmental objects, landscapes, and buildings are invested with meaning of a religious kind."[49] In this vein, Chapter 2 describes the postwar suburbanization of Toronto's Orthodox Jewish community as a historical process of creating "sacred suburban space" along Bathurst Street, Toronto's prominent Jewish corridor. The term "sacred suburban space" suggests that the Orthodox Jewish community saw suburbia as a neutral environment capable of being transformed into a religious landscape. As the chapter explains, the process of creating sacred space along the Bathurst corridor involved an initial migration into neighborhoods adjacent to Bathurst Street and the subsequent formation of a visible Jewish landscape along Bathurst itself. In so doing, the once-peripheral suburban Bathurst Street became the core both for the Orthodox and the larger general Jewish communities.

After establishing the basic historical and geographical framework of Orthodox Jewish suburbanization, the book then introduces and examines three major components of the postwar suburban Orthodox Jewish subculture: religious congregations, institutions of youth socialization, and religious consumption patterns. In each of these areas, the Orthodox Jewish community repeatedly worked to mediate the points of intersection between the styles of traditionalist religion and those of secular suburban society.

The first topic, the formation of congregations, is the subject of Chapter 3. The chapter explains the movement to suburbia and the formation of new suburban congregations as a process of "religious pioneering." Physically, the Orthodox Jewish suburbanites of the postwar period were relocating away from the established core areas of Jewish settlement to newly constructed neighborhoods in Toronto's periphery. At the same time, these suburbanites "broke new religious ground" by establishing Orthodox Jewish congregations that maintained traditionalist religious practices even as they adapted to modern styles. But as the second half of this chapter argues, Orthodox Jews became comfortable in their suburban environment and soon shed earlier models of congregational development and religious pioneering. As religious peripheries became religious cores, Orthodox Jewish suburban synagogues retreated from explicitly blending traditionalist and modern styles and instead copied older immigrant styles of congregational development. By the 1980s and 1990s, the once-peripheralized pioneering religious community had given way to a self-confident and even triumphalist traditionalist community firmly entrenched in the suburban and religious establishment.

The second component of Orthodox Jewish religious suburbanization was the socialization of youth, the subject of Chapter 4. Orthodox Jewish youth experienced religious suburbanization primarily through various institutions of youth socialization such as day schools, youth groups, and summer camps. Much as the new pioneering congregations integrated religious traditionalism and suburban styles, day schools and other youth activities reinforced this blended identity by integrating Orthodox Jewish youth into the world of suburban Orthodoxy. As this chapter explains, religious socialization had both internal and external importance: internally, through the training of newer generations of suburban Orthodox Jews, and externally, with religion serving as a mediator of the secular experiences of Orthodox Jewish youth.

Chapter 5 turns to the third component of the suburbanization of the North American Orthodox Jewish community: the development of Orthodox Jewish "religious consumerism." As suburbanizing Orthodox Jews moved up the socioeconomic ladder, they were increasingly able to participate in the consumerist trends of modern, middle-class society. Their newfound consumer power combined with their traditionalist religious needs for items such as kosher food to create a new market for religious consumerism. Both locally in Toronto and continentally in North America, a kosher food industry emerged in response to an increased demand for kosher products and an increased economic ability and willingness to pay for such products. The chapter also documents how the growth of the kosher food industry in turn spawned a broader "kosher lifestyle," as Orthodox Jews expanded their consumer tastes to a broad range of activities and goods.

In Chapter 6, the book enlarges the scale and scope of discussion from Toronto to North America by examining Orthodox Jewish religious suburbanization as a continental phenomenon. Tying together the themes of the previous chapters, this discussion shows how shared experiences of religious suburbanization at the local level—suburbanized congregations, schools and other institutions of youth socialization, and religious consumerism—translated into a broader network of suburban Orthodox Jewish communities across North America. Although happening within a broader homogenization of postwar metropolitan society, this continentalization of Orthodox Jewry remained based in a religious framework.

As the various chapters of this book show, the story of Orthodox Jewish suburbanization is fundamentally a story about community. In Chapter 7, the book considers the changing nature of community in North American life. Many observers have predicted the disappearance of community from contemporary metropolitan society, yet examples such as Orthodox Jews suggest that community is very much alive. Although stopping short of calling for an all-out return to religion, this chapter concludes that religion can and does—and perhaps even should—continue to serve as a fundamental basis for community life.

Finally, after laying out all that this book is, I must make clear to the reader what it is not. First, this story is neither a comprehensive religious history of the postwar Orthodox Jewish community nor is it a comprehensive history of postwar suburbia, although the outlines of both stories emerge in the process. I have used the history of Orthodox Jews in the second half of the twentieth century to make a particular point about the connection between religion and suburbia. If, in the process, I have glossed over internal differences within the Orthodox Jewish community, it is not because of ignorance of these differences but because they are tangential to the central themes of this book. Similarly, the concentration on religion in suburbia has meant that other aspects of the postwar suburban experience such as politics and economics are less prominent. In addition, those familiar with the specific history of Toronto and its Jewish community will find analyses of certain events or of major community leaders absent. For example, the Reichmann family is likely the most prominent Orthodox Jewish family in Toronto.[50] But as important as they have been for the suburbanization of the *ḥaredi* Orthodox Jewish community in Toronto, they have been less central to the wider story of the community's suburban expansion; thousands of individual Orthodox Jewish families suburbanized without any connection to the Reichmanns, and most of the synagogues and day schools discussed in this book developed largely outside of their financial orbit. Thus because of the orientation of this project as a "social history" of the suburban Orthodox Jewish community, I have deliberately avoided focusing on the elite few and have chosen instead to concentrate on the nonelite many.

But to concentrate on the absences in this book is to miss a fascinating story that weaves together themes of religion, community, and suburbanization. Throughout the pages, religion's mediating influence appears again and again, as it shaped Orthodox Jewish experiences in the middle-class suburban society of the late twentieth century. This fresh analysis pushes the current understanding both of traditionalist religious communities and of North American suburbia in new directions. The Orthodox Jews found in these pages present not romantic images of long beards and eighteenth-century dress but modern portraits of upwardly mobile, consumerist-driven suburbanites. Their story, then, is more than a story of the religious suburbanization of the North American Orthodox Jewish community. It is a story of how a traditionalist religious community established a religious subculture in the most secular of modern environments.

# Two

## SANCTIFYING

## SUBURBAN SPACE

In 1960, a columnist in the Toronto-based *Canadian Jewish News* reacted with some surprise to the increased "Hebrewization" of Bathurst Street, the central street on which many Jewish establishments had opened in suburban Toronto. Stores such as the Matana (Gift) Gift Shop and the Kol Toov (All That Is Good) Delicatessen testified that it had suddenly become "no novelty to see Jewish names and kosher insignia on rows of storefronts" on Bathurst.[1] Four decades later, Bathurst Street's Jewishness surprises few people in or out of the Jewish community. As one Toronto resident explained in 1995, Bathurst Street is to Toronto Jewry "what the Nile is to Egypt: a narrow strip of life with desert on both sides."[2] If anything is surprising about Bathurst Street, it is that the street's dense Jewish infrastructure is found not in an urban setting but in the sprawling geography of post–World War II suburbia. Since the early 1950s, Toronto's Jews have settled Bathurst Street in successive waves, continually pushing the Jewish frontier northward. But unlike Jewish relocation from urban to suburban areas that occurred in other North American cities during this period, the Jewish settlement of Bathurst Street in suburban North York did not follow the settlement-expansion-relocation-abandonment cycle so prevalent in other cities. That is, the development of newer Jewish areas of Bathurst Street did not come at the expense of older areas, but rather extended the existing areas of settlement northward. By the end of the twentieth century, Jewish neighborhoods strung out along Bathurst

Street like pearls on a necklace stretched for over eight miles in a progression from 1950s neighborhoods at the southern end to still uncompleted subdivisions in the middle of cornfields at the northern end.

How can one understand the evolution of this Jewish space in suburban Toronto? How did undistinguished suburban neighborhoods become transformed into vibrant landscapes of Jewish religion and culture? Or, to borrow a phrase from the geography of religion, how did these Jewish "sacred spaces" develop in the heart of postwar suburbia? Such questions are particularly appropriate to begin an inquiry into Orthodox Jewish suburbanization. Through an examination of the post–World War II creation of Bathurst Street as an Orthodox Jewish corridor, this chapter stresses the book's central theme that Orthodox Jewish suburbanization blended traditionalist religion with modern suburbia. Orthodox Jews clustered in middle-class neighborhoods adjacent to Bathurst Street and created an active and visible religious landscape along the street itself, thus defining a new sacred space in an otherwise mundane and secular environment.

In its traditional usage, "sacred space" refers to places with explicit religious sanctity such as a shrine or a holy city.[3] But there are other ways to understand sacred space. For example, the social spaces in which religious communities live also have a sacredness that, although not explicitly holy, is nevertheless essential to those communities.[4] Put differently, sacred space can include those socially and culturally constructed environments that are not necessarily associated with explicitly holy or religious events or objects.[5] Bathurst Street in postwar suburban Toronto and places like Cedar Lane in Teaneck, New Jersey, and Harvard Street in Brookline, Massachusetts, are such socially constructed sacred spaces.[6] Bathurst Street, after all, was never and still is not holy or religiously important to Orthodox Jews or any other religious group; it is a suburban traffic artery like that found in any North American city. Nevertheless, in the four-decade period following World War II, Orthodox Jewish residential concentration in the neighborhoods adjacent to Bathurst, together with the emergence of a visible Jewish landscape of synagogues, schools, and kosher food stores on the street itself, created an environment pervaded by religion and religious activities. Both inside and outside the Orthodox Jewish community, Bathurst Street became known as a Jewish space. In this process, the mundane suburban space of Bathurst was transformed into something that had symbolic meaning—a suburban sacred space. Moreover, the story of Bathurst Street makes it clear that for Orthodox Jews, suburbanization did not mean spatial dispersal and abandonment of religious practice. Rather, the creation of a new suburban sacred space consciously articulated an identity that combined adherence to tradition with a pattern of suburban mobility.

A Jewish presence in Toronto existed as early as the middle of the nineteenth century, when various Jewish individuals settled in what was then known as Upper Canada.[7] In 1832, governing British authorities granted full political and civil rights to the small community of Jews in the Canadian territories. By 1856, a Jewish community of mostly British origin had established itself in Toronto by forming a Hebrew cemetery and a synagogue, the forerunner to the present-day Holy Blossom Temple. Over the rest of the nineteenth century, the Jewish community grew slowly but steadily, although it remained a relatively marginal ethnic and religious group in an overwhelmingly Anglo-Protestant city. The community's small size precluded the development of any identifiable Jewish neighborhood, such as would emerge half a century later.

As in other cities across North America, rapidly increasing rates of Jewish immigration in the early twentieth century changed the spatial dynamics of Toronto's Jewish community. The city's Jewish population increased sixfold between 1901 and 1911 and then doubled in the next ten years (see Table 1).[8] Despite this rapid population growth, Toronto's Jews maintained compact residential patterns. In the initial wave of immigration at the beginning of the century, Jews settled in the "Ward," a few-square-block area between Yonge Street and University Avenue, just west of downtown and north of Lake Ontario. As the Jewish population grew, however, the neighborhood expanded westward, along Dundas and College Streets, across Spadina Avenue toward Bathurst Street. By the second decade of this century, the neighborhood known as Kensington had surpassed the Ward as the center of Jewish life.

Life in the Jewish district, as in many urban immigrant neighborhoods, was dense and compact and resembled classic "walking city" neighborhoods, where homes, businesses, shops, and institutions were in close proximity. No single area or street dominated the neighborhood, although certain specialized districts emerged. Kensington Market, a collection of streets just north of Dundas and Spadina, developed into the commercial center. The jumble of butchers, bakeries, dry goods stores, and other establishments made Kensington Market a vibrant Jewish street economy, similar to New York's Hester Street or Chicago's Maxwell Street.[9] Although by 1931 Jews still constituted less than 6 percent of Toronto's population, Kensington's residential, economic,

TABLE 1. Jewish Population of Greater Toronto, 1901–1991

| Year | Jewish population of metropolitan Toronto (including North York) | % of total metropolitan Toronto population | Jewish population of North York | % of total North York population |
|---|---|---|---|---|
| 1901 | 3,103 | 1.4 | – | – |
| 1911 | 18,294 | 4.5 | – | – |
| 1921 | 34,770 | 5.7 | – | – |
| 1931 | 46,751 | 5.7 | 16 | 0.1 |
| 1941 | 52,798 | 5.9 | 63 | 0.3 |
| 1951 | 66,773 | 6.0 | 3,989 | 4.6 |
| 1961 | 88,648 | 4.9 | 45,400 | 16.8 |
| 1971 | 106,000 | 5.1 | 70,635 | 14.0 |
| 1981 | 128,650 | 4.5 | 76,525 | 13.7 |
| 1991 | 162,605 | 4.6 | 67,480 | 12.0 |

*Sources*: Torczyner, Brotman, and Brodbar, *Rapid Growth and Transformation*, 7–8; DBS, *Eighth Census of Canada*, Table 38; DBS, *Ninth Census of Canada*, Table 1; DBS, *1961 Census of Canada*, Table 1; Statistics Canada, *1971 Census of Canada*, Table 1; Statistics Canada, *1981 Census of Canada*, Table 1; Statistics Canada, *1991 Census Profiles CD-ROM*.

and commercial concentration gave the Jewish community a much higher profile than this proportion would suggest.[10]

Kensington's dense Jewish life created an environment that the Orthodox Jewish community in particular considered a sacred space. All the religious, cultural, and social necessities an Orthodox Jew required could be found in Kensington. Here were the synagogues and religious schools, the kosher butchers and bakeries, the Jewish bookstores and the *mikvaoth* (ritual baths used by women following their monthly menstrual period; singular is *mikveh*). For Orthodox Jews whose lives were immersed in Kensington's religious infrastructure, any place north of Bloor Street—less than half a mile from the neighborhood's symbolic center at the intersection of College and Spadina—was "the end of the Jewish population."

The Orthodox Jews to whom the proximity of religious institutions mattered represented only a small percentage of Toronto's overall Jewish population. The majority of the city's Jews used Kensington's religious institutions on a less regular basis than did the Orthodox Jews. As such, they could religiously

*Spadina Avenue, looking north from Queen Street (just south of Kensington neighborhood), 1910. Ontario Jewish Archives.*

afford to separate themselves from the urban neighborhood and, in fact, it was the non-Orthodox Jewish population who first moved to suburbia in the late 1920s and early 1930s. In those years, demographic pressures spurred a movement away from Kensington. Continued immigration and natural population increases had made the Jewish neighborhood a "congested mass," and College Street was filled with an "almost impassable mass of human beings" on many Saturday nights.[11] In time, this bulging neighborhood began to spill northward, beyond Bloor Street and St. Clair Avenue into the newly developing municipalities of York Township and the village of Forest Hill.[12] The main traffic artery linking these new and old neighborhoods was Bathurst Street.

Between 1931 and 1951, the Jewish population in York Township and Forest Hill increased from twelve hundred to over eighteen thousand people, or almost one-third of the entire Jewish community.[13] This rapid relocation to neighborhoods around the Bathurst-Eglinton intersection occurred, however, without any significant Orthodox Jewish participation. Most Jewish institutions also remained in Kensington. By 1954 only five of the city's forty-eight synagogues lay north of St. Clair Avenue (see Map 3); the rest remained in the older downtown areas. Similarly, five of six social service agencies still maintained downtown addresses, as did six of eleven schools.[14] Although one cannot make an exact count, the majority of kosher food establishments were also located in the older neighborhoods.[15] The first wave of suburbanization in the 1940s, then, did little to restructure the geography of Toronto's Or-

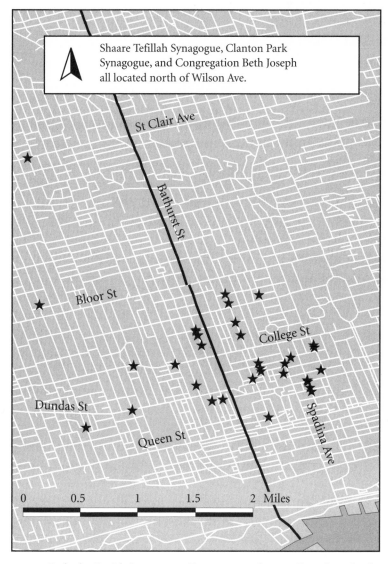

Shaare Tefillah Synagogue, Clanton Park
Synagogue, and Congregation Beth Joseph
all located north of Wilson Ave.

MAP 3. *Orthodox Jewish Synagogues, Toronto, 1954.* Source: *Rosenberg,* Study
of the Changes in the Geographic Distribution of the Jewish Population; 
Metropolitan Toronto City Directory *(1954).*

thodox Jewish community, which remained rooted in the sacred space of
Kensington.

Beginning in the early 1950s, a second wave of suburbanization to neighborhoods farther north did succeed in transforming Toronto's Orthodox Jewish religious geography. In this phase of religious suburbanization, the Ortho-

dox Jewish community moved not only its residences but its entire religious infrastructure to the new suburban environment (see Map 4). In so doing, the Orthodox Jewish community created a new sacred space along suburban Bathurst Street that replaced the declining and ultimately disappearing urban Kensington district.

In the years before World War II, few observers would have expected the township of North York to become home to a geographically and socioeconomically mobile Orthodox Jewish community. Through the mid-1940s, North York survived as a quiet, undeveloped, generally rural township a few miles north of Toronto. The community's roots as a farming center stretched back into the nineteenth century when the area was part of the larger York Township. In 1922 a contingent of rural residents voted in a plebiscite to separate from York and to incorporate as its own township.[16] Despite the incorporation, the town of North York remained relatively rural, with most of the twenty-three thousand residents concentrated in the central southern edge of the city abutting York Township and the village of Forest Hill and along the central strip of land on either side of Yonge Street. The township's population concentration was matched by its homogeneity. Like much of the Toronto area (and Canada in general), British Protestant ethnic groups dominated.[17] Religiously this translated into a heavy weighting toward Anglican and United Church affiliation, with a smaller presence of Presbyterians and Baptists. Other religious groups, including Jews and Catholics, were little represented through the 1940s (see Table 2).[18]

North York's settlement patterns derived largely from a combination of economic factors and natural geography.[19] In the late 1700s, land surveyors had created a vast checkerboard system of roads and landholdings. They spaced major north-south and east-west roads at one-and-a-quarter-mile intervals each. The grid system worked well for an agricultural economy because it granted each landholder access to at least one major transportation artery. Underneath this imposed geography lay the natural terrain, which, as might be expected, was far less rigid about its shape and format. In particular, the west and east branches of the Don River wound their way through the northern sections of North York, cutting deep ravines through the relatively flat landscape. Although streets were technically laid out across the ravines, the steep valleys often limited expansion in the spaces beyond and meant that North York's development did not occur evenly. Until the 1940s, only Yonge Street, the township's physical and economic central thoroughfare, experienced much suburban development. Streetcar and bus service on Yonge Street

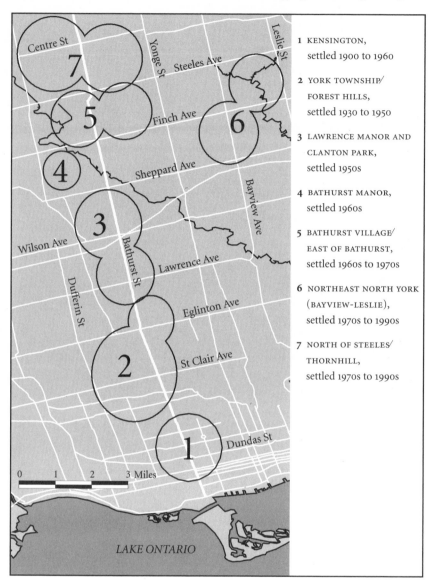

1 KENSINGTON,
  settled 1900 to 1960

2 YORK TOWNSHIP/
  FOREST HILLS,
  settled 1930 to 1950

3 LAWRENCE MANOR AND
  CLANTON PARK,
  settled 1950s

4 BATHURST MANOR,
  settled 1960s

5 BATHURST VILLAGE/
  EAST OF BATHURST,
  settled 1960s to 1970s

6 NORTHEAST NORTH YORK
  (BAYVIEW-LESLIE),
  settled 1970s to 1990s

7 NORTH OF STEELES/
  THORNHILL,
  settled 1970s to 1990s

MAP 4. *Stages of Jewish Settlement and Suburbanization, Toronto, 1900–2000*

facilitated residential development in neighborhoods just east and west of
Yonge. In contrast, most other areas of the township remained rural farmland
well into the 1940s.

North York's quietude came to an end as it emerged from the Depression
and World War II. The township found itself with a large stock of vacant land

TABLE 2. Religious Affiliation, North York, 1941–1991

| Denomination | 1941 N | 1941 % | 1951 N | 1951 % | 1961 N | 1961 % | 1971 N | 1971 % | 1981 N | 1981 % | 1991 N | 1991 % |
|---|---|---|---|---|---|---|---|---|---|---|---|---|
| Roman Catholic | 2,329 | 10.2 | 10,347 | 12.0 | 52,180 | 19.3 | 157,625 | 31.3 | 199,335 | 35.6 | 193,290 | 34.4 |
| Anglican | 8,813 | 38.5 | 26,934 | 31.4 | 56,918 | 21.1 | 77,345 | 15.4 | 58,845 | 10.5 | 39,380 | 7.0 |
| United Church | 6,403 | 28.0 | 27,193 | 31.7 | 62,564 | 23.2 | 75,810 | 15.0 | 59,125 | 10.6 | 33,715 | 6.0 |
| Jewish | 65 | 0.3 | 3,989 | 4.6 | 45,400 | 16.8 | 70,635 | 14.0 | 76,525 | 13.7 | 67,480 | 12.0 |
| Presbyterian | 2,561 | 11.2 | 8,032 | 9.4 | 18,908 | 7.0 | 29,505 | 5.9 | n/a | – | 13,640 | 2.4 |
| Lutheran | 330 | 1.4 | 1,342 | 1.6 | 9,000 | 3.3 | 15,255 | 3.0 | n/a | – | 7,970 | 1.4 |
| Baptist | 1,398 | 6.1 | 4,209 | 4.9 | 8,718 | 3.2 | 12,880 | 2.6 | n/a | – | 11,260 | 2.0 |
| Other or unaffiliated | 1,009 | 4.4 | 3,851 | 4.5 | 16,271 | 6.0 | 64,685 | 12.8 | 165,691 | 29.6 | 195,825 | 34.8 |
| Total North York population | 22,908 | 100.0 | 85,897 | 100.0 | 269,959 | 100.0 | 503,740 | 100.0 | 559,521 | 100.0 | 562,560 | 100.0 |

(n/a = not available)

Sources: DBS, Eighth Census of Canada, Table 38; DBS, Ninth Census of Canada, Table 1; DBS, 1961 Census of Canada, Table 1; Statistics Canada, 1971 Census of Canada, Table 1; Statistics Canada, 1981 Census of Canada, Table 1; Statistics Canada, 1991 Census Profiles CD-ROM.

that had been seized during the many fiscal crises of the previous decade. Township leaders recognized that this land could provide a desperately needed outlet for the growing housing shortage in Toronto and began to sell the lots to developers.[20] By 1947, North York was experiencing an unprecedented building boom, setting annual records for building permits and property assessments, which rose from $11 million in 1947 to over $40 million two years later.[21]

The building boom quickly caught up to Bathurst Street. Before the war, Bathurst had served as a secondary access road to dairy and produce farms that stretched across the northern part of North York Township. Only minimal suburban development occurred on the east side of Bathurst, but these neighborhoods were generally extensions of Yonge Street neighborhoods rather than originating from Bathurst. The rapid transformation of Bathurst Street began in 1950, when plans for the corridor's first major planned subdivision were unveiled. That spring, a consortium of the Canadian Mortgage and Housing Corporation, the Great West Life Assurance Company, and the Investor's Syndicate of Canada announced plans to build a $20 million, seventeen-hundred-unit housing complex on two farms at the northwest corner of the Bathurst-Lawrence intersection. The land, previously owned by the Mulholland family, was bought and subdivided by the CMHC and was serviced by the two insurance companies. The forty-five-foot-wide lots were then sold off to individual home builders, usually in blocks of ten. Although not as large as suburban projects elsewhere in Toronto, such as E. P. Taylor's Don Mills, Lawrence Manor showed the new direction of suburban development in the postwar era.[22] The incorporation of a twelve-acre shopping plaza into the residential project was a relatively new feature in suburban development. The neighborhood also featured other designs now commonly associated with suburbia: winding roads, a central neighborhood park, and limited external traffic access.[23]

The construction of Lawrence Manor set off a chain reaction of development up Bathurst Street. Aerial photographs, taken at yearly intervals over the metropolitan Toronto region, clearly showed the rapid progress in North York's development. For example, pictures in 1950 show the predominance of farmland along Bathurst, except for streets in Lawrence Manor that had been bulldozed and graded and awaited construction. By 1953, Lawrence Manor was completely built, and most of the lands between Lawrence and Sheppard Avenues showed signs of subdivision activity. Three years later, the Bathurst Manor subdivision north of Sheppard was well under way.[24] Within a decade and a half, virtually no large areas of undeveloped land remained in the entire

*Aerial photograph of the Bathurst-Lawrence intersection, 1969. Toronto Public Library, North York branch, Canadiana Room.*

Bathurst corridor, between Dufferin Street on the west and Yonge Street on the east, and from Eglinton Avenue to the northern North York boundary at Steeles Avenue.[25] In thirty years, this slice of North York had been transformed from a rural community of 3,400 people into a bustling metropolitan corridor of 93,000 people.[26]

The rapid growth on both sides of Bathurst Street seemed to overwhelm the street. The increase in residents brought an increase in traffic problems. Only after several accidents—one of them a hit-and-run killing of two schoolgirls—did the township install proper sidewalks along Bathurst.[27] By 1957, the street had become the third busiest traffic artery in metropolitan Toronto, with approximately thirty thousand vehicles traveling daily on only four paved lanes.[28] The newly built Toronto bypass highway (now known as Highway 401) added to the congestion with an interchange at Bathurst Street. The increased flow of traffic also magnified a major parking shortage on Bathurst. Curbside parking was simply not an option. Compounding the parking problem south of Wilson Avenue, many of the existing commercial

*Looking north on Bathurst Street at the intersection with Drewry Avenue, May 1958. Photograph by E. S. (Ted) Chirnside.*

properties fronting the street were built without any parking facilities, either in front of or behind the structures. Zoning regulators sought to encourage developers to build new strip mall–type properties with small parking areas, although such regulations concerned some Bathurst Street businessmen who thought that a "strung-out corridor" of stores would prevent the street from becoming a central business center.[29] Their fears were largely realized but not only because of the ribbonlike development. Uncoordinated zoning bylaws created an unregulated patchwork of storefronts, apartment houses, and mostly vacant lots. Hasty development forced zoning regulators to make quick decisions permitting a variety of uses with little regard for the street as a whole.[30] Such a mishmash of growth meant that, in the 1950s at least, a pre-suburban transportation route was being overrun by new forms of suburban commercial and residential development.

Into this reluctant and somewhat unprepared suburb, Toronto's Orthodox Jews, together with their non-Orthodox coreligionists, moved in the 1950s. To be sure, some Jewish settlement had occurred along the southern edges of the

*Looking north on Bathurst Street at the intersection with Drewry Avenue, June 1999. Leo Snowbell.*

township's border with Forest Hill and York Township in the 1940s. The 1951 census reported, for example, that the two southernmost census tracts along Bathurst Street contained two-thirds of the township's four thousand Jews.[31] But although they formally lived in North York, Jews in these areas formed no new religious institutions and remained tied to neighborhoods in Forest Hill and York Township and further south.

A more accurate starting point for the development of the Bathurst corridor is 1951, when Orthodox Jews formed the first suburban Jewish institution in North York. That year, a group of Jewish residents who had recently moved to the Lawrence Manor subdivision organized a small minyan for prayer services. Two of the congregation's founding members had canvassed the area to assemble enough men for services, which were initially held in the home of one of the members. As the congregation grew, it moved to a rented storefront, and by the late 1950s, Shaarei Tefillah Synagogue had hired a rabbi and had undertaken plans to construct a permanent synagogue building.[32] Shaarei Tefillah's success was followed in the next two decades by the formation of at least eight other built-from-scratch synagogues—Orthodox, Conservative, and Reform—in the neighborhoods adjacent to Bathurst. The success of these new congregations spurred many of the older synagogues located downtown to join the suburbanizing Jewish population up north, some merging with another congregation and others moving to their own location in the corridor.[33]

That North York's first Jewish congregation was Orthodox immediately highlights some of the differences between this wave of suburbanization and earlier migrations into York Township and Forest Hill, when Orthodox Jews did not actively relocate out of Kensington. Several factors accounted for the Orthodox presence in this second generation of suburbanizing Jews. In the four decades preceding World War II, Toronto's Orthodox Jewish community displayed a tendency to remain spatially tied to the established religious institutions in Kensington. They had little incentive or desire to recreate a new religious infrastructure in new suburban neighborhoods. In the years immediately before and after World War II, however, Toronto received a large influx of European refugees. This group had neither sentimental ties to particular neighborhoods nor any preconceived notions about the community's religious geography. Moreover, as a socioeconomic group they moved into the middle class soon after they arrived. Although this pattern contrasts with the stereotype of immigrants, one should not be surprised at this group's rapid upward mobility. Many of the Hungarian Jewish refugees had been highly successful businessmen and professionals before the war. Although many were stripped of their possessions by the tragedies of Europe, they came to Toronto with business acumen and a familiarity with financial success. Their relatively quick movement into the middle and upper-middle class, then, should be seen more as a return to an earlier way of life than as any drastic shift in socioeconomic status.[34] The prominent Reichmann family might be the best example of this experience, as they used business and family connections from Europe to build a global real estate empire based in Toronto.[35]

Presented with the opportunity to obtain new suburban housing, this group had no qualms about leaving their temporary residences in downtown neighborhoods for the fresh suburbs of North York, and in fact these nonnative Torontonians made up many of the early Orthodox Jewish suburbanites of the 1950s. For example, the founders of Clanton Park Synagogue included a large contingent of Hungarian and German Jews who came to Toronto immediately after the war, quickly established themselves in businesses or professions, and bought homes in the new neighborhoods along Bathurst Street.

Several of them also facilitated Jewish suburbanization as well by entering the construction and development business. Many of the houses in the neighborhood were built by synagogue members, and a survey of Clanton Park Synagogue shows that about one-quarter of members in the 1950s and 1960s were involved in the construction industry, including the Hofstedter and Rubinstein families, two Hungarian Jewish families who later built their firm into one of Toronto's leading real estate development companies.[36]

Toronto's native Orthodox Jews (those who had been in the city for at least a couple of decades) saw the recent immigrants' settlement and realized that movement away from the Jewish core was religiously possible. They recognized this at a time when other pressures, such as rising rents and an aging housing stock, were pushing Jews of all types out of Kensington. The suburban periphery offered a spacious environment and affordable housing; only the most stalwart of urbanites would have been able to resist the lure of the new neighborhoods. But moving to newly constructed subdivisions was a double-edged sword for Orthodox Jewish families because Jewish halakhah forbids any form of vehicular travel on the Sabbath and permits only travel by foot. Leaving the downtown neighborhoods meant that Orthodox Jewish families would move beyond walking distance of their former congregations. Still needing to attend services on the Sabbath, they had no choice but to create new congregations as soon as they settled in their new environment. By contrast, Conservative and Reform Jews whose Sabbath observances permitted vehicular driving could travel to their former neighborhoods to attend synagogue services. Thus, throughout the postwar period, non-Orthodox Jewish congregations generally formed only after suburban neighborhoods had been established, rather than as part of the initial settlement process.

By 1961, after only ten years of Jewish suburbanization, the overwhelming Jewishness—both Orthodox and non-Orthodox—of the Bathurst corridor had already become evident. That year, the census reported that the eleven census tracts abutting Bathurst Street contained forty-two thousand Jews, an increase of over 800 percent from a decade before. On the west side of Bathurst, four of the five tracts were more than 50 percent Jewish, and one of these tracts registered as more than three-quarters Jewish.[37] Despite their residential domination, Jews were not evenly scattered throughout the neighborhoods. A review of property assessment records from the 1950s shows that Jews tended to concentrate on certain streets in specific neighborhoods. For example, in the Clanton Park neighborhood on the west side of Bathurst between Wilson and Sheppard Avenues, Jewish families lived in 124 of 127 houses on Palm Drive and its adjacent side streets. Only two blocks to the north, however, Jewish households were entirely absent. In general, Jewish families tended to move to newly built streets and avoided moving onto blocks of existing homes. Between Finch and Steeles Avenues, for example, far more Jews moved into the newly constructed subdivisions on the west side of Bathurst than moved into the slightly older streets on the east side.[38]

By 1971, Jews had staked for themselves an even more clearly defined corridor along Bathurst Street, where they constituted the single largest ethnic or religious group in the Bathurst corridor.[39] Their dominance continued through the 1970s and into the 1980s, when Jews filled new Bathurst neighborhoods in Thornhill, the suburban municipality to the immediate north of the North York boundary at Steeles Avenue. Thornhill was home to the first subdivision conceived from the start to be a Jewish space. The Spring Farm community, built by developer Joseph Tannenbaum beginning in 1981, included a large Orthodox Jewish synagogue-cum-community center, a shopping plaza with kosher food stores, and a Jewish book and gift store.[40] By the late 1980s, forty-five Orthodox Jewish congregations were located on or adjacent to Bathurst Street.[41] In fact, in the five decades since World War II, only three new Orthodox Jewish congregations have been located outside the Bathurst corridor. Of these three, two failed to develop into major congregations, while the third was formed as an Orthodox Jewish outreach congregation targeted at non-Orthodox Jewish families.

Orthodox Jewish residential settlement in neighborhoods adjacent to Bathurst and the formation of local congregations were a first step in creating a sacred space along Bathurst Street. But homes and congregations alone did not create sacred space. For that to occur, other religious institutions were needed, institutions that would add to the visible religious activity of the district and to the sense that *this* was a Jewish neighborhood. This second stage of sacred space creation began in 1954, when the Jewish Old Folks Home (now Baycrest Center) moved to its present location at Bathurst and Baycrest Avenue. A year later, a branch of the Associated Hebrew Day School opened a block away at Bathurst and Neptune Drive. In time, other institutions joined these pioneers, including the Viewmount Street branch of Eitz Chaim Day School, which began operations in 1958; the community *mikveh* on Sheppard just west of Bathurst; and the city's first kosher restaurant, which opened just south of Baycrest and the Associated school that same year. As would be expected, these and other institutions increased the level of visible Jewish activity on Bathurst Street. A passerby on Bathurst could not help but see Jews of all types—and particularly Orthodox Jews—going to school, doing their shopping, or, on the Sabbath, walking to synagogue.

The visibility of this developing Jewish landscape was aided by a pattern of clustering among Jewish commercial establishments. Clustering was particularly important on a street such as Bathurst, which was generally inhospitable to the automobile. Because of parking difficulties on Bathurst itself, customers had to park on side streets and walk from store to store. By clustering, stores enabled shoppers to run their errands without having to return to their cars between stops.[42] The importance of store clusters, however, ran deeper than merely providing an easier shopping environment. Life in Kensington had bred a Jewish community geographically and culturally accustomed to a dense and compact religious infrastructure; the typical suburban pattern of dispersed commercial activity was foreign to many former urban residents. The commercial clusters along Bathurst, then, worked to integrate urban and suburban patterns of communal activity. After driving to the cluster and parking on a side street—a suburban pattern—Jewish shoppers could stop and chat with store owners or other shoppers in a manner common to urban environments. Moreover, because many of the stores had been previously located downtown, shoppers were already familiar with the shopkeepers and felt a continuity between Kensington and the new centers along Bathurst. By transplanting some stores, opening new ones, and mixing them with schools and synagogues, Toronto's Orthodox Jewish community recreated an infrastructure that serviced its religious and cultural needs, all in a geographic pattern commonly absent from main suburban roads. The result was a suburban-oriented road with urbanlike pedestrian activity, a religious landscape filled with "the business types in the pinstripes, the *chassid* with his *streimel* [large, black hat] and *capote* [black coat], the Orthodox matrons with their fashionable *sheitels* [wigs], the bicycle-riding yeshiva students with earlocks flapping in the wind—and the majority, the ordinary Jewish man and woman, shopping, conversing, going about their daily tasks."[43]

Given the large Jewish population in Kensington, it is surprising that the massive relocation of people and institutions northward to Toronto's suburbs provoked as little reaction as it did. In reviewing the *Canadian Jewish News* and the *Jewish Standard*, the two local Jewish newspapers, one finds very little critical analysis of what the personal and institutional abandonment of Kensington would do to the neighborhood. A rare comment was made by the editor of the *Canadian Jewish News* in 1961, in an editorial that focused on Toronto's suburbanization as a whole (not just that of the Jews.) The most recent census reported that the city of Toronto's population was only 40 percent British in heritage, down from 70 percent in 1951. The Jewish community had a dual role in this shift. As part of the "old guard" of ethnic groups with a long history in the city, second- and third-generation Jews were part of the northward migration into suburbia. At the same time, more recent European immigration from Hungary made Jews a large part of the "new guard" that moved downtown, at least initially. Because of this continual turnover of population in Kensington, the "Jewish community has much to gain by maintaining its identity with the 'historic' part of Toronto." Furthermore, the editorial continued, Toronto's Jews should avoid as much as possible becoming "linked exclusively with the outer ring of suburbs." In this last point, the editorial contrasted Toronto Jewry's connection to Kensington with Cleveland, where black migration into the inner city had made those neighborhoods "virtually *Judenrein* [free of Jews]."[44]

This comment was the exception. Synagogue records and newsletters and newspaper articles betrayed little feeling of hesitation or regret at suburbanization. Oral interviews with participants in the suburbanization process expressed similar feelings. Bathurst Street represented space, newness, and modernity, three characteristics lacking in the immigrant neighborhoods of Kensington. Perhaps it was the seeming inevitability of suburbanization, or perhaps it was the absence of conflict pushing Jews out of Kensington. As the editorial alluded to, Toronto had no influxes of African Americans to push Jews out of inner-city neighborhoods, as happened in New York, Boston, Cleveland, Indianapolis, and almost every other American city.[45] Moreover, unlike Protestant and Catholic communities undergoing suburbanization in the same period, the Jewish community lacked any institutional ties to the urban neighborhood.[46] Absent the perceived threats from inmigrating African Americans and any sense of "mission" to the neighborhood, there was little reason to express concern for those being "left behind." It was unstated, but likely felt, that eventually everyone in the Jewish community would come "up north," simply because that was where everyone was going.

Of course, not all Jews who left Kensington went to Bathurst Street. For some of Toronto's Jews, Bathurst was too Jewish. They interpreted the clustering of synagogues, schools, and stores and the extent to which Jews' daily lives overlapped with one another as insularity and cliqueishness rather than cohesion and community. In an open letter to the rest of the Jewish community, one Jewish housewife proudly described her family's decision not "to live in a self-made ghetto" such as Bathurst, but rather in a non-Jewish environment in Toronto's western suburbs. The advantages were many. For example, her children could be exposed to other cultural groups; her daughter attended Christmas parties and hosted non-Jewish friends at her Ḥanukkah parties. Moreover, when her Jewish friends got together, they did not fill their conversations with "daily trivia." "Perhaps we have to work a little harder to preserve our Jewish identity," she explained, "but we feel we have made the proper choice." Despite the letter's defiant tone, other comments hint at a yearning for Bathurst that the author may not have even realized. She noted the lack of good Jewish delicatessen and the need to chauffeur children to Jewish activities. Although the few Jewish families in the area formed a three-day-a-week Jewish education program, she recognized that Jewish education "could be another problem." Finally, she had few Jewish companions in her circle of friends. Such comments suggest the extent to which Bathurst had become embedded in the minds of Toronto's Jews. Even when portraying the neighborhood negatively, such critics could not help but recognize the community-building qualities of Bathurst Street.[47]

Bathurst's Jewishness did not go unnoticed in the non-Jewish world. Various sociological and demographic studies of Toronto's ethnic population noted the Jewish community's tendency to concentrate along the Bathurst Street corridor.[48] Bathurst's Jewishness was even mentioned in official North York planning documents. A 1985 study of the development needs of Bathurst described the corridor as one of the few "street-oriented" commercial strips behind which, both east and west, lay low-density, stable residential neighborhoods. The study noted that most of these street-oriented commercial uses "cater to the particular needs of the area's and the city's Jewish community. Jewish bookstores, kosher markets and delis are visible on virtually every block."[49]

One might have thought that in a predominantly Anglo-Protestant community as North York was in the 1950s and 1960s the rapid influx of Jews and the construction of a visible Jewish infrastructure along Bathurst Street would have raised anti-Jewish issues. In general, however, religious and political relations with other groups remained positive. At least nothing happened in Toronto that resembled the antisuburban synagogue lawsuits or zoning board controversies that occurred in suburban Cleveland in the 1950s or in Rockland County, New York, in the 1990s.[50] Instead, one finds examples of cooperation between Jews and non-Jews. For example, when it was initially founded, the Reform Temple Sinai rented space from the Asbury and West United Church on Bathurst Street. Later, after it moved into its own building, the synagogue occasionally joined with the church for combined ecumenical services.[51] When the Wilson Heights United Church closed in 1968, it transferred its building to Congregation Beth Meyer, a small Conservative Jewish synagogue in the area.[52] Jews integrated into North York's political world as well. Within a decade of their settlement in North York, Jews were being elected to the township's political bodies, and in 1972, voters chose the brash Mel Lastman as mayor, a job he held continuously for more than two decades.

Still, cordial and even friendly relations between Jews and Christians did not preclude occasional problems. One Friday night in November 1966, for example, a group of youths in North York beat up an Orthodox Jewish teenager who was walking home from a friend's house.[53] More prominent was the "Leiner Affair" four years earlier. One Friday night in January 1962, Rabbi Norbert Leiner, a teacher at the Orthodox Jewish Ner Israel Yeshiva, was stopped by police in the Bathurst–St. Clair neighborhood in York Township. The police in the area had been put on alert for a suspicious person whom neighborhood residents claimed was stalking the area. Although Rabbi Leiner looked nothing like the suspected stalker, the police nevertheless confronted him, used abusive language, and demanded that he enter their automobile. Rabbi Leiner refused, citing the Jewish Sabbath's prohibitions against riding in a vehicle. The officers pushed the rabbi into their car, drove him to the police station, and held him overnight. At the station, officers slapped Rabbi Leiner after he again refused to cooperate with fingerprinting and other procedures because of his Sabbath observances. Rabbi Leiner was released the next day when authorities admitted that he had been mistakenly apprehended.[54] Both the Jewish and non-Jewish press attacked the police for their actions, and a specially convened royal commission condemned the authorities for the incident. Although the arrest was not deemed anti-Semitic, the commission admonished the police for failing to understand or be sensitive to Rabbi Leiner's religious observances. At the same time, the commission did not spare Rabbi Leiner, criticizing him for not cooperating to the extent that he might have.[55] The "Leiner Affair," and other occasional assaults, reminded Jews that, though they might have dominated Bathurst Street, they were still a minority in an Anglo-Protestant environment.

Although many inside and outside the Orthodox Jewish community saw Bathurst as distinctly Jewish, it must be made clear that Bathurst's "sacredness" was neither universal nor universally relevant. The clusters of Orthodox Jewish neighborhoods, synagogues, schools, and stores created a sacred space that was meaningful only to those whose lives were connected to those neighborhoods, synagogues, schools, and stores. Throughout the entire postwar period, thousands of individuals—both non-Orthodox Jews and non-Jews—lived along Bathurst and remained generally unaffected by the Orthodox Jewish subculture. In fact, throughout the entire postwar period, only a small proportion of all stores, businesses, and other institutions on the street were Jewish. Even the dense clusters of Jewish bakeries, butchers, and restaurants shared their street frontages with non-Jewish enterprises. The street's many synagogues were joined by several churches situated on or immediately adjacent to Bathurst. For those who frequented these stores and institutions, Bathurst was a suburban traffic artery and little more; the Orthodox Jewish infrastructure had little real or symbolic value. The same was true for Orthodox Jewish centers in other metropolitan areas. For example, in Rockland County, New York, which developed in the 1970s, 1980s, and 1990s into one of the largest concentrations of suburban Orthodox Jews, Jews accounted for less than one-quarter of the county's population. Even in dense urban neighborhoods such as Brooklyn's Crown Heights, Jews were a minority. In fact, as late as 1990, only one county in the United States even had a plurality of Jews, that being Palm Beach County in South Florida.[56] The point, then, is that sacred space is neither exclusive nor all-encompassing. The same spaces that some people—usually insiders—recognize as "Jewish" might have absolutely no relevance to someone else. As Vivian Klaff noted in 1987, "We need to be careful not to confuse the concentration of Jews in an area with the Jewishness of an area. In fact, in most areas for which the data point to a concentration of Jewish population, the population is generally a minority in the area."[57] But the presence and even predominance of non-Jews and non-Jewish institutions on Bathurst and in the many other centers of suburban Orthodox Jewry does not negate the concentration of Orthodox Jews and Orthodox Jewish institutions in those same places. The fact remained that, in all of Toronto, Bathurst Street was where Orthodox Jews lived and practiced their religion. For the hundreds of families who moved into houses in the neighborhoods adjacent to Bathurst Street and for the dozens of store owners who located their businesses on the street itself, the sacredness was obvious even though it was not universal.

But the clustering of Orthodox Jewish families and businesses along Bathurst Street is not the only evidence that Bathurst Street held special significance for the Orthodox Jewish community. Another source can be found in the ways urban synagogues undertook the process of relocation to suburbia. When it was founded in the early 1930s, Shaarei Shomayim Synagogue was located at the northwestern edges of Jewish settlement on St. Clair Avenue between Bathurst and Dufferin Streets. After some financial delays, the congregation built an imposing edifice on Winona Avenue in the mid-1940s and established itself as the dominant Orthodox Jewish synagogue in Toronto. Its prominence was helped by the membership of many of the Jewish community's elite and by its location near upper-middle-class neighborhoods just north of the synagogue. Unfortunately for Shaarei Shomayim, the Jewish exodus to suburbia began only a few years after the congregation had dedicated its sanctuary. The newer suburban neighborhoods in North York and the new Orthodox Jewish congregations in the Bathurst corridor attracted many young, religiously observant families who years before might have moved into the Shaarei Shomayim area.

For the most part, Shaarei Shomayim weathered this initial northward push through the 1950s. By the end of that decade, however, it had become clear to the synagogue's leadership that because of its location on St. Clair, Shaarei Shomayim was losing its viability as a Jewish center. The congregation, through its executive board, actively began to debate the question of congregational relocation. The possibility of relocating was first broached at an April 1957 board meeting. Some at the meeting questioned the need for moving, especially when most members had not moved northward yet. In addition, the membership had a "vested interest" in the present St. Clair location, where, as one board member trumpeted, the synagogue had given "inestimable service and value to the general Jewish community and to its own members." On the other side, those favoring a move pointed to the success of the Orthodox Jewish synagogues that had emerged north of Wilson Avenue. In particular, this faction saw the Bathurst-Sheppard area as "fertile ground" for the "expansion of Orthodox ideology" through a "progressive, modern Orthodox synagogue." Unstated but implicit in this argument was the inevitability of northward migration along Bathurst Street; the congregation simply *had* to move.[58]

Over the next four years, the issue of relocation arose several more times. Board members repeatedly stressed that a "prestigious" congregation like Shaarei Shomayim needed to move northward to ensure access to a "middle class" and "relatively well-to-do" membership and to maintain its place as the community's "leading" Orthodox Jewish synagogue.[59] By the fall of 1962, however, the board's discussion had clearly changed from a matter of "if and why" to "where and when." The answers to both questions came quickly, when the synagogue obtained a large lot on Glencairn Avenue, just east of Bathurst, about three miles north of the existing St. Clair building. After a dis-

*Groundbreaking ceremony, Shaarei Shomayim Synagogue, 13 September 1964.*
*Shaarei Shomayim Synagogue.*

pute with a local neighborhood group over the presence of a synagogue was resolved, construction began in September 1964. The first Shabbat services were held on 10 September 1966, and within a year, the St. Clair branch closed and all synagogue activities relocated to the Glencairn and Bathurst site.[60]

Shaarei Shomayim's relocation experience reflected the extent to which Bathurst Street had become the core space for Toronto's Orthodox Jewish community. From the start, Shaarei Shomayim's leaders recognized that if they had to relocate, there was only one place to do so: suburban Bathurst Street. The presence of other successful Orthodox Jewish congregations and of other Jewish institutions such as schools and kosher food stores convinced Shaarei Shomayim's leaders that the future of the Orthodox Jewish community was rooted in Bathurst Street. There was no discussion of Shaarei Shomayim moving elsewhere in suburban Toronto and hoping then to attract Orthodox Jews. Instead the congregation looked to the growing numbers of young, middle-class, religiously observant families who had settled in the Bathurst corridor and knew that that space would be the backbone of the Orthodox Jewish community for decades to come.

Just as Shaarei Shomayim's relocation to Bathurst Street highlighted the Orthodox Jewish community's sacred space, the experiences of other Orthodox Jews who moved away from Bathurst told the same story. In the early 1970s, when the Bathurst Street corridor was fully built to the North York border at Steeles Avenue, the Orthodox Jewish community faced a bit of a problem. The disappearance of available land meant that housing costs began to increase.[61] Now, many young families, who had been the Orthodox Jewish community's backbone of settlement along Bathurst Street, had to look elsewhere for affordable housing. A small portion of them looked eastward to the northeast part of North York where non-Orthodox Jewish settlement had been occurring for some time. Although removed from the sacred space of Bathurst Street, these families assumed that despite their divergence from the corridor, they could create a new religious infrastructure that would extend the sacred space eastward. As their story showed, they were wrong.

In September 1971, a group of Jewish families who had moved to neighborhoods along Leslie Street between Finch and Steeles Avenues began to hold Orthodox services in the home of one of the group. Two years later, the now-named Shaare Zion Congregation moved to a portable trailer that sat on the lawn of one of the members. Expecting continued growth, the group began to look for a more permanent home and in March 1975 received permission from the local residential association to erect a building. Neither the growth nor the building ever came. In 1981, the congregation had expanded to only forty-four members and still met in the trailer. Even the hiring of a rabbi in 1980 and the affiliation with the National Council of Young Israel, a North American Orthodox synagogue organization, failed to spur growth. By the mid-1980s, the congregation moved into space in a new building of the Associated Hebrew Day School on Leslie Street, but despite the efforts of a small but dedicated core of membership, the congregation remained far smaller than its founders had originally anticipated.[62]

One major street closer to Bathurst on Bayview Avenue, a second Orthodox Jewish congregation developed with a marginally better outcome. In the mid-1970s, a small contingent of South African Jews moved to Toronto and settled, not in the Bathurst corridor but east of Bathurst around the intersection of Bayview and Sheppard Avenues. Wanting to preserve the traditions of the community left behind, this group organized a regular Friday evening Shabbat service that soon became known as the "South African minyan." By the fall of 1979, the congregation held High Holiday services in one of the apartment complexes where some members lived. One year later, the Kehillat Shaarei Torah, as the South African minyan became known, hired a full-time rabbi.[63] As had Shaare Zion, the congregation worked to find a permanent building so they would not have to meet in a nearby junior high school. Despite disagreements with local neighborhood groups over the noise and traffic a synagogue building was expected to generate, the congregation completed a new sanctuary by 1986.[64] Despite its building, however, Shaarei Torah never attracted a large enough membership to make it a major force in the Orthodox Jewish community.

There would seem to be nothing out of the ordinary in the history of these congregations that precluded their success. Most new synagogues in the suburban environment were built-from-scratch congregations that started with a small group and grew into more complete institutions, a model that fit both of these synagogues. Yet neither synagogue made that step from small congregation to mature institution. Moreover, a broader religious infrastructure never developed in North York's northeast neighborhoods; not a single kosher butcher, bakery, grocery store, or restaurant opened in the area, and the only day school to be built attracted a largely non-Orthodox Jewish student population. In contrast, the other stages of Toronto's Orthodox Jewish suburbanization brought with them new stores and schools to serve the expanding population.

The explanation for this failure was, to quote many a real estate agent, location. Simply put, the northeast neighborhoods were not in the Bathurst corridor. All of the earlier waves of Orthodox Jewish suburbanization had occurred along Bathurst Street. The string of neighborhoods that developed along this corridor was seen as a single entity. One might have lived further north or south but at least one lived *on* Bathurst. In the terminology of the urbanist Kevin Lynch, Bathurst Street acted like a "path" that connected various "districts" or neighborhoods into a single community.[65] The northeast congregations, located parallel to Bathurst on Bayview Avenue and Leslie Street, lacked this geographical connection to the central community space. Even though the northeast neighborhoods were physically closer to the religious infrastructure on Bathurst Street than the original Orthodox Jewish suburbanites had been to Kensington downtown, the distances were perceived as being much greater. Living parallel to Bathurst meant that one had to travel in an east-west plane to reach the religious infrastructure, a psychologically difficult prospect in a city where a north-south mentality had long dominated growth. In Lynch's terms, the north-south streets between Bathurst and the northeast neighborhoods acted as "edges" dividing neighborhoods rather than as "paths" joining them. To live in northeast Toronto and to drive to Bathurst meant to leave one neighborhood and go to another; one felt no sense of continuity between the two places. To a degree, the Orthodox Jews who moved to the northeast anticipated some of these problems. In September 1981, for example, Rabbi Eliot Feldman of Shaarei Torah admitted that his Orthodox congregation "is itself a great wonder, for the area of Leslie and Sheppard is not known for being a place for observant Jews."[66] As it happened, it did not become one either; the attraction of Bathurst Street proved too strong.

A final example of the Orthodox Jewish community's relationship to Bathurst Street is found in the history of Toronto's *eruv*. According to Jewish religious law, an observant Jew is forbidden to carry any object in public property on the Sabbath. Carrying is permitted only in private space. This restriction can be circumvented, however, with the construction of an *eruv*, a fence or enclosure that encircles the public space and, in religious legal terms, transforms that space into private property. A proper *eruv* permits a range of activities on the Sabbath that would otherwise be prohibited, such as carrying food and pushing baby strollers. While to those not familiar with the Sabbath prohibitions, being able to carry a tissue to synagogue might seem trivial, for others the presence of an *eruv* is more serious. For example, an Orthodox Jewish woman in Twin Rivers, New Jersey, explained, "I have a 17½ year-old son who has to be pushed in a wheelchair. To go to synagogue [without the *eruv*] I have to hire a nurse at $30 an hour with a four-hour minimum. That's $120 if I want to go to the synagogue."[67]

Although an *eruv* is entirely irrelevant to those outside the Orthodox Jewish community (excepting the small numbers of non-Orthodox Jews who observe the Sabbath prohibitions against carrying), the presence of an *eruv*, or proposals to build one, can spark controversies. Opponents often reject an *eruv* for practical reasons such as lower property values or aesthetic reasons. But other feelings have simmered close to the surface and occasionally have bubbled over. For example, a historic preservationist in London, England, claimed that a proposed *eruv* in the Golder's Green neighborhood "affronted every other sect by insisting on imposing a series of poles and wires" on the area. But, perhaps betraying his true feelings, the same man wondered whether a "totem pole" would be next. In Twin Rivers, New Jersey, in 1997, one protester explained his opposition to the *eruv* quite rationally: "You might have a legal right to put it up but not a moral right," he said. But he quickly lost credibility when he asked, "What happens when the black community wants to put Kwanzaa around the community? What do we do then?" Opposition came not only from outside the Jewish community. Sometimes non-Orthodox Jews expressed concern that the *eruv* would result in too many "visible Jews" moving to the area. One Holocaust survivor feared that the *eruv* would create another "Williamsburg," referring to the Ḥasidic Jewish neighborhood in Brooklyn. Another likened the *eruv*'s posts and wires to those in the Auschwitz concentration camp.[68]

This last reaction, a rejection of an *eruv* because of the presence of unsightly wires and poles, is not uncommon. Many people who hear about a proposed *eruv* fear that it will "fence them in." One woman in London was horrified by the thought that a post would go "right next to" her neighbor's house. Were these opponents to know how an *eruv* is actually constructed, they would realize how laughable their fears were. In reality, an *eruv* is a rather mundane and unexciting technology. Often, the *eruv* is "built" with existing utility wires around the perimeter of an area. In some cases, religious authorities have allowed major highways or train tracks to be considered part of an *eruv*, since they can act as enclosures of a particular space.[69] Where existing wires or other natural boundaries are absent, new wires and poles have to be erected, usually in consultation with utility companies, which permit wires to be attached to their poles. However the construction, an *eruv*'s structure is almost always unnoticeable except to those who know the locations of the particular poles and wires.

But even if most Orthodox Jews do not know the exact dimensions and location of their local *eruv*, they recognize that its very existence is an essential part of Orthodox Jewish community life. Because an *eruv* delineates the area where carrying is permissible on the Sabbath, its boundaries will generally parallel the boundaries of Orthodox Jewish settlement. Orthodox Jewish families will usually seek to live only within an *eruv* because doing so makes Sabbath observances easier than they would be outside the *eruv*. Furthermore, if enough Orthodox Jewish families live outside an existing *eruv*, the *eruv* is often expanded to include this contingent. The erection of an *eruv*, then, involves the literal creation of sacred space, since it demarcates the area within which—and outside of which—certain religious behaviors are permissible or prohibited.[70]

In Toronto, the *eruv*, as initially set up by Rabbi Abraham Price before World War II, extended only as far north as Bloor Street. This boundary sufficed because an overwhelming majority of the observant community lived south of Bloor and would have had no reason to carry objects on the Sabbath north of the *eruv*. Throughout the postwar period, however, the *eruv* was extended as necessary to encompass the areas of Orthodox Jewish settlement.

For example, in 1951, the *eruv* was extended to Wilson Avenue, at that point the northern limit of Jewish settlement. Over the next decade, Orthodox Jews moved further north, and in 1966, another adjustment brought the boundaries all the way north to Steeles Avenue, the outer edge of North York. Later, when Orthodox Jews began to move into neighborhoods in northeast North York and in Thornhill directly north of North York, the *eruv* was extended again.[71] With each extension, the *eruv* eased certain Sabbath difficulties for Orthodox Jewish families. More important, each extension repeated the process of spatial sanctification; each new area became integrated into a single "religious space." Not coincidentally, at the core of this space stood Bathurst Street, with its blend of middle-class subdivisions full of Orthodox Jews and their synagogues and strip malls full of kosher food stores and restaurants.

As much as it organized the sacred space of Toronto's Orthodox Jewish community along Bathurst Street, the *eruv* also became a point of conflict within that community in the 1980s. Although most of Toronto's Orthodox Jews abided by Rabbi Price's *eruv*, those within the *ḥaredi* community tended not to, both out of a specific concern for the correctness of Rabbi Price's *eruv* and a more general practice of not relying on any *eruv* to permit carrying on the Sabbath. Through the 1980s, this division remained generally unarticulated and simmered below the surface of intra–Orthodox Jewish community relationships. The status quo changed, however, when Rabbi Jacob Sofer, a rabbi brought in by the Reichmann family to lead one of the synagogues that they supported, publicly announced that Rabbi Price's *eruv* was faulty and to carry on the Sabbath within his *eruv* would violate Sabbath law. Immediately, Rabbi Price's defenders, and Rabbi Price himself, published defenses demonstrating the halakhic reliability of the *eruv*. Most of Toronto's Orthodox Jews did not stop carrying on the Sabbath because of Rabbi Sofer's pronouncement, but the damage was already done. Although not declaring Rabbi Price's *eruv* invalid, the Va'ad HaRabbonim, one of Toronto's Orthodox Jewish rabbinical councils, ruled that Rabbi Sofer could erect his own *eruv*.[72] By the early 1990s, soon after Rabbi Price died, a new *eruv* was constructed with the backing of the *ḥaredi* community. The irony of the entire episode was that the differences between the two *eruvim* were minor and mostly concerned the outer boundaries where few Orthodox Jews lived. In both cases, the central Bathurst Street corridor and the adjacent neighborhoods were squarely inside. But if it articulated the cleavages between the *ḥaredi* and centrist Orthodox Jewish communities in Toronto, it also pointed to their spatial similarities. Both groups lived along that same narrow suburban corridor and, despite the differing interpretations of the margins of the community's sacred space, neither showed any hint of loosening those spatial ties.

The debates within the Orthodox Jewish community over the definition of sacred space, as well as Bathurst Street's invisibleness, or at least its irrelevance, to a large proportion of Toronto's population suggest the extent to which the Orthodox Jewish community has blended into the broader suburban society. Although they had built a thriving religiously traditional subculture, they had done so in the context of the secular host culture. The postwar Orthodox Jews in suburban Toronto chose not to isolate themselves in an insulated enclave, away from the city or in some way independent from the city. Instead, they built their religious infrastructure right in the heart of postwar suburbia, in neighborhoods that were never exclusively composed of Orthodox Jews and on a street that was never exclusively populated by religious institutions and businesses. Their lives were suburban as much as they were Orthodox Jewish, and the space of Bathurst Street was both suburban *and* sacred.

Ultimately, the sacredness of Bathurst Street derived not from any intrinsic holiness but from the institutions and activities of Toronto's suburbanizing Orthodox Jewish community. The new congregations that formed, the schools that were built, the kosher food stores and Jewish bookstores all contributed to Bathurst's Jewish identity. In each of these areas—the formation of congregations, the development of institutions of religious socialization, and the creation of a religious consumer infrastructure—Orthodox Jews combined an adherence to traditionalism with an acceptance of modern secular styles, although each developed at its own pace with its own historical peculiarities. It is to the first of these processes, the formation of new suburban Orthodox Jewish congregations, to which we turn in the following chapter.

# *Three*

## RELIGIOUS

## PIONEERING ON

## THE SUBURBAN

## FRONTIER

"Suburbia may not seem like much of a place to pioneer, but for young, religiously committed Jewish families, it's open territory."[1] These words, spoken in the early 1970s by an Orthodox Jew who had helped to found a new synagogue in suburban Toronto, might bring to mind some bizarre image of Gene Wilder's *Frisco Kid* transplanted to the front lawns of Levittown. But strange as it might seem, the experience of Orthodox Jewish suburbanization fits a long historical pattern of North Americans using religion to help tame the frontier, wherever that frontier may have been. In seventeenth-century New England, Puritan colonists made religious congregations central to their settlement. In the 1800s, Methodist circuit riders brought periodic bursts of religion to isolated settlements in the American West, setting up makeshift churches and offering an assortment of religious services for the surrounding population, including baptisms, conversions, marriages, funerals, and general religious instruction. In so doing, circuit-riding preachers made life on the frontier ever so slightly more bearable for the scattered pioneers.[2]

But if religious groups have historically helped to pioneer the frontier, they also have historically lost their religious zeal once the hardships of isolation have been overcome.[3] Hard-line seventeenth-century Puritans evolved into liberal nineteenth-century Congregationalists, and those same frontier Methodists settled down within a few decades into a respectable mainstream denomination that lacked the religious fervor of an earlier generation. As described by Roger Finke and Rodney Stark, the combination of affluence, higher levels of education, and professionalization of the clergy almost always led successful religious movements to "shift their emphasis toward this world and away from the next, moving from high tension with the environment toward increasingly lower levels of tension." Or, as Cotton Mather eloquently wrote two centuries earlier, "Religion brought forth prosperity, and the daughter destroyed the mother." [4]

Although not quite as romantic as the forests of colonial New England or the mining towns of Colorado, the suburbs of major North American cities have been the frontier lands of the late twentieth century. [5] And although less well known than the Puritans or the Methodist circuit riders, Orthodox Jews were important religious pioneers in these new environments. These parallels end abruptly, however, when one compares the different trajectory taken by Orthodox Jews and by earlier pioneers in their respective new environments. Whereas most religious pioneers declined in religious intensity and fervor as their cultural entrenchment increased, suburbanizing Orthodox Jews proceeded in the exact opposite direction. For this group, cultural entrenchment led not to a softening of religious practice but to an increase in religious observance. After the first generation of pioneering suburban Orthodox Jews adapted their religious congregations to new suburban styles, subsequent generations of *suburbanized* Orthodox Jews retreated from those initial adaptations and sought instead to root their congregations and communities within older traditions. More important, they did so even as they were achieving considerable material success and gaining communal strength. Thus, rather than "destroying the suburban mother," as Cotton Mather might have predicted had he lived in the late twentieth century, the suburban Orthodox Jewish community, through its religious congregations, retained and strengthened its sense of traditionalist religious observance even as it became more integrated into the suburban environment.

As discussed in the previous chapter, the opening of North York to suburbanization in the 1950s provided a welcome outlet for thousands of Torontonians looking for more modern and spacious homes than could be found in older urban neighborhoods. In a string of neighborhoods running north along Bathurst Street, as well as along other major north-south arteries in the suburban township, new subdivision construction seemed to emerge overnight. [6]

The speed with which many of these new neighborhoods were built con-tributed to a pioneering atmosphere on the suburban periphery. In many cases, new homeowners lacked even the most basic amenities. In exchange for an affordable house, suburbanites often had to forgo paved streets and side-walks, sodded lawns, or phone service for a period of time. Stories of this hard-ship were many. Lillian Silverberg, an early resident of the Palm Drive sub-division, recalled walking several blocks just to pick up her mail. One of her neighbors, Bill Rubinstein, found out that his wife gave birth only when the nurse called him on the street's single public pay phone. Max Neuberger re-membered the "swamp" along Faywood Avenue, where baby carriages were submerged in the mud and dust of unpaved sidewalks.[7] The difficulties of sub-urbanization were confirmed repeatedly in articles in North York's local pa-per, the *Enterprise*, which reported in 1950, for example, how moving trucks on Southgate Avenue had to be extricated from the mud-filled street.[8] Despite these difficulties, Torontonians poured out of urban neighborhoods and into the newly erected subdivisions along Bathurst Street and elsewhere in North York. Like millions of their anonymous counterparts in major metropolitan regions across North America, North York's new residents relocated to the suburban periphery, seeking affordable and spacious homes and participating in the new middle-class, consumerist, suburban way of life of the 1950s.

Among the thousands of suburban pioneers in North York were members of Toronto's Orthodox Jewish community, lured by the prospect of a new home and open space. For this community, however, suburbanization pre-sented a religious challenge. Bound by religious prohibitions against driving to synagogue on the Sabbath or Jewish holidays, Orthodox Jewish families would not have wanted to move too far from their existing synagogues back in Kensington. Moreover, Toronto's *eruv*, which eased Sabbath observance by permitting carrying, had not yet been extended to the northern neighbor-hoods of Bathurst Street. Those who moved to the new suburban neighbor-hoods had, in a religious sense, expanded beyond the Jewish community's boundaries. Having relocated themselves to a religious wilderness but com-pelled by religious needs to maintain a nearby synagogue, Toronto's subur-banizing Orthodox Jews in the early 1950s worked to create new congre-gations. In the three main neighborhoods of Orthodox Jewish settlement, three large Orthodox Jewish congregations were formed: Shaarei Tefillah Synagogue, Clanton Park Synagogue, and Torath Emeth Jewish Centre (see Map 6). Each shared roughly the same formation experiences, meeting ini-tially in members' homes, moving to larger rented premises as the congrega-tions grew, and finally raising enough money to erect a permanent synagogue

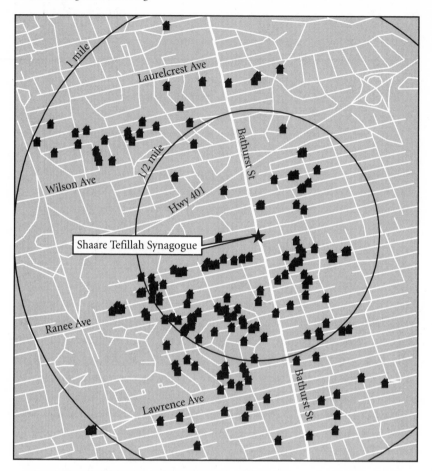

MAP 5. *Shaarei Tefillah Synagogue Membership, 1957.*
Source: *Shaarei Tefillah Synagogue.*

building. Because of their similarity of origin, a brief history of one of them, Clanton Park Synagogue, will suffice in representing this trajectory.

In the early 1950s, an Orthodox Jewish businessman opened a Hebrew school at the corner of Bathurst and Edinburgh Road. Wanting to add a synagogue to the institution, he organized a small weekly minyan with participants from Orthodox Jewish families who had moved to the new subdivisions on either side of Bathurst Street. As the informal minyan grew, a disagreement erupted in the group over payment of rent. One faction broke away in 1954 and began to convene for services in the basement of Sam and Sarah Kideckel's home on Southgate Avenue.[9] Within a year, this minyan formally constituted itself as Clanton Park Synagogue, named for a neighborhood

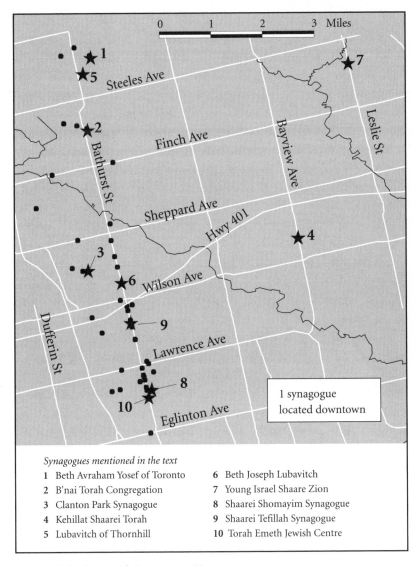

0    1    2    3  Miles

Steeles Ave

Finch Ave

Bathurst St

Bayview Ave

Leslie St

Sheppard Ave

Hwy 401

★4

3

★6  Wilson Ave

Dufferin St

★9

Lawrence Ave

8

10

Eglinton Ave

1 synagogue
located downtown

*Synagogues mentioned in the text*

| | | | |
|---|---|---|---|
| 1 | Beth Avraham Yosef of Toronto | 6 | Beth Joseph Lubavitch |
| 2 | B'nai Torah Congregation | 7 | Young Israel Shaare Zion |
| 3 | Clanton Park Synagogue | 8 | Shaarei Shomayim Synagogue |
| 4 | Kehillat Shaarei Torah | 9 | Shaarei Tefillah Synagogue |
| 5 | Lubavitch of Thornhill | 10 | Torah Emeth Jewish Centre |

MAP 6. *Orthodox Jewish Synagogues, Toronto, 1995.*
Source: *Toronto Jewish Orthodox Community Directory, 5755.*

park. That year, the congregation held its weekly services in the Kideckels'
basement and its High Holiday services in the Wilson Heights Gardens Social
Hall. A sense of permanency was reinforced with the hiring of Rabbi Morris
Gorelick as a full-time rabbi in 1956.[10]

After a few months of meeting in the Kideckels' basement, the congregation realized that it would soon outgrow its premises. Members of the congre-

gation worked with North York Township officials to obtain an available plot of land on Lowesmoor Avenue, in the heart of the Clanton Park neighborhood.[11] The purchase of a building site and the erection of a building were two entirely separate matters, however. A shortage of funds constantly plagued the new congregation's efforts to construct a permanent building. "None of us had any money," recalled Sandy Hofstedter, one of the synagogue's earliest members.[12] The congregation devised numerous fund-raising activities, including Monte Carlo Casino nights and a "Buy a Brick" plan, through which members bought symbolic bricks for the new building. Nevertheless, the congregation often found itself short of cash. According to Sol Edell, one of the synagogue's founders, construction was sometimes arranged on a day-to-day basis. The congregation "paid the workmen by COD, by the day. We used to drive around at night, we picked up $50, $100, $25. If we didn't have the money, they didn't come to work." In this financial bind, Clanton Park Synagogue was able to build only its social hall by 1958. Three more years passed before the congregation raised enough money to erect its sanctuary.[13] The founding of Clanton Park fit well with the spirit of the 1950s suburbia. After all, here were thousands of new homeowners, who were engrossed in domesticating their new homes and new neighborhoods; transferring this pioneering spirit to a new religious congregation seemed a logical next step.

The "do-it-yourself," grassroots style of Clanton Park's founding and its reliance on internal dynamics to organize and finance its growth also fit into the historical model of Jewish synagogue development, which emphasized congregational independence and the absence of ecclesiastical or denominational oversight. For much of Jewish history, and particularly in North America, each congregation was free to develop as it wanted, to choose its own rabbinical leaders, and to create its own organizational structure. Such congregational freedom differed from the more systematic approach to suburban church expansion found in many Christian denominations that were more denominationally centralized, bureaucratic, and hierarchical. In general, Christian denominations approached suburban church expansion from a religious belief in mission and from a denominational desire to increase membership. At times, the latter concern seemed to overwhelm any religious imperatives of church growth. In the 1949 Report of the Toronto Home Missions Council, the Reverend J. C. Torrance, the council's secretary, reported, "Greater Toronto is bursting at the seams . . . [and] unless the Church gets into each of these new developments at its initial stages, it discovers later that the most desirable sites [are] taken" by other denominations.[14] In 1951, a representative of the Presbyterian Church's Synod of Toronto lamented his denomination's slow effort at church extension. "There is an urgency about the extension projects," he wrote. "If the need is not met now—it may be questioned whether it will ever be met—we will have failed because of too little too late." [15] Two years later, he worried that a failure to respond to suburban growth would "jeopardize the future in Canada" of the Presbyterian Church.[16]

To ensure a presence in suburbia, most denominations established official church extension committees to oversee the development process. The Presbyterian Church in Canada maintained an active "Christian Outreach" program, while the United Church of Canada established a Toronto Home Missions Council as a local parallel to international foreign missions activities. By establishing centralized church extension committees, Christian denominations created a top-down planning approach to congregational formation that was absent in Jewish congregational planning. This top-down approach was far more natural for churches than it was for synagogues, given the tradition in many denominations of a strong centralized church hierarchy. Both the Anglican Church and the Catholic Church purchased church sites in advance of the suburbanizing population. Then, when a sufficient population settled the neighborhood, the diocese installed a parish priest and organized a service, often in a home, a local school, or portable trailers.[17] Over time, the congregation assumed the financial responsibility for planning a permanent building, although all decisions were ultimately approved by the central office. The central offices of the Lutheran Church, United Church, and Presbyterian Church also helped to organize congregations but usually did so only after a neighborhood was developed rather than before.[18] Most of these centralized denominations also maintained standards for congregational development, including minimum lot sizes, proper parking space-to-member ratios, and pew-to-member ratios.[19]

Although the process of new suburban congregational formation was different for Orthodox Jews than it was for many Christians, the populations of the two suburbanizing groups were quite similar. In general, the suburbanizing Orthodox Jews who attended these new synagogues matched the profile of the young, upwardly mobile, middle-class, consumerist population that came to dominate North American suburbia in the 1950s. For example, like many suburbanites at that time, most of North York's Orthodox Jews came directly from urban neighborhoods.[20] In 1957, of the twenty-two Clanton Park member families for whom a previous address is known, eighteen had moved from Toronto or York Township, and most hailed from Kensington downtown. This proportion matched that found in the larger population in the Clanton Park neighborhood; seventeen of twenty-three families who moved to nearby Palm

Drive in 1957 also came from Toronto or York Township addresses, although not all originated in Kensington.[21] For this population, the neighborhoods of north Bathurst Street offered a chance to own a cheaper and more spacious home than could be found in the older areas.[22] It was, as one Orthodox Jewish suburbanite stated simply, "less expensive here [in North York]."[23] Housing costs were important to an Orthodox Jewish community that was planted squarely in the middle and professional occupational classes. In 1957, more than half of Clanton Park Synagogue's 127 members worked in middle-class fields such as sales, accounting, pharmacy, and insurance or owned their own businesses (see Table 3).[24] Even among those working in lower-status occupa-

TABLE 3. Occupations of Congregation Members, Clanton Park Synagogue, 1957

| | |
|---|---:|
| Professional / business / self-employed | |
| Merchant | 18 |
| Salesman | 8 |
| Chartered accountant | 5 |
| Manufacturer | 5 |
| Manager | 4 |
| Insurance agent | 3 |
| Pharmacist | 3 |
| Dentist | 2 |
| Real estate agent | 2 |
| Scrap metal dealer | 2 |
| Bookkeeper | 1 |
| Cattle dealer | 1 |
| Chartered accountant / builder | 1 |
| Engineer | 1 |
| Executive director | 1 |
| Manufacturer's agent | 1 |
| News agent | 1 |
| Office manager | 1 |
| Officer | 1 |
| President | 1 |
| Rabbi | 1 |
| Sales manager | 1 |
| School principal | 1 |
| Teacher | 1 |
| Total professional / business / self-employed | 66 |

TABLE 3. (*Continued*)

| | |
|---|---|
| Building and construction | |
| Builder | 11 |
| Contractor | 5 |
| Owner/construction firm | 3 |
| Carpenter | 2 |
| Plumber | 2 |
| Brick manufacturer | 1 |
| Foreman | 1 |
| Plasterer | 1 |
| Total building and construction | 26 |
| Garment industry | |
| Furrier | 6 |
| Owner, garment firm | 3 |
| Tailor | 3 |
| Cutter | 2 |
| Operator | 2 |
| Total garment industry | 16 |
| Other occupations and trades | |
| Butcher | 4 |
| Retired | 3 |
| Jeweler | 2 |
| Printer | 2 |
| Appraiser | 1 |
| Baker | 1 |
| Bookbinder | 1 |
| Costume jeweler | 1 |
| Gemologist | 1 |
| Metal spinner | 1 |
| Packer | 1 |
| Projectionist | 1 |
| Silver plater | 1 |
| Taxi driver | 1 |
| Upholsterer | 1 |
| Total other occupations and trades | 22 |
| Total members | 130 |
| Total occupations | 52 |

*Sources*: Clanton Park Synagogue, Membership List (1957–58), SEPP; *1957 Toronto City Directory*; City of North York, *1957 for 1958 Property Assessment Rolls*.

tions, such positions were often stepping-stones to bigger and more successful careers. In one case, three families had come from Europe following World
War II to work as furriers. Within a decade of their relocation to Toronto, they
began one of the most successful real estate development companies in the
city.[25] A similar occupational pattern was found in Washington, D.C., where
members of one suburban Orthodox Jewish congregation were "professionals," with a "larger than usual proportion of scientists and engineers" working
in government-related occupations.[26]

The clustering of Orthodox Jewish men in positions such as independent
businessmen and self-employed professionals stemmed largely from a historical tradition of urban, immigrant Jews who worked in independent enterprises such as peddling. Social factors also played a part in the choice of occupation. Working for oneself allowed a person to avoid exposure to potentially
anti-Semitic work environments, which through the 1950s were not uncommon in a Protestant-dominated corporate culture. Self-employment also permitted one to create a work schedule that did not conflict with the Orthodox
Jewish observances of the Sabbath and Jewish holidays. Even with the general
secular movement to the five-day workweek, Sabbath observance still posed
hardships in the winter months, when sundown came well before the work-
day ended. Although a Sabbath-observant worker might well make up the
work by staying late on other days or by working on Sunday, in many cases
leaving early engendered resentment and distrust in the office. To help Orthodox Jews circumvent possible clashes between work and religion, a 1952 article
in the national Orthodox Jewish magazine, *Jewish Life*, titled "Careers for the
Sabbath Observer," suggested careers such as architecture, optometry, engineering, social work, and teaching, all of which offered flexibility of scheduling. For example, because optometrists regulated their own hours and rarely
faced emergencies, "the *Shomer Shabboth* [Sabbath Observant Jew] should encounter few difficulties" in this career path. Similarly, because teaching and
clerical work both operated on five-day workweeks, it was suggested that observant Jews consider those areas as well. Of course, finding a religiously compatible career choice was only half of the equation. Orthodox Jewish men, like
their non-Orthodox counterparts throughout middle-class suburban society, wanted jobs that offered economic growth potential. Thus the *Jewish
Life* article on careers made sure to note that, in 1952, skilled architects could
earn from $15,000 to $25,000 a year, optometrists from $4,000 to $20,000 (depending on location and practice), and religious functionaries such as rabbis
and cantors began at $4,000 to $5,000 a year.[27] The message was clear: being

a religiously observant Jew need not interfere with socioeconomic upward mobility.[28]

Finding a well-paying occupation was particularly important because, as was the case in most suburban middle-class families, suburban Orthodox Jewish men were expected to be the primary income earners in their families. In Clanton Park Synagogue, not a single female head of household reported herself as employed outside the home; every one listed her occupation as "housewife."[29] The pervasiveness of stay-at-home wives and mothers fit into a communal mentality that made clear that men "have their job, and we have ours. It is our duty to take care of the home, cope with children, and be able to face whatever emergency there is."[30] Cynthia Gasner, an Orthodox Jewish woman in Toronto, recalled that in many suburban neighborhoods in the 1950s, women's work was not only uncommon, it was almost taboo; "you embarrassed your husband" if a woman worked, "you made it look like he couldn't afford to support you."[31] To be sure, as the changing realities of middle-class life necessitated second incomes, Orthodox Jewish women entered the workforce in increasing numbers in the 1960s and 1970s. But even when they did, they generally remained the secondary income earner in their families.

In short, the suburbanizing Orthodox Jews in Toronto and elsewhere fit into the general mold of postwar suburbanite, albeit with a religious twist. In Far Rockaway, Long Island, a suburb of New York City, the Orthodox Jewish community had adopted "middle class suburban practices as sports coat and cap, the outdoor patio barbecue, and keeping up with the Joneses."[32] The membership of Congregation Shomrai Emunah in suburban Washington reflected the fact that "in the 'Space Age' one can be at the same time a fervent Torah-true Jew and a capable, or in fact an outstanding, scientist," lawyer, or any other occupation.[33] This adherence to traditionalist religion stood out from the overwhelming lack of observance among non-Orthodox Jewish suburbanites of the 1950s. In most suburban Jewish communities, "there is little mention of those who come to the synagogue because this is the place where Torah lives. These are the minority in Suburbia," wrote one essayist in 1954.[34] Adamant in their desire to remain faithful to the halakhic tradition yet eager to partake of the modern suburban dream, Orthodox Jews in Toronto and across North America had begun to create a new image of Orthodoxy different from both the socioeconomic stereotypes of urban Orthodox Jews and the religious stereotypes of other suburban Jews. In their typical middle classness, this religious population had become religious pioneers.

Although the focus thus far has been on the broader pioneering experience of religious suburbanization and congregational formation among suburban Orthodox Jews in the 1950s, the pioneering experience did not end with the creation of a congregation and the erection of a synagogue building. What went on *inside* the synagogue was also part of the religious pioneering process, as suburbanizing Orthodox Jews searched for the forms that their new congregations should take. Having grown up in urban neighborhoods, Orthodox Jewish suburbanites had only the urban immigrant synagogue as a reference point. These congregations, known as *shteiblakh* (plural of *shteibel*), generally reflected Old World synagogue styles; they were usually informally run, with little sanctuary decorum or architectural niceties. In a sense, *shteiblakh* paralleled the urban Jewish neighborhood itself, with its noisy, cramped quarters and lack of socioeconomic polish or flair. While the *shteibel* model was the most familiar form of congregation, Orthodox Jews of the 1950s saw new congregations as an opportunity to express their newly achieved suburban, middle-class status even while remaining faithful to Orthodox Jewish practice and ritual. They wanted to demonstrate that "a strictly traditional Jewish congregation could meet present-day Jewish requirements without diluting any of its essential characteristics." [35] These "present-day Jewish requirements" included an emphasis on aesthetics and congregational socialization, two trends that were clearly influenced by middle-class suburban culture.

In striking a balance between old and new, in creating new suburban Orthodox Jewish congregations that layered modern suburban aesthetics onto a strict foundation of Orthodox Jewish religious law, Orthodox Jewish suburbanites became religious pioneers—explorers of new "religious territory." In four main areas they moved the suburban synagogue away from lower-class, urban, immigrant models and toward those that reflected the new attitudes, behaviors, and styles of the suburban middle class: the development of the congregation as social center; the bureaucraticization of the synagogue; the introduction of middle-class styles of decorous worship; and the construction of architecturally modern sanctuaries. [36] As the suburban Orthodox Jews integrated these new styles into their congregations, they broke new ground as religious pioneers.

The development of synagogue centers had, by the 1950s, been under way for several decades in North American Jewish life. The historian David Kaufman has traced the evolution of the "shul with a pool" to the late nineteenth century, when many Jewish leaders sought ways to Americanize the immigrant synagogue. [37] Although the idea of explicitly adding social programs and other nonreligious activities caught on mostly among Conservative Jewish synagogues, several Orthodox Jewish synagogues on the East Coast developed center-oriented programs as a way to broaden the appeal of Orthodoxy to a second generation of American Jews. Despite its earlier growth, the concept of a synagogue-cum-social center blossomed even further with religion replacing ethnicity as an important badge of social identification in postwar suburban society.[38] Congregations of all religious types increasingly sought to be more than merely houses of worship; they wished to be places of formal and informal social interaction—community centers with a bit of God thrown in. Orthodox Jewish leaders, many of whom had rejected any tampering with the synagogue styles in the prewar period, recognized that the small ethnic *shteibel* of the immigrant neighborhood would no longer suffice for a suburbanizing population who wanted more from their synagogue than just religious services and classes in religious texts. What was needed was a new form of Orthodox Jewish synagogue, which, "under modern conditions, [would] be equipped to provide for both religious *and* secular needs in order to serve its community with undiminished vigor." To be sure, "the religious aspect of the functions of the community [could] not be disregarded or slighted in any manner," but as long as the religious practices remained Orthodox, more modern social practices would be acceptable.[39] In other words, suburban synagogue centers were fine, as long as they were built as *Orthodox Jewish* synagogue centers.

Toronto's new suburban Orthodox Jewish congregations demonstrated that such religious/social centers could in fact succeed. Both Clanton Park and Shaarei Tefillah, for example, constructed their social halls before their sanctuaries. Although both congregations did so in part because of financial imperatives, erecting the social hall first made a clear statement as to the synagogue's socializing function. For these congregations, synagogue buildings could be multipurpose environments that provided a range of religious and social activities for the congregation and the community. Thus religious activities, such as weekly Torah and Talmud classes and lectures on Jewish topics, shared the calendar with activities more associated with the suburban middle class, such as Boy Scout troops and Monte Carlo nights.[40] Torath Emeth even went a step further, explicitly calling itself a "Jewish Centre" rather than "congregation" or "synagogue." But whatever the wording, these congregations did not abandon their religious obligations; the content of the religious activities that occurred in these new Jewish congregations remained Orthodox in practice.

The growth of religious and social congregational activities increased the opportunities for leadership within the congregation and led to the second major transformation of suburban Orthodox congregations: the bureaucraticization of the synagogue. As congregational members increasingly worked in professional and other middle-class occupations, bureaucraticization enabled this suburban membership to transfer its occupational skills to the operation of the synagogue, a pattern that was typical of newly founded suburban churches as well.[41] For example, members who worked in the construction industry usually headed the building campaigns, while many of the adult education classes were conducted by members who taught in the community's Jewish day schools.[42] The changing internal organization soon gave these synagogues the appearance of well-run businesses, often resembling a big corporation more than a religious congregation. Suburban congregations developed dozens of committees, each with a chairman and each with its own particular bureaucratic niche. In 1960, Clanton Park Synagogue's extensive bureaucracy included ritual, building, house, publicity, membership, special funds, cultural, and Talmud Torah (Hebrew School) committees. One year later, Shaarei Tefillah's building campaign included a separate building committee, budget and finance committee, and campaign committee.[43]

Although men were primarily involved in running these suburban Orthodox Jewish congregations, women and children found opportunities for participation in congregational organizations. For women, virtually none of whom worked outside the home, the main congregational activity was the sisterhood. Congregational sisterhoods had long been a part of North American synagogue life, providing a forum for women's participation that did not contravene the Orthodox Jewish halakhah.[44] Serving largely as social coordinators for the congregation, as well as offering educational programs such as lectures and films, congregational sisterhoods replicated in the synagogue the same roles women played in the suburban home.[45] In Clanton Park Synagogue, the sisterhood sponsored fashion shows, afternoon teas, and casino nights. Sisterhoods also usually provided the Sabbath morning congregational kiddush, setting up and serving the light snack of cakes and beverages that follows Sabbath services.[46] Sisterhood activities were not all social events. Those interested in furthering their organizational skills could participate in national sisterhood organizations such as the Women's Branch of the Union of Orthodox Jewish Congregations. Such participation created sisterhood "career tracks," so those with particular expertise could move up the ranks of the national groups.[47]

These new institutional outlets for women occurred only in the secular realm of the synagogue. Women's activities inside the sanctuary rarely if ever were modernized in suburban Orthodox Jewish congregations. Unlike their counterparts in Conservative and Reform Jewish synagogues, for example, women in Orthodox Jewish synagogues did not gain equal status in worship; they were still not counted in a minyan and did not participate in the service as prayer leaders or Torah readers. The only modernization that one might have pointed to was the rearrangement of the *mehitsah*, the barrier that divided men and women in an Orthodox Jewish sanctuary. This rearrangement, however, was one of placement—not replacement—in the sanctuary. But even if women remained less empowered than men in the synagogue, congregational activities formed only a small part of Orthodox Jewish life. Unlike in much of Christianity or even in other forms of Judaism, Orthodox Judaism had as much to do with the private, daily activities of individuals as it did with weekly worship services. It was the religious modernization of these private areas, rather than the more public issues of worship, that was the focus of an Orthodox Jewish feminist movement that emerged in the 1970s.[48] Debates over the halakhic validity of all-women's *tefillah* (prayer) groups and women's megillah (lit., scroll, refers here to the Book of Esther, which is read on the holiday of Purim) readings widened out to discussions over women's personal mourning rituals, expanded participation in wedding ceremonies, and even the possibility of women rabbis. By the late 1990s, the movement had grown strong enough to warrant the formation of the Jewish Orthodox Feminist Alliance (JOFA), which held its first annual conference in 1997.[49] One of the most passionate debates for JOFA and other Orthodox Jewish feminists was over the issue of *agunoth*, women whose husbands refuse to grant religious divorces, thus prohibiting them from remarrying. Here, pressure from Orthodox Jewish women's groups forced the hand of the Rabbinical Council of America to begin including prenuptial agreements in Orthodox Jewish marriages.[50]

The suburban congregation also provided opportunities for youth involvement. New suburban neighborhoods were typically full of children, and the neighborhoods in which these congregations sat were no exception; member families were young and often had three or four children each. Children's congregational participation began in junior congregations, which provided a setting for children to lead and take part in services while not distracting their parents in the main sanctuary. Junior congregations proved popular. In 1961, Clanton Park's junior services averaged fifty to sixty participants.[51] In Washington's Congregation Shomrai Emunah, the junior services "literally catered to the children," holding special kiddushes for the children, who "often out-numbered the adults."[52] As children grew accustomed to praying in their own setting, they graduated to teen or youth services. Sometimes the main sanctuary held special youth services in which high school students led prayers for the entire congregation.[53] Youth groups were another way to involve children in the congregation. These groups, with their elected boards and various committees, provided a setting in which teenagers could take part in congregational life and could learn through copying the organizational styles of their fathers on the synagogue board.

The third major pioneering transformation of the suburban Orthodox Jewish synagogues was the increased demand for synagogue decorum. The problem of noisy and undignified behavior in Orthodox Jewish congregations was legendary.[54] Older, immigrant *shteiblakh* were famous for the incessant socializing among worshipers as well as for the circuslike atmosphere associated with the selling of congregational honors via auction, a practice known as *shnoddering*. Such behavior contrasted with the more staid and dignified styles of Protestant churches and was derided by many Reform and Conservative Jewish leaders, who preferred the decorum of Christian services. Quiet, orderly services were a selling point for many non-Orthodox Jewish synagogues, a fact not lost on the Orthodox Jewish leadership in the immediate postwar years. Many pointed "enviously at the greater decorum and dignity of a Reform service" and saw a correlation between congregational styles and success in the suburban environment.[55]

In time, Orthodox Jewish congregations began to work to create a more dignified atmosphere during services. For example, a guide to High Holiday services at Clanton Park Synagogue included a list of rules for services; ushers would seat worshipers only at certain times in the services. All forms of social mingling were strongly discouraged even in the synagogue lobby outside the sanctuary.[56] These and other efforts seemed to pay off. One commentator described Orthodox Jewish congregations in the mid-1950s as places that "pride themselves upon their decorum. Worshipers remain in their seats throughout the service, which is not over until the congregational singing of *Adon Olam* [hymn sung at conclusion of Sabbath evening and morning services], and do not jump around all over the synagogue as some people are prone to do in a '*shteibel.*'"[57]

The final area of suburban Orthodox Jewish pioneering involved a movement toward modern sanctuary design. In the years following World War II, the suburban synagogue became "not only a Jewish house of worship but a symbol of suburbia itself. . . . Aesthetically, it embodied a sense of newness in everything from furniture and light fixtures to Torah covers and candelabra." In the new suburban synagogue, the social hall became an architectural focal point, both as a space for the overflow of worshipers on High Holidays and for bar mitzvah and wedding receptions. Many new synagogues also incorporated a large educational wing to house the often bulging religious school and a main administrative center that reflected "both the bureaucratic needs of the suburban congregation and the important role of office work in post–World War II society." Even the rabbi's study was remodeled into a "showcase of professionalism." [58]

Orthodox Jewish congregations had to balance the lure of modern architecture with the halakhic requirements of synagogue design. Toronto's Torath Emeth Jewish Centre succeeded in combining "the most modern of architectural designs with the hallowed traditional style" of a sex-separating *meḥitsah* (barrier separating men and women in an Orthodox Jewish sanctuary) and a central *bimah* (prayer stand). [59] Shaarei Tefillah's sanctuary was a similar balance of modernity and tradition, although this did not emerge easily. In his original sanctuary proposal, Shaarei Tefillah's architect had designed an upstairs women's gallery, as was common in older traditional synagogues both in Toronto and in Europe. The synagogue members, however, preferred a more modern *meḥitsah* where men and women sat separated on the same level. In the architect's eyes, an odd role reversal had occurred. As he explained, "Here I was, not a *shul* [synagogue]-going Orthodox Jew, trying to convince these fellows who walked to *shul* and who chose their house location so that it was not too far to walk on the Sabbath" that they should accept a sanctuary style that was even more "faithful to tradition" than they wanted. [60] In the end, a compromise was worked out. The balcony stayed but was used only for High Holiday services. The rest of the year, the women sat on the main floor of the sanctuary in a separate and slightly raised gallery located around the perimeter of the round room.

The disagreement between Shaarei Tefillah's architect and his congregational clients pointed to perhaps the most crucial aspects of the religious pioneering experience. The architect believed there was a need to remain "faithful to tradition." As he saw it, there had been a strong custom, extending back to Europe's great synagogues, for Orthodox Jewish congregations to have an upstairs women's gallery. Surely, he thought, this was how a synagogue *should* be built. But whereas the architect thought in terms of historical tradition, Shaarei Tefillah thought in terms of the religious law—the halakhah—which, in fact, did not require a sanctuary balcony. Thus there was nothing religiously wrong with shifting the *meḥitsah* to the floor level. Shaarei Tefillah could rearrange its sanctuary seating plan for financial reasons and still remain well within the bounds of Orthodox Jewish religious practices.

Other changes in Orthodox Jewish congregations were similar. New congregational bureaucracies, social functions, and sanctuary decorum might have moved the suburban Orthodox Jewish congregation away from tradition and toward more modern suburban religious institutional styles, but none abandoned the actual religious obligations. In the words of the sociologist Steven Cohen, these congregational transformations were "beyond the purview of the mandatory *halacha*" and could thus give way to modern styles without violating any explicit religious law.[61] From this perspective, then, the religious pioneering qualities of the suburbanizing Orthodox Jewish community of the 1950s becomes clear. For the first time in the North American Jewish experience, Orthodoxy had moved not only into new physical and geographical areas on the suburban periphery but also into previously unexplored aesthetic and social realms. For this decidedly suburban, middle-class community, nothing less than a decidedly suburban, middle-class synagogue was acceptable. Yet this decidedly suburban, middle-class community was decidedly Orthodox, and it demanded that its synagogues reflect this fact. Modernizing the Orthodox Jewish congregation could not be enacted willy-nilly. Adherence to the religious halakhah was still necessary; pioneering had its limits.

It was this tension between halakhah and modernity that threw perhaps the biggest challenge to new suburban Orthodox Jewish congregations of the 1950s, in the form of the *meḥitsah* debates. Unlike Shaarei Tefillah, which argued over where to put the separation, many other North American Orthodox Jewish congregations questioned whether even to have a barrier. Most of those who wanted to remove the *meḥitsah* drew on modern conceptions of worship for their argument. For the enlightened, middle-class, suburban family, the argument followed, the segregation of women to a separate section no longer seemed appropriate. Family pews were the only proper alternative, a logic that took literally the popular slogan "The Family That Prays Together Stays Together." Many congregations introduced mixed seating, even while trying to maintain an Orthodox Jewish structure in the rest of the service.[62]

The question of replacing separate seating with family pews was not new to postwar suburbia. As Jonathan Sarna has demonstrated, the debate over mixed seating extended back into the early nineteenth century. There were even occasional court cases, usually brought by dissident congregants who disapproved of a decision to remove the separation.[63] But in the immediate postwar suburban period, when so many new synagogues were being built by new or relocating congregations, the *mehitsah* issue seemed to have become magnified. *Mehitsah* debates in three different Orthodox Jewish congregations went to secular courts within a five-year period. In Cincinnati in 1952, in suburban Detroit in 1955, and in New Orleans in 1957, members of Orthodox Jewish congregations fought attempts by fellow congregants to alter their sanctuary's separate seating structure. The case of *Davis v. Scher* in Mt. Clemens, Michigan, illustrates the main issues. After Congregation Beth Tefila Moses voted to remove its *mehitsah*, an opposing member, Baruch Litvin, sued the congregation for breaching its charter that forbade any deviation from Orthodox Jewish tradition. Moreover, Litvin argued that removing the *mehitsah* would deprive him of his rights to use the synagogue because it violated his religious beliefs. The Union of Orthodox Jewish Congregations of America (UOJCA), the national association of Orthodox Jewish synagogues, supported Litvin's claim and provided evidence and statements declaring that mixed seating clearly violated Orthodox Jewish norms. The initial court ruling favored the congregation, but an appeal to the Michigan Supreme Court favored Litvin's claim that the congregational majority could not override a minority's religious rights. The *mehitsah* was returned. A few years later, after Litvin died, however, the congregation once again removed the separation. Soon, Beth Tefila Moses, like most other congregations that removed their *mehitsah*, changed its affiliation from Orthodox to Conservative and the matter was soon forgotten.[64]

For those who wanted to keep the *mehitsah*, then, the issue was clear. The halakhah might have been silent on the specific placement of the *mehitsah*, but it shouted vociferously about its necessity. As the *mehitsah* supporters perceived the issue, it was "the acid test for distinguishing an Orthodox from a non-Orthodox congregation."[65] Any congregation that removed its *mehitsah* had pushed itself outside the halakhic framework and could no longer be considered Orthodox. But for many, the fight over the *mehitsah* was as much a symbolic fight over the future of suburban Orthodox Jewry as it was a tangible debate over sanctuary structure.[66] Throughout the 1950s, leading Orthodox rabbis and laypeople pressed congregations not to change their sanctuaries. In 1958, Moses Feuerstein and Samson Weiss, the top two executives of the UOJCA, offered legal and other aid to members of an Orthodox Jewish synagogue in Atlanta that had removed the *mehitsah*. The two men also appealed to synagogue sisterhoods and other Orthodox Jewish women's organizations in the hope that these groups would influence the direction of their congregations.[67] Some leading Orthodox Jewish rabbis even permitted rabbis to take pulpits in non-*meḥitsah* congregations solely for the purpose of persuading the membership to install or reinstall the sanctuary barriers and retain their adherence to Orthodoxy. Rabbi Jeffrey Bienenfeld, of the Young Israel of St. Louis in suburban University City, recalled how Rabbi Joseph B. Soloveitchik, the leading rabbinical figure in Orthodoxy for most of the postwar period, permitted him to accept a position with a non-*meḥitsah* congregation in Oshawa, Ontario, for a limited period of time. At the end of the two years the membership voted to reintroduce a *meḥitsah* into the sanctuary. When Bienenfeld later lost a similar vote in another congregation in New Orleans, he felt compelled to leave altogether rather than continue to serve in a non-*meḥitsah* setting.[68]

Thus just as the suburban Orthodox Jewish community of the 1950s recognized that certain areas of congregational life were beyond halakhic authority, they equally recognized that the halakhah remained primary. They resisted the trend in the larger Jewish community to move entirely away from the halakhah and chose instead to remain faithful to the legalistic religious rulings from centuries past; the *meḥitsah* would stay. Although this resistance to change represented an almost opposite approach from the congregational transformations discussed earlier, it nevertheless was an equally important part of the religious pioneering of the suburban Orthodox Jewish community. These changes not only brought suburban qualities into Orthodox Jewish life, but they brought Orthodox Jewish practices into the suburban environment.

In December 1963, Shaarei Tefillah Synagogue, the first of Toronto's three original suburban Orthodox Jewish congregations, became the last of the three to dedicate its sanctuary. With this dedication, Orthodox Jewish suburban pioneering had achieved a sense of closure. The initial frontier atmosphere had disappeared as newer subdivisions were developed further north on Bathurst Street. Moreover, the new congregations confirmed for the suburban Orthodox Jews the compatibility of their religious practices with their new suburban environment. They might have been sitting in technologically modern structures, but they were nevertheless sitting in the same sex-separating arrangement as dictated by the religious halakhic tradition. If they admired their congregation's artistically designed *aron kodesh* (Holy Ark), they knew that it contained the same Torah scrolls as it always had. And if they developed special junior congregations for their children, those children recited the same traditional prayers that worshipers had recited for two thousand years. In short, the suburban Orthodox Jewish community of the 1950s built congregations that were religious replicas of their new life in the middle-class metropolitan peripheries, where "the historic sanctity of Judaism and its authentic religious expression" was presented in equally authentic expressions of modern suburbia.[69] After a decade of Orthodox Jewish pioneering, the religious wilderness of suburbia had been tamed.

By the early 1960s, the Orthodox Jewish community in the neighborhoods along suburban Bathurst Street found itself no longer living "way out in the sticks." In religious terms, Bathurst Street's Orthodox Jews had developed an infrastructure that provided almost all the amenities needed for an observant Jewish life. In addition to synagogues, the Bathurst Street neighborhoods had Orthodox Jewish day schools, Jewish bookstores, kosher butchers and bakers, and even the city's only kosher restaurant. In just fifteen years, Toronto's suburban Orthodox Jewish periphery had become the city's religious core. The Bathurst Street neighborhoods that were settled in the 1950s had by the 1960s become well integrated into the metropolitan fabric. Many neighborhoods were already experiencing population turnover, as the first wave of homeowners sold their homes to newer families. Newer subdivision activity was occurring along Bathurst Street north of Sheppard Avenue toward Finch Avenue and even the northern boundary of North York at Steeles Avenue. As in the previous decade, large tracts of farmland were being subdivided and sold off to small builders for development. In short, a new suburban frontier was emerging.

The events of the previous decade convinced developers and builders that Bathurst Street's newer neighborhoods would continue to attract the Jewish community. A planning report prepared for the Forest Hills Golf Club, north of Finch Avenue on the west side of Bathurst, observed "that the Bathurst Street area is the center of suburban development for Toronto's Jewish community. . . . It may therefore be stated that these lands will supply a housing market predominantly for Toronto's Jewish community."[70] These predictions proved more than accurate. Jews accounted for 7,000 of the 9,200 people enumerated in the 1961 census for the Bathurst Manor census tract, between Sheppard and Finch Avenues.[71] Similarly, Jews represented over 90 percent of new homeowners between 1962 and 1965 in Bathurst Village subdivision, just north of the Forest Hills Golf Club. The demographics of this second wave of suburbanization roughly paralleled earlier migrations, dominated by families with young children and with fathers who worked in professions or business.

TABLE 4. Occupations of New Homeowners, Bathurst Village Subdivision, North York, 1963

| | |
|---|---|
| Professional / business / self-employed | |
|     Chartered accountant | 4 |
|     Clothing merchandiser | 1 |
|     Executive | 3 |
|     Insurance agent | 1 |
|     Manager | 1 |
|     Merchant | 7 |
|     Pawnbroker | 1 |
|     Pharmacist | 5 |
|     Proprietor | 1 |
|     Sales manager | 1 |
|     Salesman | 7 |
|     Technical sales engineer | 1 |
|         Total professional / business / self-employed | 33 |
| Other occupations | |
|     Construction superintendent | 1 |
|     Contractor | 2 |
|     Plumber | 2 |
|     Printer | 1 |
|     Upholsterer | 1 |
|         Total other occupations | 7 |
| Total homeowners | 40 |
| Total occupations | 17 |

*Source*: City of North York, *1963 for 1964 Property Assessment Rolls.*

More than three-quarters of the forty men who moved to Bathurst Village subdivision in 1963 worked in white-collar jobs, including seven salesmen, five pharmacists, and four accountants (see Table 4).[72]

In contrast to the suburban migration of the previous decade, many of these young, professional families were quite familiar with the suburban environment and with Bathurst Street. Of the 120 households for whom the place of former residence is known, over half (67 households) moved to Bathurst Village from another residence along the Bathurst corridor. Thus these families were not new to the suburban experience of living in a house rather than in an apartment; 70 percent of the families who moved from another North York residence had exchanged one house for another. Although the

physical hardships of a new suburban neighborhood were not entirely eliminated by this familiarity, there was clearly a lessened sense of isolated pioneering among those who had already experienced the suburban environment.

For observant Jews, moving to a new neighborhood regardless of the actual
distance involved still meant separating one's family from existing religious
congregations. As before, the Orthodox Jewish population worked quickly
to reduce its religious handicaps by forming new congregations in the new
neighborhoods. But although the actual grassroots process of congregation
formation still resembled earlier efforts, there was nevertheless a shift away
from the religious pioneering styles of the 1950s. Rather than turn to consciously new suburban models of congregational development, Orthodox
Jewish suburbanites of the 1960s sought to root themselves in the traditions of
older, urban congregations.

In late summer 1961, a small number of Orthodox Jewish families sought to
organize High Holiday services for residents in the Bathurst Street neighborhoods between Finch and Steeles Avenues.[73] After the services attracted over
150 people to worship in a rented public school auditorium, a core group of
families began to meet on a weekly basis. Sometimes the new minyan enlisted
the help of Ner Israel Yeshiva, which had opened on Finch Avenue about a
mile and a half away, to send two or three students to complete the necessary
quorum for prayer services. The group first met in the apartment of one of the
founders, but after only a few months the minyan had grown too large for an
apartment-sized living room and moved to a nearby storefront on Transwell
Avenue, just east of Bathurst Street and south of Drewry Avenue. Striking a
deal with the landlord who had wanted to rid himself of an unrented property, the minyan agreed to pay for the upkeep and utility expenses, and, in return, the landlord permitted them to meet rent-free.[74]

Over the next few years, the congregation now known as B'nai Torah grew
to "unexpected proportions."[75] The presence of a new congregation in an affordable part of North York proved attractive to young Orthodox Jewish families. The northern location did have one drawback, however. These same families had young children who needed day care and nursery school. The existing
Orthodox Jewish schools were too far south on Bathurst, although ironically
those very schools had located where they did in the 1950s in response to
the earlier suburban migration. To fill their need for a local religious Jewish
school, several parents in the congregation formed a nursery branch of the
Eitz Chaim Day School, which was still located further south on Bathurst. (As
the children grew, newer grades were added and the school became a full

branch.) Sharing the same storefront, the synagogue and the school complemented each other; the school used the storefront during the weekdays and
the congregation met on the weekends.

By the mid-1960s, the storefront was in constant use and the landlord demanded rent money from his tenants. Seeking a new location, the minyan
found an undeveloped lot at the corner of Bathurst and Patricia Avenue, just
one block north of its location on Transwell. With representatives from Eitz
Chaim negotiating, the land was obtained from the North York government
and was subdivided between the congregation and the school. For the rest of
the decade, B'nai Torah met in a portable trailer, affectionately known as "the
Shack," and developed an active congregational life, including a sisterhood, a
children's junior congregation, and an adult Jewish education program.[76]

To this point, B'nai Torah's development seemed to follow the pioneering
patterns of the first generation of suburban Jewish Orthodox synagogues. The
congregation had been formed in the same manner as the earlier ones had,
and in fact, one of the synagogue's first members proudly claimed that B'nai
Torah was always a grassroots congregation, developed from within and supported by its own membership. Living on Toronto's northern fringe—the
"sticks," as one participant described it—also contributed to a pioneering
mentality. Finch Avenue had only recently been paved and Steeles Avenue was
still a "country road" in the early 1960s. Ruth Lane, who moved with her husband, Mark, to what was then the northernmost apartment building on Bathurst Street, recalled that "you looked north and all you could see was farms."
Even kosher butchers located downtown did not initially deliver to the northern neighborhoods because of the distance.[77]

Despite the similarities to the religious pioneering experiences of the
previous decade, B'nai Torah represented a new phase in suburban Orthodox Jewish congregational development. Rather than introducing suburban,
middle-class styles into the traditionalist congregation, B'nai Torah's founders
consciously drew on the traditionalism of older, urban models of congregational development. For example, like Clanton Park and Shaarei Tefillah,
B'nai Torah's financial situation forced it to erect its synagogue building in two
phases. But unlike the earlier suburban congregations, B'nai Torah chose to
erect its sanctuary before it built a social hall. As Marvin Wenner, one of B'nai
Torah's founders, explained, "we'd *davened* in social halls all our life," a reference to the fact that most of the congregation's members had grown up in
Clanton Park or Shaarei Tefillah. Tired of the temporary nature of social hall
services, "we said 'no, we're going to *daven* in a *shul*.' " In part, the sanctuary-

first decision was a concession to the presence of Murray House, a large kosher catering hall located less than a mile away on Steeles Avenue. Wenner and his fellow congregants realized that they could not compete with the established caterers for social functions and built only a small meeting room in the building's basement for minor social functions.[78] More important, the decision to build the sanctuary before the social hall declared that the new congregation was a religious community first and a social community second. This mentality contrasted, of course, with the "suburban Jewish center" view of Shaarei Tefillah and Clanton Park in the decade before.

A similar contrast was found in the choice of B'nai Torah's *meḥitsah* style. According to Wenner, the congregation chose a gallery-style women's section specifically because "we want[ed] a balcony like Shaarei Shomayim" had in its building on St. Clair Avenue, and not like the floor-level *meḥitsahs* of Shaarei Tefillah and Torath Emeth.[79] The choice of seating in the sanctuary also harkened to a presuburban tradition because B'nai Torah's pews had originally been used in Shaarei Shomayim and were obtained when that congregation moved out of its St. Clair location. Even the question of decorum was downplayed in B'nai Torah, which always maintained an informal *shteibel*-like atmosphere. As one congregational bulletin noted in the early 1970s, an announcement of a birth to a synagogue member was usually met with "catcalls of '*kiddush, kiddush*' from the assembled congregation." In an odd way, talking almost became a point of pride for some in the congregation, who seemed to dare synagogue officials to chastise them publicly during prayer services. The problem was so great that in 1986, the synagogue board was forced to authorize that services be stopped whenever the "decibels become intolerable."[80]

In drawing on older traditionalist styles, B'nai Torah's founders reacted against the pioneering efforts of their suburban congregational predecessors, yet, at the same time, they directly benefited from those very same pioneers. The founders of suburban congregations of the 1950s had, after all, succeeded in establishing Orthodox Judaism as a legitimate option in suburban Jewish society. They showed that traditional religious observance could be intertwined with contemporary suburban, middle-class styles. Because this first generation had planted Orthodox Jewish roots in the suburban landscape, the second generation—B'nai Torah's founders—had the luxury of being able to look back to an older tradition. They did not have to be religious pioneers because the suburban Orthodox congregations before them already were.

In general, B'nai Torah's confidence in drawing on older congregational traditions and rejecting newer suburban pioneering ones reflected the wider

*Interior of the B'nai Torah Congregation. Ontario Jewish Archives.*

maturation of the North American Orthodox Jewish community that had occurred between the 1950s and early 1970s, a period in which conservative
groups of all religious stripes were among the fastest-growing denominations
in North America.[81] As Orthodox Jews made the geographical and socioeconomic transition to suburbia, they realized that they need not sacrifice religious practice for material success. Their ability to merge the two propelled
the suburban Orthodox Jewish community from being the weakest of Judaism's religious denominations in the immediate postwar period to the most
vibrant and vocal Jewish community by the early 1970s. This vibrancy translated into a movement away from explicit syntheses of modernity and halakhah and toward greater insularity and isolation. Moreover, as Orthodoxy's
self-confidence rose, the community was less and less willing to make even external—and in many cases entirely permissible within the grounds of the halakhah—modifications that smacked of "modernity."

At the congregational level, that unwillingness translated into the development of traditionalist-oriented synagogues such as B'nai Torah.[82] At the communal level, it translated into a more central role for Orthodox Jews within
the Jewish community structure. In Toronto in 1962, for example, extensive
Orthodox Jewish lobbying succeeded in having kosher food served at the annual convention of the Canadian Jewish Congress. That same year, pressure
on the congress also led to a campaign to help Sabbath observers deal with

employment hardships, particularly the holding of civil service exams only on Saturday, when Orthodox Jews could not take part. In 1966, a group of Orthodox Jewish college students organized a public demonstration against the congress's lack of initiative on the question of public funding for Jewish day schools. Two years later, Toronto's Orthodox Jewish rabbinate issued an open letter to the community criticizing the city's Jewish Community Center for opening on the Sabbath and for operating a nonkosher snack bar.[83]

The rise in Orthodox Jewish self-confidence also meant that the community was willing to remove itself from communal issues when it deemed necessary. Thus in 1970 a group of suburban Orthodox Jewish congregations formed the short-lived Orthodox Jewish Community Council, which was "dedicated to the survival of Judaism in halakhic expression." Two years later, this organization, together with the Rabbinical Council of Ontario, the community's main Orthodox Jewish rabbinical organization, held a Holocaust memorial service separate from a community-wide service. That twelve suburban Orthodox Jewish synagogues cosponsored the event clearly testified to the self-confidence and communal strength of the Orthodox Jewish community. Such organizational isolation was a long way from the scene of the 1950s, when Shaarei Tefillah and Clanton Park had joined with suburban Conservative and Reform congregations to form the North York Synagogue Council, an aborted attempt at suburban communal organization.[84] By the 1970s, the days of intrareligious bonding were long gone, and even these original pioneering congregations had undergone a transformation. The suburban Orthodox Jewish community had grown large enough and strong enough to stand on its own—when it chose to.

Although this self-confidence empowered the suburban Orthodox Jewish community, it did not particularly help to foster positive relationships with the wider Jewish community. Non-Orthodox Jewish leaders perceived that the Orthodox Jews looked down on them because of their nonobservance. This was particularly manifest when Orthodox Jewish groups did not participate in communal activities, especially those held in non-Orthodox synagogues. Interestingly, the strained relationship between the Orthodox and non-Orthodox Jewish communities generally applied to institutional relationships and did not extend to individuals. This unevenness had a religious explanation. For official Orthodox Jewish organizations, and synagogues in particular, working with non-Orthodox Jewish synagogues lent a degree of legitimacy that would have contradicted their own religious outlook; the Orthodox Jewish halakhic framework simply has no room for religious pluralism.

The issue of institutional relationships sparked not only interdenominational tensions but also *intra*denominational tensions within the Orthodox Jewish world. Specifically, *haredi* Orthodox Jewish groups began to frown on any interaction with the non-Orthodox Jewish world, while centrist and left-wing Orthodox Jewish groups hoped for some collaboration and interaction. From the right, the feeling was quite clear-cut: there *is* no room for religious pluralism. From the center and left, the feeling was that Reform and Conservative Judaism was a reality that must be addressed and dealt with, even if it was not the preferred state of Judaism. The tensions within Orthodoxy became clearest around issues of rabbinical alliances and other organizational groups. In New York, the Synagogue Council of America was the battleground. Initially, representatives of Orthodox Jewish groups participated in this interdenominational group. A 1956 decree from various other Orthodox Jewish groups, including the Union of Orthodox Rabbis (different from the more centrist Union of Orthodox Jewish Congregations) and the Rabbinical Alliance of America (different from the more centrist Rabbinical Council of America), declared the SCA to be antihalakhic and forbidden. Moreover, any Orthodox Jewish group or individual participating in the group was to be put in *herem* (excommunication). To be sure, the declaration of *herem* bore little weight outside of the constituents of those declaring groups; it was a far cry from the more enforceable excommunication edicts issued by Latter-day Saints and Amish groups. Enforcement aside, the statement nevertheless made clear that participation with non-Orthodox Jewish groups was beyond the pale of acceptable behavior. In the three decades following the SCA controversy, interdenominational activities declined precipitously among even the centrist Orthodox Jewish groups, for fear of invoking the wrath of the more right-wing elements.

To a degree, the "rise of the right" in Orthodox Judaism parallels the broader rise of the conservative Protestant right in North America and the rejection by those conservatives of any ecumenical cooperation with liberal denominations. But whereas right-versus-left culture wars represented a rupture in denominational relations, the rightward shift in Orthodox Jewry should be understood more as a correction of course, to use a navigational metaphor. That is, the interreligious cooperation demonstrated in the 1940s and 1950s reflected the relative weakness and institutional immaturity of North American Orthodox Judaism; cooperation *had* to occur for Orthodoxy to survive. By the 1960s, however, the retention of younger generations of Orthodox Jews and the maturation of Orthodox Jewish institutions enabled the observant Jewish community to stand apart from the Jewish organizational establishment. Cooperation was no longer a necessity and not even a luxury. It was antithetical to the tradition and to the halakhah.

By the 1970s, then, the original model of Orthodox Jewish religious pioneering had become outdated. The image of a few newly suburbanized Orthodox Jews knocking on doors of neighbors to find a minyan no longer held true. Similarly, the idea of a new Orthodox Jewish congregation explicitly blending modern secular styles with religious traditional had become a thing of the past. Yet the demise of the traditional (if one can consider thirty years traditional) model of suburban Orthodox Jewish congregational growth did not mean that new suburban Orthodox Jewish congregations no longer were established. To the contrary, as the history of North American Orthodox Jewry shows, suburbanization continued well into the 1980s and 1990s. Moreover, the material success that permeated many Orthodox Jewish communities led to the construction of many new synagogues in newly developing suburban areas across North America. By the 1980s, Orthodox Jews had become fully entrenched in their suburban environment without losing any of their religious vigor. As if to confirm the Orthodox Jewish success in fusing suburban success with religious vitality, one can look to suburban Toronto, where an Orthodox Jewish land developer sought to concretize the Orthodox Jewish suburban dream.

The northward momentum of suburban development seemed to halt when it reached the North York border at Steeles Avenue around 1970. North of Steeles was the village of Thornhill, part of the larger Vaughan Township. In many ways, Thornhill in the 1970s and early 1980s was an environment similar to that of North York in the 1950s. The landscape was mostly farmland, with occasional pockets of development near Yonge Street. Religiously, Thornhill and Vaughan were dominated by a heavily Anglo-Protestant population.[85] The suburban similarity between Thornhill and North York notwithstanding, Jewish suburbanization followed a different track. Whereas North York's Jewish families immediately formed congregations and established the basic community structures, the initial Jewish settlement of Thornhill consisted largely of "young and loosely affiliated" families who showed little of the religious organizational abilities or desires exhibited by earlier suburban pioneers.[86]

That Orthodox Jewish suburbanization would be different in Thornhill became clear in 1981, when land developer Joseph Tannenbaum unveiled his plans for a comprehensive residential community just east of Bathurst on Clark Avenue. As early as the 1960s, Tannenbaum had realized that the ultimate direction of the Jewish community was northward. After developing a smaller subdivision on the south side of Steeles Avenue, he bought over two hundred acres of farmland north of Steeles and waited until the market and the demographics were right for a new residential community. That time was the early 1980s. In the rustically named Spring Farm project (and misleadingly named because there was neither a spring nor a farm in the development), Tannenbaum proposed to build over seventeen hundred homes, a small shopping center, a community center, and several small parks. The centerpiece of Spring Farm was a large, all-in-one Orthodox Jewish synagogue and religious community center. As Tannenbaum trumpeted, his project would be the "first time a synagogue [was] being built right along with a housing project, anywhere in North America and probably in the world." Tannenbaum named the congregation Beth Avraham Yosef (House of Abraham Joseph) of Toronto after his father and himself. In 1987, BAYT (both the English abbreviation of its name and the Hebrew word for "House of") moved into its permanent building on Clark Avenue.[87]

Tannenbaum's hope of creating an "instant community" around his congregation was met several times over. A shopping plaza just west of the synagogue emerged as a mini-Jewish center, with a Jewish bookstore, a kosher pizza shop and two other kosher restaurants, and a grocery store with a large kosher bakery and meat department. In addition, branches of Toronto's three Orthodox Jewish day schools opened within a mile of the synagogue. Because housing prices were considerably lower than in neighborhoods further south in North York and the religious infrastructure was practically put in place from the start, Thornhill quickly became the location of choice for young Orthodox Jewish families, as well as for many older families looking for cheaper land to build newer and bigger homes.

Tannenbaum's Spring Farm and BAYT represented the new style of Orthodox Jewish suburbanization. In the past, Orthodox Jewish settlement occurred on a small scale and at a slow pace. Individual families bought homes from individual builders. The neighborhoods they bought in had nothing particularly distinguished about them, nothing to point to that said, "This should be an Orthodox Jewish neighborhood." Rather, the few Orthodox Jewish families who moved into the same area formed a neighborhood minyan which they hoped would mature into a larger congregation. In short, neighborhood settlement and congregational development were grassroots, bottom-up endeavors. With Thornhill's BAYT, the scale and pace of earlier congregations were turned on their heads. Here, a single developer erected an entire neighborhood on a scale larger than any of the Bathurst neighborhoods further south and from the start intended it to be an Orthodox Jewish neighborhood. The preplanned nature of BAYT meant that it skipped over the "basement shul" experience to become immediately a full-service congregation. The entire BAYT and Spring Farm project, then, represented an externally imposed process with virtually none of the pioneering individualism of the previous four decades. Other new synagogues that sprung up in Thornhill in the years after BAYT's formation continued this pattern. New synagogues were attached to organizations such as Aish Hatorah, Lubavitch, and Or Sameyach, three outreach-oriented groups. Congregations could also be found in Thornhill's new Orthodox Jewish schools, including Ner Israel Yeshiva, the Or HaEmet Sephardic elementary day school, and the Thornhill branch of the Associated Hebrew Day School.

But if the formation of these new congregations differed from the experience of earlier decades, they maintained two important, if not essential, continuities. The first continuity was Bathurst Street. Joseph Tannenbaum understood Bathurst's importance and, by locating his Spring Farm development just east of the street, integrated it into the Orthodox Jewish community's sacred space. The Orthodox Jewish community began to refer to Thornhill simply as "up north," just as they had referred to the city's northernmost neighborhoods in previous decades. The neighborhood around BAYT and the other synagogues became just one more Orthodox Jewish neighborhood along Bathurst Street, as B'nai Torah's neighborhood was and as Clanton Park's, Shaarei Tefillah's, and Shaarei Shomayim's were. The sacred space of Bathurst Street—eight miles of suburban settlement and synagogue development—provided a geographical anchor for an ever-lengthening religious community.

A second continuity between the first and last generations of Orthodox Jewish synagogues was religion. At the core of all of these congregational experiences was the Orthodox Jewish halakhah. Although the degree of interaction between this halakhah and suburban styles might have fluctuated over time—like B'nai Torah, BAYT was built with a balcony, yet like Shaarei Tefillah it had a large (even dominant) social hall—the adherence to traditionalist religious practice remained central. Thus, unlike with many religious denominations, which often reduced demands on adherents as affluence and social integration increased, the suburban Orthodox Jewish community's integration into the suburban establishment occurred without much loss in the group's religious content.[88] Its halakhic content stayed firm even as Orthodox Jews grew comfortable in their socioeconomic status.

The four-decade journey from the consciously modernizing congregations of Shaarei Tefillah and Clanton Park, to the consciously traditional B'nai Torah, to the suburban developer's self-created BAYT, tracked an Orthodox Jewish community that grew undeniably suburban while remaining adamantly traditionalist. As such, postwar suburban Orthodox Jewish congregations represented the formal expressions of interaction between religion and the secular suburban world. Here, the styles of worship, the sanctuary design, and the various synagogue activities and programs were among the many ways congregants publicly blended their suburban values with observance of religious law. But suburban Orthodox Jewish congregations were not the only arenas in which the religious-suburban contacts were mediated and expressed. As the following chapter explains, the formal and informal institutions of youth socialization, including day schools, youth groups, and summer camps, worked side by side with religious congregations to transmit the cultural worldview of suburban Orthodox Jewry.

# *Four*

## DAY SCHOOLS AND THE SOCIALIZATION OF ORTHODOX JEWISH YOUTH

"What Does Jewish Youth Really Want?" asked the Orthodox Jewish magazine *Jewish Life* in 1963.[1] Aimed though it was toward Orthodox Jews, this question was essentially the same one that millions of North American parents were asking in the early 1960s: how to understand their children, the baby boom generation of postwar society. Throughout the 1950s and 1960s, North American society was obsessed with understanding and catering to the needs of children and teenagers. The great medium of television targeted children. Teenagers, often rebellious or on the verge of rebellion, were the subjects of dozens of movies in this period. Study after study sought to document the youth phenomenon. One of the most famous of these sociological studies, the 1956 Crestwood Heights study of Forest Hill, Ontario, emphasized how the education, development, and cultural socialization of youth dominated the activities and concerns of middle-class suburban society.[2] That the Orthodox Jewish community faced these same issues reflected the extent to which this religious group had integrated into the broader culture of middle-class suburbia. How they responded, however, reflected the extent to which religious traditionalism continued to be central to this religious community.

For Orthodox Jews, the centrality of youth derived not only from broader secular suburban influences but also from a religious tradition that histori- cally valued the transmission of cultural and religious knowledge from one generation to another. For example, the Talmud notes that providing an edu- cation is a basic religious obligation of a parent to a child.[3] The twelfth-cen- tury scholar Moses Maimonides forbade a person from living in a city that lacked, among other things, a "teacher of children."[4] The itinerant *melamed* (teacher), traveling from town to town to tutor children, remains a striking image from the premodern European shtetl. Because relatively few children were formally educated, religious socialization occurred predominantly in- side the home through informal means of education. Haym Soloveitchik has argued that children learned the ins and outs of religious observance by watch- ing and copying their parents; for centuries, this "mimetic" style of education and socialization provided a crucial link in the continuity of the Orthodox Jewish religious and cultural heritage.[5]

Two separate but parallel forces pulled the North American suburban Orthodox Jewish community. A historical religious tradition made youth so- cialization essential to communal continuity, while a more recent secular tradition made youth socialization essential to cultural integration. The two traditions came together for postwar Orthodox Jewry in a variety of settings, but none more important than the Orthodox Jewish day school. This "most important bulwark of American Orthodoxy" played two key roles in the emer- gence of a vibrant postwar Orthodox Jewry.[6] First, day schools provided an arena for the expression of Orthodox Jewish religious suburbanization and thus mediated the acculturation of the first generation of suburbanizing Or- thodox Jews into their new environment. Second, the day school culture was crucial in transmitting the styles of religious suburbanization to the second and third generations of suburban Orthodox Jewish youth, thus facilitating expansion of this suburban religious community. These two factors ensured that the suburban Orthodox Jewish day school and the youth culture that sur- rounded it would become the "most significant factor in the revival of Ortho- doxy" in the late twentieth century.[7]

The methods and styles of socializing youth in presuburban Orthodox Jewry were generally informal. In European communities, children received their religious education from *melamdim* (teachers, plural of *melamed*), inde- pendent educators who supported themselves by tutoring groups of students. The boys who showed educational promise were sent to larger yeshivoth (academies, plural of yeshiva) in major cities, where they would study Jewish texts for a period of several years. Most yeshiva students returned to their villages in their late teens or early twenties, but a small elite would remain in residence at the academy to lead a life of Torah and to become the teachers of the next generation.[8] In all of these settings, secular education was minimal to nonexistent. The education of girls paralleled that of boys in the early years, but formal education for daughters stopped in early adolescence. That is not to say that Jewish girls received no education after they stopped learning with a *melamed*. Rather, according to Haym Soloveitchik, the education of girls primarily occurred in the home in informal and unstructured ways. For example, girls learned the rules of *kashruth* (Jewish religious dietary laws) not by reading texts but by watching their mothers keep a kosher kitchen. This mimetic mode of watching and learning followed the daily, weekly, and yearly cycle of the Jewish calendar to provide a comprehensive, if not textually based, education for girls.

When they came to North America, European Jewish immigrants left the formal *melamdim* system and the informal, mimetic educational styles of the shtetl. In their place, they emphasized more formal schooling patterns, with the *ḥeder* (lit., room, refers to afternoon Hebrew schools common in Eastern Europe and American immigrant neighborhoods), also known as the Talmud Torah, becoming the dominant mode of Jewish education.[9] In some cases communally sponsored and in others operating under the auspices of a specific congregation, Talmud Torahs taught a basic Jewish curriculum, focusing on prayers, sacred texts, Jewish holidays, and the Hebrew language. Depending on the religious outlook of the sponsoring organization, Talmud Torahs varied in the religious demands placed on students. An Orthodox Talmud Torah, for example, might have spent more time teaching the specific details of halakhic (religious legal) observance, whereas a Reform or Conservative Hebrew school would have focused on Jewish history or Bible stories.

Generally, Talmud Torahs met in the late afternoon or evening hours and on Sunday mornings. Meeting at these times ensured that the schools would not conflict with hours of public school instruction, which was vitally important to most North American immigrant Jews. For the generations of Jewish immigrants in the late nineteenth and early twentieth centuries, the free, accessible, and (in theory) religiously neutral public schools were important institutions of acculturation and Americanization. In the public school, immigrant children learned about their new home, its history, and its language. There, the old-fashioned ways of the old country would be replaced by the modern and progressive ways of the new one. By academically and socially succeeding in the public school, immigrant Jewish children would, their parents hoped, ultimately achieve "full integration into American life." [10]

While most Jews followed the public school / Talmud Torah method of secular and Jewish education, many in the Orthodox Jewish community bemoaned the state of religious education. Even though Orthodox Jewish ḥeders generally met for more hours during the week than non-Orthodox Jewish schools, and even if Orthodox Jewish home life reinforced observances to a greater degree than non-Orthodox Jewish homes, the overall impact of Orthodox Jewish education remained low. The second and third generations of immigrants seemed to be moving to other forms of Jewish affiliation, and especially Conservative Judaism, whose blend of tradition and modernity attracted many children and grandchildren of immigrants. [11]

If the current state of Jewish religious education was not impetus enough, an influx of more traditionalist European immigrants in the 1930s prompted Orthodox Jewish leaders to develop alternative educational models. The new immigrants were coming from a society where a yeshiva-based education was far more common than in North America and, as newly arrived immigrants, they lacked any historical connection to the public school /ḥeder model of education common to North American Jewry. What was developed, then, was an entirely new model of Jewish religious education: the all-day Jewish school. Structured around a dual Judaic/secular studies curriculum, the all-day Jewish school was promoted as having two distinct advantages over the more popular public school / Talmud Torah method of Jewish and secular education. First, day school students would receive more hours of Judaic instruction than they would in the afternoon Talmud Torah. This quantitative increase in Judaic instruction also meant a qualitative improvement because classes would not occur after public school, when students were tired and their attention focused elsewhere, but in the morning, when students were at their freshest. A second advantage of the all-Jewish school lay in the elimination of religious conflicts that Jewish students faced in the public school. Despite being officially secular, public schools impressed upon students a generally Christian perspective. In some cases, this religious viewpoint was overt; in Ontario, for example, Bible reading and school prayers reminded students of the public schools' Methodist origins. In other cases, the conflicts were more subtle but equally difficult for Orthodox Jewish students. Several times a year, observant Jewish students were forced to miss classes on days when Jewish holidays fell during the week. The problems were multiplied by the fact that non-Orthodox

Jewish students often did not skip school on certain less prominent holidays, such as *Shavuoth* (Jewish holiday, falling in late spring, celebrating God's giving the Torah to the Israelites on Mount Sinai) or *Sukkoth* (Jewish thanksgiving festival, falling in midautumn). For a non-Jewish teacher unaware of Orthodox Jewish observances, the absences appeared to result from laxity rather than from religious necessity. Christmas celebrations presented another annual conflict for Orthodox Jewish students. Typically, Jewish students would either participate uncomfortably in Christmas pageants or would be excused rather conspicuously from participation. In either case the situation highlighted the fact that the students were *not* Christian.[12] Orthodox Jewish day schools removed these obstacles. Whatever prayers were recited in the day school were Jewish prayers, and the Bible that was read was the Jewish Bible, not the New Testament. Because day schools shut down for Jewish holidays, students would be afforded the "indispensable opportunity for Jewish holiday observance in a natural fashion" without "injuring [their] scholastic standing."[13] Furthermore, Christmas and other religious celebrations ceased to be a problem because Jewish day schools did not observe these holidays.

From just a handful in the 1920s, the number of day schools increased to over 30 by the beginning of World War II, almost all of them located in urban centers along the Atlantic seaboard. In 1944, a group of Orthodox Jewish community leaders and educators united to promote Jewish day schools as a viable educational alternative to the Talmud Torah. Within a short period of time, this highly active group, named Torah Umesorah (Torah and Tradition), experienced considerable success.[14] Five years after Torah Umesorah's founding, the number of day schools in the United States and Canada had increased to 132 in forty-eight communities. By 1960, this total had doubled to 265 schools in ninety-five cities. By the 1980s, over 550 Jewish day schools operated in almost every Jewish community in the United States and Canada, 86 percent of which were under Orthodox Jewish auspices.[15]

More important, a large percentage of these schools were established in the growing suburban neighborhoods of North America's metropolitan areas. In the New York metropolitan area, for example, suburban day schools experienced a sevenfold increase in enrollment between 1951 and 1964, a period when enrollments in urban day schools only doubled. In other cities, older day schools and yeshivoth opened new branches in the growing areas of suburban Jewish settlement, while simultaneously reducing and eventually closing the size of their existing urban branches. In St. Louis, the H. F. Epstein Hebrew Academy moved from an urban location to the suburb of Olivette in the late 1950s, while in Boston, the Maimonides Day School dedicated its new campus in suburban Brookline in 1962.[16]

This trend of older schools opening new branches or relocating altogether to suburban neighborhoods was evident in Toronto, which had two elementary day schools that dated to 1942. That year, the city's two largest afternoon Talmud Torahs, the Associated Hebrew School and Eitz Chaim School, opened day school branches in their main buildings in the downtown neighborhood of Kensington, then the heart of Toronto's Jewish community. Initially, the financial constraints imposed by World War II limited both schools to opening only nursery and kindergarten classes, but more classes were added in the higher grades after the war's conclusion. Over the next decade, both Associated and Eitz Chaim attracted enough students to grow slowly and steadily; by 1954, the former had over four hundred students.[17] By the early 1950s as well, both day schools faced a changing Orthodox Jewish landscape. More and more Orthodox Jewish families with children in the day schools were leaving Kensington for the newer neighborhoods of North York. For these suburbanizing students, going to school now meant a time-consuming trip that was often dependent on the still irregular system of public transportation that linked north Bathurst Street with Kensington. Recognizing that their future enrollment was relocating northward, both Associated and Eitz Chaim undertook plans to relocate to suburbia as well.

Associated made the first move into North York in 1952, when it created an all-day first grade class at Bathurst Street and Brooke Avenue. Two years later, the school purchased a four-and-a-half-acre site at Bathurst and Neptune, just south of Wilson Avenue. After considerable fund-raising efforts, the building's cornerstone was laid in 1956, and the day school opened for classes in the fall of 1957. Eitz Chaim soon followed suit, obtaining land at the corner of Bathurst and Viewmount, at the southern edge of North York. By 1959, the school opened its new building adjacent to the Torath Emeth Jewish Centre. The new locations worked well for both schools. Within two years of opening its new building, Associated undertook a large expansion project to almost double its space. In 1961, only a couple of years after beginning operations on Viewmount, Eitz Chaim began its own expansion plans. Both schools also shut down their downtown branches not long after they relocated the bulk of their classes to suburban North York.[18]

By moving to the metropolitan periphery, Toronto's day schools and those in other cities helped to root the suburbanizing Orthodox Jewish community

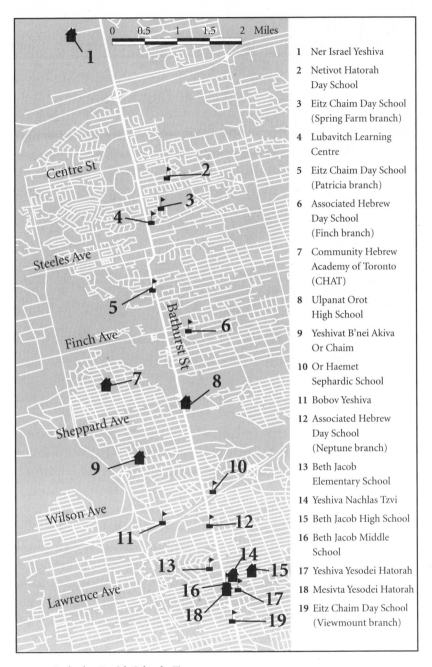

MAP 7. *Orthodox Jewish Schools, Toronto, 1995.*
Source: Toronto Jewish Orthodox Community Directory, 5755.

*Associated Hebrew Day School classroom, 1950s. Aaron Weisblatt personal collection.*

to its new sacred spaces. In Toronto, the suburban branches of both Associated and Eitz Chaim were located on or immediately adjacent to Bathurst Street, adding to the growing visible Jewish activity of the main suburban road and its nearby neighborhoods. Within two blocks of the new Associated school, for example, were built the Shaarei Tefillah Synagogue, the Jewish Old Folks Home (later renamed Baycrest Center), and several kosher food stores, bakeries, and restaurants. Further south, Eitz Chaim shared a property with the Torath Emeth Jewish Centre and was within four or five blocks of several other Orthodox Jewish synagogues. Even the immediate participants in the suburban expansion of Toronto's day schools recognized the spatial connections between school and community. At Associated's sod-turning ceremony for its new building in 1956, one speaker declared that the new Bathurst Street building showed that "history repeats itself." Four decades earlier, when the Associated Talmud Torah had bought land north of College Street, the area had become the "new Jewish center." With Associated once again moving northward to the new Jewish center along Bathurst, "the vision and foresight of these pioneers of old is now being emulated by the generation of today, a large number of whom are the sons of these very pioneers." [19]

The pioneering imagery was appropriate, for the new suburban day schools embodied many of the same elements as did the pioneering religious congregations discussed earlier in the book. Although Jewish day schools were not initially conceived as suburban middle-class institutions—Torah Umesorah's founders saw their organization's goal simply to "disseminate the Torah True spirit" throughout North America—Jewish day schools became increasingly tied to the spatial and social suburbanization of the middle-class Orthodox Jewish community.[20] Seeking to appeal to a suburban middle-class population with traditionally religious needs, the day schools pushed the boundaries of Jewish education in new directions by bringing together religious and secular styles in a single educational institution.

This "modernization" of Jewish education can be seen in four areas. First was the inclusion of girls in a formal setting. Although girls were minimally educated in the shtetl Talmud Torahs, they were excluded from the higher yeshivoth in Europe and in the United States. To be sure, the Bais Ya'acov (House of Jacob) movement, a network of girls-only religious schools, did exist in Europe, having been founded by Sarah Schenirer in 1918.[21] But this movement did not extend to the United States or Canada until the middle of the century. The question of teaching boys and girls religious studies in a coeducational setting was not always uncontroversial, however. In Boston in the 1930s, for example, the new Maimonides Day School, founded and headed by Rabbi Joseph B. Soloveitchik, introduced coeducation over the concerns of certain factions who opposed such a concept. In Boston, as in other smaller communities, coeducation was a necessity because a community could rarely support two separate-sex institutions.[22] Where communities could afford to support separate schools, as in many New York City neighborhoods, such separate schools existed. But even in the larger cities, by the 1950s coeducation had become a nonissue for the upwardly mobile, suburbanizing Orthodox Jewish community.

In addition to promoting Jewish education for girls, new day schools modernized Jewish education by promoting an image of professionalization that had been generally absent in prewar schools. Although founded with a small staff and limited resources, Torah Umesorah quickly developed into a larger, corporatelike bureaucracy that addressed a comprehensive range of issues relating to day schools. Torah Umesorah's programs included teacher training and certification; centralized teacher placement services; curriculum development; principal training and certification; parent-teacher associations; and *Olameinu* (Our World), a monthly magazine for students.[23] At the local level,

Torah Umesorah encouraged day schools to develop similar bureaucracies to operate the programs. Such a professional image positioned the day schools as educational complements to the middle-class, "organization man" orientation of the suburbanizing Orthodox Jewish community. The corporate, administrative atmosphere showed parents that their children were being educated in an institution in tune with the modern, technocratic methods of postwar suburban society. In this way, the professionalization of Jewish education paralleled the bureaucraticization of suburban congregations, which, as discussed in Chapter 2, saw synagogue members applying their business expertise to the religious congregation.

Of course, the professional image promoted by day school principals and administrators often exceeded the reality in many schools. Financial troubles were a particular problem, and stories of teachers not being paid on time were not uncommon. In most cities, teachers were not unionized and lacked professional bargaining power. In smaller schools, the provision of extracurricular or enrichment programs was an elusive goal, limited by the lack of finances or personnel (or sometimes both). Despite these inadequacies, however, many day schools could be considered an improvement over what had existed before.

A third modernization occurred inside the classroom. Promotional literature often emphasized the physical differences between the new suburban day schools and older urban structures. No longer would Jewish education be associated with the inadequate facilities of the downtown neighborhood, where the congregational Talmud Torah might have been held in an unrenovated basement of an old synagogue building. Instead, suburban day schools would be like Eitz Chaim's new Viewmount Street building, constructed with "modern steel and masonry" and containing spacious classrooms and multipurpose facilities.

Finally, the new suburban day schools represented "modernity" by incorporating secular holidays and personalities into the general studies curriculum. In 1954, one parent from a New York suburb noted that his daughter's day school had "no lack of emphasis on American holidays and songs." For his daughters, "Thanksgiving is as happy an event as Chanukah, and there is no tendency to place Herzl and Weizmann [two prominent Zionist leaders] on higher pedestals than Washington or Lincoln."[24] Stories of Abraham Lincoln freeing the American slaves were connected to biblical stories about the Israelite Exodus from Egypt. Connecting religious traditions to contemporary secular examples fit into the overall goal of day schools to promote the "harmonization of American living with genuine Judaism," a process that would result in the "enriching" of "American democracy."[25]

Obviously, not every new suburban Orthodox Jewish day school followed the same trajectory in modernizing the religious educational experience. Some schools struggled financially, while others faced a continual teacher shortage. Successful schools faced parents who were suspicious whether the all-day Jewish school could provide an education up to standards for a self-consciously upwardly mobile community. It should not surprise, then, to read how one administrator at Toronto's Eitz Chaim touted his school's ability to provide "an adequate Torah and Hebrew education that is traditional in spirit yet modern in method and approach."[26] That he left undefined his meaning of "modern" did not matter; the hope was that his suburban middle-class Orthodox Jewish audience would read into it whatever they chose.

At the same time that schools touted their modern outlook (however it was interpreted), certain aspects of "modernity" remained beyond acceptable boundaries for suburban Orthodox Jewish day schools. For one thing, Christmas and Easter and even less explicitly religious holidays such as Valentine's Day, St. Patrick's Day, and Halloween were entirely absent from Orthodox Jewish day schools. Certain other components of the general studies curriculum were also removed when they clashed with religiously traditional viewpoints. Many day schools excised those parts of elementary English texts which contained "excessive references to Christian celebrations" and beliefs.[27] In addition, science classes avoided topics that directly opposed Orthodox Jewish beliefs about biblical creationism, such as evolution, dinosaurs, and the origins of the universe. For a period of time, Torah Umesorah proposed to commission new textbooks that eliminated such references, although a lack of adequate funding ultimately kept this project from reaching fruition. Still, wherever possible, Orthodox Jewish day schools generally sought to maintain "harmony in the curriculum between general and religious studies," and differences between the two were decided in favor of religion.[28]

For all their efforts to promote religious traditionalism in the classroom, day school leaders recognized that Orthodox Jewish education could succeed only if the lessons of school were being reinforced in the home and the community. Throughout the late 1940s and 1950s, national publications such as Torah Umesorah's *Jewish Parents Magazine* and the Union of Orthodox Jewish Congregation's *Jewish Life* printed articles with titles such as "Ways to Religious Growth in the Home" and why "Parents Too Grow through Day Schools."[29] These articles argued that, as students brought home their lessons about the observance of the Sabbath or keeping a kosher kitchen, their parents would become more observant themselves. Moreover, the experience of seeing parents perform a ritual at home reinforced what a child learned in class. In the words of the president of Torah Umesorah, "One Sabbath beautifully experienced is worth a hundred learned dissertations on the Jewish day of rest." [30] Another author suggested ways to include children in Sabbath preparations, such as having them make dessert for the Sabbath meal or sing songs they learned in school. By bolstering "the Jewish spirit of our homes," Orthodox Jewish parents provided "a fertile climate for our children's intellectual and emotional growth in the Hebrew Day School." Invoking the language of contemporary popular psychology, this author noted that by not making home life compatible with school, parents risked creating a "conflict situation" that could have "serious repercussions on the child's developing personality and on his ability to learn in school." [31]

The relationship between day schools and the community was also strengthened through the suburban congregation. Synagogues incorporated children and youth into the community through programs such as youth *minyanim* and junior congregations. Such specialized youth services allowed students to put the skills they learned in school to a practical test by leading the prayers or reading from the Torah. Seeing their children use their education also engendered pride in parents and congregations, so much so that they would publicly report the occasions in the Jewish press. In January 1960, for example, the *Canadian Jewish News* proudly noted that Aaron Weisblatt, a junior high student in the Associated Day School, participated in the school's Sabbath morning services. [32] The next year, the newspaper described in glowing terms how students from the new Ner Israel Yeshiva led services for the entire congregation at Clanton Park Synagogue. [33]

The day schools and the suburban congregations were also linked through youth groups and summer camps. In Toronto, for example, the religious Zionist B'nei Akiva youth group had chapters in Clanton Park Synagogue and other smaller congregations and attracted many Orthodox Jewish youth who attended the religious Zionist Associated Day School. Many students from the religious non-Zionist Eitz Chaim participated in the Agudath Israel youth groups at the Torath Emeth Jewish Centre. These extracurricular programs, which often consisted of a Friday night Sabbath *oneg* (party) or a Sabbath afternoon *shiur* (class or lecture on Jewish texts), provided an opportunity for Orthodox Jewish youth to interact socially and religiously outside the classroom. During the summer months, when school was not in session, the ex-

*"Hanging out" on Roberta Lane in North York, September 1957. Aaron Weisblatt personal collection.*

tracurricular educational process continued at youth-group-sponsored summer camps. Many of the same Eitz Chaim youth involved in the Agudath Israel programs during the school year attended Camp Israel during the summer, while the B'nei Akiva crowd filled the bunks at Camp Moshava. Following the day schools' lead, camps appealed to both religious and secular tastes in the suburban Orthodox Jewish community. Camp Moshava, for example, promoted the fact that it combined Torah study and a "positive" religious atmosphere with more traditional camping experiences such as sports activities and arts and crafts. Each spring, when camp registration began, short articles in the *Canadian Jewish News* reported the latest camp innovation, such as a new woodworking shop and improved waterfront facilities.[34]

That the new suburban Orthodox Jewish day schools sought to emphasize their modernity, relevance, and centrality to the Orthodox Jewish community was largely rooted in economic necessity. Most Orthodox Jewish day schools had a financial incentive to show that they fit into the Orthodox Jewish community's overall religious way of life. Parents would be willing to pay the high tuition fees charged by private day schools only if they understood the reli-

gious and academic benefits of these institutions. Garnering economic support from the Orthodox Jewish community was particularly necessary for day
schools because they had few funding alternatives. As private schools they received no public funds, although since the 1960s, various Orthodox Jewish organizations have fought for legislative support for funding proposals such as
vouchers for private schools. Unlike in the United States, where opponents of
parochial school funding can fall back on the constitutional separation of religion and state, Canada had a somewhat fuzzier arrangement. The founding
document of the Canadian confederation, the 1867 British North American
Act, permitted public funding of Catholic schools (and Protestant schools in
Quebec). Making an argument for equality in support, Jewish educational
proponents in some Canadian provinces succeeded in obtaining provincial
funding for Jewish schools. Other efforts, notably in Ontario, failed to convince courts and legislatures that Jewish schools deserved public monies as
much as did Catholic schools.[35]

The lack of public funding might have been less important had Orthodox
Jewish schools succeeded in obtaining support from the broader Jewish community. But these schools found little backing from Jewish communal federations, which were usually staffed by non-Orthodox Jews. In fact, the question
of community funding of Orthodox Jewish schools developed into one of the
prime sources of tension between the Orthodox and non-Orthodox Jewish
communities in the late twentieth century. In the minds of communal leaders, Orthodox Jewish day schools were targeted to a narrow clientele and did
not appeal to the broader Jewish community. Since few non-Orthodox Jewish
children would attend these schools, communal Jewish funds should not go to
support them, reasoned many federation leaders. Although usually hidden
below the surface, underlying anti-Orthodox attitudes sometimes emerged
during these funding struggles. In 1964, when the Indianapolis Jewish Welfare
Federation was approached to support the national network of Beth Jacob
high schools (girls schools aimed at Orthodox Jewish families), the federation's
executive director refused to give as much as he had authorized in earlier
years. "Because of special relationships in the community," he wrote, "there
has always been pressure to give [Beth Jacob schools] more than I feel such an
organization should receive." To show that he was "convinced that the organization should not receive as much as they are," he was "ready for a 'show-
down' with local friends of the institutions."[36] Such antagonistic attitudes
meant that by 1964 only thirty-seven out of three hundred day schools across
the United States received federation assistance.[37] Over the next three decades,

these tensions did not dissipate, even as the number of non-Orthodox Jewish students began to attend day schools and even as study after study suggested that day school education was crucial to "Jewish continuity." In Indianapolis, noted for its federation's distaste for parochial education, the Hebrew Academy was founded in 1974 despite having little access to communal funds. Twenty-five years later, when the school attracted students from all types of Jewish households, the federation was including the Hebrew Academy in its allocations, although the amount still represented less than one-seventh of the school's entire budget.[38]

Although they could not always convince Jewish communal leaders to offer financial assistance, those who founded, administered, and supported Orthodox Jewish day schools did succeed in convincing many in the Jewish community of the merits of the all-day Jewish school.[39] Writing in the *American Jewish Year Book* in 1958, Arthur Hertzberg, a Conservative Jewish rabbi, admitted that there was "reasonable evidence that the Orthodox school both retained its students longer and was attended by more of the children of Orthodox parents than were the schools of [Conservative and Reform] groups."[40] By the mid-1960s, educational leaders in those Conservative and Reform groups also saw the connections between the blossoming of suburban Orthodox Judaism and their day schools. In the words of one Conservative Jewish educator, the Orthodox Jewish system of combining religious instruction with academically advanced secular education had contributed to the "meaningful survival of Judaism in America."[41] This admiration soon translated into imitation, as non-Orthodox Jewish groups began to establish day schools under their own auspices. In Toronto, for example, three non-Orthodox Jewish day schools opened in the 1960s and 1970s. In 1961, a group of Conservative Jewish synagogues sponsored the United Synagogue Day School (USDS) marketed primarily to members of the city's Conservative synagogues.[42] That same year, a group of parents affiliated with the secular Jewish Labor–Zionist movement opened the Bialik Day School on Viewmount Avenue and Bathurst Street.[43] The trend toward private Jewish education even extended to Toronto's Reform Jewish community in 1974, when the Leo Baeck School offered a Judaic studies curriculum "consistent with the principles of the Liberal Reform movement."[44]

The entry of non-Orthodox Jewish groups into the day school market did not hurt Toronto's existing Orthodox Jewish schools. The right-wing schools were obviously not affected because none of their students came from non-Orthodox backgrounds. But even Associated and Eitz Chaim, with a mixture of students, saw their enrollment expand through the late 1950s and 1960s. From 440 students in 1954, Associated's enrollment had grown to over 1,200 students in 1968. By that same year, Eitz Chaim was educating more than 550 students.[45] By the end of the 1960s, both schools had established newer branches to "serve the educational needs of the rapidly expanding Jewish population" in the northern stretches of Bathurst Street.[46] In other communities as well, the number of students in Jewish day schools continued to rise, although the overall proportion of Jewish students in day schools remained less than 20 percent across North America.[47] Instead of hurting the existing Orthodox Jewish day schools, then, the new non-Orthodox Jewish schools helped them by making day school education more popular among a wider range of the Jewish community. The growth of non-Orthodox Jewish schools also suggested that Orthodox Jewish religious suburbanization had begun to move into the Jewish communal mainstream. It was no longer religiously strange to maintain one's religious orientation while simultaneously immersing oneself in the suburban middle-class world of educational achievement and youth development.

By the 1960s, an increasing number of youth were passing through Orthodox Jewish schools, youth groups, and summer camps. A decade's worth of suburban Orthodox Jewish children had grown up in an environment that reinforced the compatibility of religious and suburban ways of life. But as the Orthodox Jewish community reveled in its successes—and as those outside the community began to emulate them—a structural weakness in this model of socialization became apparent: the absence of postelementary educational institutions. Without reinforcement at the secondary school level, much of what the day schools taught was likely to be lost. In Toronto and in other communities that lacked Jewish high schools, graduates from local day schools could choose to attend public school during the day and study Jewish subjects independently or in a Talmud Torah after school or leave home and attend a Jewish high school in another city. A popular local option was the Rabbi Abraham Price's after-school yeshiva, where many Orthodox Jewish high school students studied in the afternoon or evening. Alternatively, many students left home to attend a Jewish high school in Chicago, Cleveland, or Detroit, all of which had yeshivoth programs for out-of-town students. To all but the most dedicated families, however, this latter choice was less favorable because it meant separating children from their parents during their adolescent years.

The lack of Orthodox Jewish high schools magnified a broader problem within the Orthodox Jewish community and across North American suburban society in general regarding the future of youth. As the baby boom generation was moving into adolescence, scholars and laypeople alike expressed concern over a growing "teenage tyranny." [48] The spirit of youth discontent manifested itself in religious terms by the widespread abandonment of traditions among a younger generation. The popularity of Eastern religious styles among teenagers and young adults stemmed from an overwhelming dissatisfaction with the religious styles of their parents; suburban churches and synagogues seemed too sterile and uninspiring. [49] Leaders of the North American Orthodox Jewish community feared that religious alienation would strike their community, and, as the opening quotation of this chapter stated, sought to find out "What Does Jewish Youth Really Want?" [50] Thus, caught between the micro-problem of the lack of local high school facilities and the macro-problem of the religious future of youth, many Orthodox Jewish communities turned in the 1960s to expanding the secondary school options for their teenaged children.

In Toronto, the first efforts to fill this educational gap began in 1959, when a group of Eitz Chaim parents began to work with representatives of the Ner Israel Yeshiva in Baltimore to establish a Toronto branch of the Yeshiva. Beginning in the fall of 1960, the all-boys school combined an intensive Orthodox Judaic program with a secular studies program designed for university preparation. The following year, the Beth Jacob High School for Girls opened, oriented primarily to the daughters of families whose sons attended Ner Israel and other *haredi* yeshivoth. [51] A second group of Orthodox Jewish parents, centered more around the Associated Day School, also wanted a Jewish high school but did not like the sex-segregated, non-Zionist, *haredi* orientation of Ner Israel and Beth Jacob. Working with the United Jewish Welfare Fund, the central organization that dispersed educational funds in Toronto, this group founded the Community Hebrew Academy of Toronto (CHAT) in 1960 as a coeducational school. Although as a "community" school CHAT attracted students from across the religious spectrum, it maintained a generally religious environment, largely because of its proximity to Associated; the two schools shared the same building, administration, and teachers, and most of CHAT's students were graduates of Associated. Within two years, then, Toronto's Orthodox Jewish community went from having no high schools to having three.

The development of the new high schools paralleled that of the earlier Orthodox Jewish day schools. As in the previous two decades, the new high schools consciously appealed to suburban middle-class concerns about the modernity of Jewish education. Advertisements in 1966 for Beth Jacob's new building, for example, proudly noted that the school incorporated "all the latest and most up-to-date features in school design." The schools also emphasized their academic qualities to reassure middle-class parents concerned about their children's university success. When Beth Jacob's first graduating class passed its Ontario matriculation exams, their achievements "demonstrated that it was possible to be deeply rooted in Jewish tradition and practice while, at the same time, successfully pursue academic studies." Other articles in the local Jewish press also reported the names of universities attended by graduates of local Jewish high schools.[52]

Even more than providing a "modern traditional" education similar to that of the day schools, the new Jewish high schools in Toronto and elsewhere established a continuity that helped to reinforce the Orthodox Jewish religious identity among a restless generation of youth. No longer would the intensive Jewish education of the elementary years have to be followed by a sharp decrease in religious learning when a student entered a public high school. Instead, he or she could stay in an all-Jewish environment, learning Jewish texts, practices, and values, and continue to receive a secular education. The impact of this expansion of Orthodox Jewish education on the religious identity can be seen in the ways that suburban Orthodox Jewish youth experienced the 1960s culture of protest. While a secular spirit of youth discontent coursed through the Orthodox Jewish community, the *content* of this discontent remained decidedly traditional. In 1966, for example, a group of Orthodox Jewish college students in Toronto staged a typical public protest against a major "establishment" organization. Their focus was to criticize the Canadian Jewish Congress's lack of initiative on obtaining provincial funding for Jewish schools. In 1969, a rally in New York City attracted Orthodox Jewish teenage girls from up and down the Atlantic seaboard. Their cause was to protest against the miniskirt and to demand greater adherence to the laws of *tsniuth* (modesty). Two years later, teenage members of a Vancouver chapter of the Orthodox-affiliated National Conference of Synagogue Youth (NCSY) echoed the spirit of the times by publicly declaring their desire for a "purposeful" Jewish life. They did so, however, not by rejecting the status quo of their parents but by rejecting marijuana and other drugs, which were seen as a "violation of basic Jewish law." That same year, at the annual national convention of NCSY, over eight hundred delegates passed several resolutions promising to "forge a social revolution with Torah principles." In short, the popular youth desire to change the world meant, for Orthodox Jewish youth, to change the world in a religiously traditional manner.[53]

The reaction of Vancouver's NCSY chapter against drug use was also important, for it emphasized the limits of Orthodox Jewish involvement in the youth counterculture. To be sure, drug use and abuse found its way into religious communities in the 1960s and early 1970s. Various reports on the general social problem of drugs noted that abuse was not uncommon even among members of various *Hasidic* Orthodox Jewish groups; the "stifling" conformity of these religiously traditional communities was said to drive teenagers to rebellion.[54] But even if Orthodox Jews were counted among the tripped-out hippies in Haight-Ashbury or Greenwich Village, they were a tiny minority in a much wider social phenomenon. As much as the radical transformation of suburban youth society had made its presence felt in the Orthodox Jewish community, the community's religiously traditional ways of life retained their hold over its youth. Unlike in other communities where the youth had rebelled *against* the religious traditions of their parents, these teenagers did not; when all was said and done, they remained part of the suburban *Orthodox* Jewish community.

Still, having grown up in a suburban middle-class world, Orthodox Jewish youth shared the same dissatisfactions with the "establishment" as did their non-Orthodox and non-Jewish peers. Thus, like their more famous counterparts at Columbia University, students at New York's Yeshiva University, further north on Amsterdam Avenue, participated in protests against their school's association with "big science," military research, and the Vietnam War.[55] The general opposition to the war was also manifested by draft avoidance. One Yeshiva graduate recalled that many students entered rabbinical school as a way to get out of draft eligibility. Furthermore, upon graduation, many chose to become educators rather than pulpit rabbis to avoid once again being eligible for draft status.[56]

The effects of another four or five years of Orthodox Jewish education at the high school level carried over to the university experience. Beginning in the 1960s, increasing numbers of religiously observant youth began to attend college. Like their non-Orthodox peers, Orthodox Jewish students from middle-class homes expected to attend university. Acceptance at a good college, the sociologist Samuel Heilman has argued, "had become the single most important theme of Jewish adolescence and adulthood." Parents as well pushed their children to "acquire more education than they had and reach even greater heights."[57] But the pride parents felt about their children's secular academic achievements was tempered by concerns about the nonreligious environment their children were entering. How would Orthodox Jewish students react to the secularism of college life?[58] As one observer commented, living in a college environment was a "trying experience for the observant youth at an age when he is developing intellectually."[59] Adding to the challenges of campus life, many Orthodox Jews perceived that the existing Jewish campus institutions, in the form of B'nai Brith-sponsored Hillel Houses, did not particularly cater to the religious needs of Orthodox Jewish students.[60]

For some students, the solution was to attend the Orthodox Jewish–sponsored Yeshiva University or its sister school, Stern College for Women, both of which were located in Manhattan. There, one could be immersed in a religious environment and could continue his or her religious studies while pursing a secular degree. For others who attended secular universities, the solution was to form campus groups specifically for Orthodox Jewish students. At Columbia University, for example, Jewish religious students established the Yeshurun Society; other campuses developed chapters of Yavneh, the Religious Students Association. Sometimes working within the Hillel structure and other times outside of it, these groups arranged for the provision of kosher food, scheduled lectures on religious topics, and generally operated in loco communitas for students living away from home in a secular atmosphere. By the 1970s regular kosher food service could be found on almost two dozen campuses across the United States and Canada.[61] Moreover, Orthodox Jewish students had integrated into the Hillel Houses by serving on student boards and running their own Sabbath services. By this time, an Orthodox Jewish student could attend some of the finest secular universities in North America and remain immersed in an active religious community.[62]

The development of Orthodox Jewish campus life capped a progression that had begun with the first suburban day schools in the 1940s and 1950s. A seamless system of Orthodox Jewish education, proceeding from nursery school through college graduation, had produced a postwar generation of youth that had never left the social milieu of suburban Orthodoxy. As members of this generation married and settled down, they returned—not surprisingly—to the same suburban Orthodox Jewish communities in which they had grown up (or identical ones elsewhere in North America). Before long, they produced a new generation of children who would begin the same process of education, socialization, and immersion in the religious and cultural world of suburban Orthodox Jewry. But this next generation did not merely continue what their parents and grandparents began. Rather, they carried with them a self-confident traditionalism that matched their entrenchment in suburban middle-class society. Just as they returned to more traditionalist styles in their congregations, the generation of suburban Orthodox

Jews in the 1960s and 1970s similarly transformed their educational experiences. In some cities, such as Toronto, this new attitude was expressed through the development of newer schools that appealed more exclusively to the Orthodox Jewish community.

From its inception in 1960, the Community Hebrew Academy of Toronto had been linked to the Associated Hebrew Day School. Housed in the same building, both schools shared administrators, teachers, and students. For all intents and purposes, CHAT was an Orthodox school even though it was supposed to be a "community" school. For parents and administrators in Toronto's non-Orthodox Jewish schools, such as Bialik or USDS, the relationship between CHAT and Associated conveyed the message that non-Orthodox and non-Associated students were unwelcome in the high school. As a result, when its first classes prepared to graduate in 1968, USDS formed the Independent High School (IHS) as a non-Orthodox alternative to CHAT.[63] For three years, IHS and CHAT operated simultaneously. In the fall of 1971, however, leaders of the United Jewish Welfare Fund (UJWF), the communal organization that sponsored CHAT, sought ways to reduce the competition between the schools; from the UJWF's perspective, if community funds were going to support CHAT, and if CHAT and IHS were merely duplicating services, then something should be done to reduce duplication and save money. One year later, a special committee recommended that IHS and CHAT merge and that a nonreligious stream be integrated into the community school.[64]

Almost immediately, the Orthodox Jewish families with students in CHAT reacted negatively to the recommendations. They had sent their children to CHAT specifically because it provided an academically advanced program in a generally religious environment. Integrating a large number of non-Orthodox Jewish students from IHS and from the secular Jewish Bialik School would do nothing but "water down" this religious atmosphere.[65] Unhappy with the alternative of Ner Israel or Beth Jacob, this group of disaffected CHAT parents, together with Orthodox Jewish families from Eitz Chaim, proceeded to create the Yeshiva B'nei Akiva Or Chaim. Modeled after Israeli yeshiva high schools, Or Chaim espoused a religious Zionist perspective combined with a strong college preparatory program.[66]

On one level, the reaction against CHAT's integration and the speed with which the new Orthodox Jewish high schools were formed can be taken at face value: the addition of non-Orthodox Jewish students would change the religious atmosphere. Practical problems might have emerged, such as the possibility of nonkosher food being brought to school or the scheduling of a non-

Orthodox Jewish classmate's party on the Sabbath. But even if this were to be true, it did not necessarily warrant a formal separation and formation of a new high school. Perhaps a solution could have been found in-house, such as through the formation of separate "religious streams" for more observant students. At a deeper level, the Or Chaim/CHAT split represented the new traditionalist direction of this second generation of suburban Orthodoxy. There was not, after all, anything religiously impermissible about attending school with non-Orthodox Jewish students, yet the Orthodox Jewish community felt something was psychologically wrong with the prospect. The integration with IHS and the inclusion of students from the secular Jewish Bialik school smacked of too much integration, of legitimizing the alternative religious perspectives of the non-Orthodox Jewish community.

To be sure, these problems existed in earlier decades when Orthodox and non-Orthodox Jewish students were educated together. But whereas a decade or two previous, the suburbanizing Orthodox Jewish community was still in its pioneering mode, by the 1970s its religious self-confidence and, more important, its economic self-sufficiency had increased to the point that it was willing and able to break away and to form a new school. In this vein, in the mid-1980s, a split similar to the CHAT/Or Chaim situation occurred at the elementary school level in Toronto. Then, a group of parents, dissatisfied with the increasing nonreligious atmosphere of Associated Day School, broke off and formed the Netivot Hatorah Day School. As with Or Chaim's split from CHAT, the opening of Netivot resulted in the draining of Orthodox Jewish students from Associated, which, by the late 1980s, had virtually no Orthodox Jewish enrollment. In a sense, then, the suburban Orthodox Jewish community was victimized by its own educational successes. At the outset of the postwar period, its private institutions ran counter to the historical models of Jewish and secular education. Over time, however, the broader Jewish community came to recognize the benefits accrued by combining intensive Jewish study and secular academic achievement. But as more non-Orthodox Jews entered the day school educational system, the Orthodox Jewish community realized that its monopoly on religious instruction no longer held and retreated into its own institutions.

The new traditionalist attitude of the suburban Orthodox Jewish community was expressed in other ways, such as the increased visible religious identification among Orthodox Jewish youth. The yarmulke (skullcap, also known in Hebrew as *kippah*), once reserved for synagogue services, Jewish study, and eating, became a normal part of the daily fashion ensemble of Orthodox Jewish males.[67] In contrast to an older generation who were raised in a climate of not publicly displaying one's Judaism and often wore caps or hats, the younger generation had been schooled in ethnic pride and visibly paraded their Judaism on their heads.[68] Initially, the head coverings provoked controversy, as newspapers reported problems faced by students wearing yarmulkes in public school or witnesses refusing to remove their skullcaps in court.[69] Over time, however, the sight of Orthodox Jewish men wearing yarmulkes in school, at the office, or at the ball game became less and less strange. To a degree, the visible religious symbol of the yarmulke reflected a general cultural acceptance of religious and ethnic identification. The civil rights movement of the 1960s heightened social awareness of visible minorities and by the end of the decade, universities had developed a multiplicity of black and ethnic and even Jewish studies programs. The popularity of identifiably ethnic clothing styles, such as various African robes and Indian saris, made the yarmulke just another piece of fashion worn by a minority group.

While the wearing of a yarmulke served to identify religiously observant Jews to the outside world, it also took on significance as an internal identifier within the Orthodox Jewish world. The *type* of head covering one wore made a statement about one's Orthodoxy. Religious Zionists, for example, wore colorful knitted ones, while more traditionalist Orthodox Jews preferred black velvet. *Kippoth* (plural of *kippah*) also played a socializing role, particularly in centrist Orthodox Jewish circles, where boys and girls interacted on a social level. A girl's ability to crochet a *kippah* with intricate designs and multiple colors was often a key to popularity and friendship. Conversely, a certain status was accorded to boys who collected many handmade *kippoth*.

According to Edward Shapiro, "The wearing in public of skullcaps and other distinctive Orthodox clothing [indicated] greater confidence in American pluralism."[70] But even more than confidence in American pluralism, these public displays of religious identity reflected the influence of four decades of Orthodox Jewish education and socialization in the world of suburban Orthodoxy. Study after study showed the impact of day school and yeshiva high school education on Jewish religious identity.[71] Having passed through a seamless educational system, in which lessons learned at one stage were reinforced at the next and in which religious traditionalism was shown to be compatible with the cultural values of the suburban middle class, Orthodox Jews found little reason to hide their religious identity. To wear a yarmulke in public stated that one was an *Orthodox* Jew and that one continued to be so even outside the sacred space of the suburban Orthodox Jewish neighborhood.

In the end, that day schools and other institutions of youth socialization were vital in transmitting the suburban Orthodox Jewish way of life from one generation to another was confirmed not only by the actions of Orthodox Jewish youth but by formal studies. Steven Cohen, for example, showed in 1974 that intensive religious education provided "attitude maintenance" for Jewish youth.[72] In 1998, the first full study of alumni of the National Conference of Synagogue Youth was completed. In that study, over a thousand former NCSY participants responded to a survey of religious behaviors and attitudes. The results showed that participation in the Orthodox youth group was linked to a variety of other indicators of Jewish involvement later in life. More NCSY alumni observed Shabbat, maintained kosher homes, prayed on a regular basis, studied Jewish texts, and sent their own children to Jewish day schools than did the broader Jewish community. Even though most of the participants in NCSY started out as Orthodox Jews (that is, most had not moved from one denominational affiliation to another), the study made clear that NCSY reinforced the socialization process that was crucial to the expansion of the Orthodox Jewish subculture.[73] In short, institutions such as day schools and youth groups complemented the informal learning that occurred in the Orthodox Jewish synagogue and home and reinforced to Orthodox Jewish youth that one could flourish in the suburban middle-class world without losing one's traditionalist religious lifestyle. More important, these were not merely academic lessons; the everyday reality of the suburban Orthodox Jewish world brought this message home to an entire postwar generation. As the next chapter discusses, the development of a religiously based consumer culture among suburban Orthodox Jews represented most clearly this effort to unite suburban and religious ideals and behaviors.

# *Five*

## FAKE BACON:

## ORTHODOX JEWISH

## RELIGIOUS

## CONSUMERISM

In the May 1952 issue of *Commentary* magazine, Morris Freedman wrote an extended essay on the phenomenon of Barton's Chocolates. Established in the late 1930s by Stephen Klein, a European Jewish immigrant, Barton's almost single-handedly created a market for gourmet chocolates. Its boutiques—not stores—were "all show window, frivolously decked with tinsel and ribbon," and designed to give customers a "pleasure" from entering the premises. When they did enter a Barton's store, they found an assortment of some of the finest chocolates available presented in elegant style. As Klein explained, the goal was "to make each piece of candy attractive. All the pieces should look good. You should keep wanting to eat more and not get tired." But for the reporter Freedman, Barton's success lay not in its ability to make chocolate a luxury item but in the fact that it did so while having its chocolates produced under the strict supervision of the Orthodox Union (OU), the kosher certifying agency of the Union of Orthodox Jewish Congregations of America. Such certification meant that every piece of Barton's chocolate—down to the chocolate Santa Clauses and Easter bunnies—could be eaten by Orthodox Jews who observed the religious dietary laws known as *kashruth*. Although Jews who observed the religious dietary laws were in the minority,

Barton's owner Klein recognized the value of gourmet kosher chocolate. Orthodox Jewish businessmen, for example, could give boxes of chocolates as gifts without worrying that they were giving something not kosher. For Orthodox Jews, or for those visiting Orthodox Jews, a box of Barton's had also become "one of the habitual choices for the ritual gift picked up on the way to dinner at a friend's home, or for one's week-end suburban hostess, or for the weekly gathering of the *mishpocha* [family]." Kosher chocolate could even bridge the generations, since "a child may be supplied with a box to present to grandpa because it is *kosher* chocolate; grandpa, for his part, may bring a box to grandson because it is kosher *chocolate.*"[1]

For Freedman, Barton's chocolates represented a "classic example of how Orthodoxy can be subtly attractive to the modern world," where "increased substance and status has found expression [among Orthodox Jews] as often in elegance of cuisine and dining ritual as in the greater modishness of matters pertaining to the synagogue."[2] Together with the changing synagogue structure and a renewed emphasis on youth and education, this sense of religious materialism that Freedman describes was one of the key developments in the suburban Orthodox Jewish experience of the post–World War II period. The physical movement of Orthodox Jews into suburbia was accompanied by their socioeconomic movement into a middle-class and upper-middle-class world of consumerism, epitomized by the land-consuming sprawl of suburban subdivisions and the material consumerism of shopping malls. It should not surprise, then, that such secular consumerist styles influenced the development of a religious consumerism that dominated postwar suburban Orthodox Jewry. In this period, Orthodox Jewish homes became filled not only with kosher chocolates like Barton's but also with thousands of new kosher grocery products, award-winning (and expensive) kosher wines, and a range of artistic (and expensive) Jewish ritual objects for display and for use. Moreover, the Orthodox Jewish individuals in those homes listened to Jewish rock music on CDs and *divrei torah* (lit., words of Torah, refers to short sermons on a scriptural or religious legal topic) and *shiurim* (classes or lectures) on tapes. To be sure, Jews of all religious backgrounds became increasingly interested in a Jewish "objects culture" in the postwar period. As the sociologist Herbert Gans noted in 1956, "A relatively large amount of business is now done in things whose main function is to be 'Jewish' or portray something Jewish: doilies and tablecloths with the Star of David [and] pictures, books, and records depicting Jews (usually conspicuously pious ones)."[3] But whereas for most Jews, this interest in Jewish objects masked the absence of actual ritual—owning a decorative silver kiddush cup sufficed even if one never recited the kiddush on Friday nights—for suburban Orthodox Jews, consumerism was wrapped in religious observance.

The suburban Orthodox Jewish community's embrace of religious consumerism should not be seen as a departure from or rejection of religious tradition. To the contrary, Jews have historically valued special "items of luxury" such as silver candlesticks and cups for kiddush.[4] But although the Orthodox Jewish halakhah rejects the ascetic lifestyle, it does not condone unbridled consumerism. Instead, the halakhah demands that consumption occur within religiously appropriate boundaries. For example, the halakhah requires that one must recite a blessing before eating as an articulation of appreciation of God as the source of all food. In another vein, one of the most widely known customs of a Jewish wedding ceremony, the breaking of a glass by the groom, has its roots in a rabbinical warning against too much ostentation at the reception.[5] For traditionalist Judaism, then, consumption is a value-neutral, religiously mediated activity that if done properly can be infused with holiness, or, if not, can be degraded with excess. Such a middle-ground approach to material consumption stands in contrast to the attitudes of other groups in the history of North American religion. At one extreme, groups like the Amish and the Shakers have championed asceticism, or at least the minimalization of material goods. At the other end, groups such as seventeenth-century Puritans viewed material accumulation as a sign of divine blessing; the more one had, the more one was favored by Heaven. Contemporary "gospels of wealth" continue this theme, seeing socioeconomic upward mobility as evidence of religious "success." For example, the televangelist Frederick Price uses his television ministry to promote a prosperity theology, based in part on Mark 12:24, in which Jesus declared that "what things so ever you desire, when you pray, believe that you receive them, and you shall have them." For Price, this verse clearly demonstrates that material accumulation is a sure sign of proper Christian faith.[6]

Although not always expressed in as blatant terms as those used by Price, this sense of material consumerism has seeped into much of the North American religious world. Overt religious holidays such as Christmas have been shaped by a "material Christianity" and other quasi-religious holidays such as Thanksgiving, Valentine's Day, and Halloween have a clear material component.[7] In many cases, the religious materialism focuses on food, such as the tradition of Christmas fruitcakes, Thanksgiving turkeys, chocolate Easter bunnies, and the numerous Halloween candies. But in their religious guise, food habits also serve as vehicles for group identification and as barriers to so-cial integration.[8] For example, participation in the food ritual of the commu-nion or Eucharist brings Christians together and serves in many churches as a marker of in-group status (only confirmed members or those who have been "saved" may partake, for example). Conversely, food can exclude, such as when an observant Muslim businessman attends a lunch meeting at which pork is served or when an Orthodox Jewish secretary is excluded from an office celebration that includes nonkosher food.[9] More than simply prevent-ing Orthodox Jews from eating ham or pork, the religious system of *kashruth* is perhaps the best example of religious consumerism. In fact, the story of the development of the kosher food industry and of a broader "kosher" lifestyle among suburban Orthodox Jews symbolizes the broader story of suburban Orthodox Jews in the postwar period. The professionalization and standard-ization of the kosher food industry, the commodification and commercial-ization of kosher food, and the emergence of a broader kosher lifestyle, all represented an infusion of strict religious practices with modern suburban consumerist styles. For suburban Orthodox Jews, in short, religious consum-erism in the form of the kosher lifestyle was yet "another striking example of the historical adaptability of an ancient tradition to totally new conditions." [10]

It is important to clarify a number of issues about the concept of *kash-ruth*, or of "keeping kosher," which is among the most fundamental—but also misunderstood—parts of the Orthodox Jewish subculture. To start, kosher food is *not* food that is blessed by a rabbi. Rather, the laws of *kashruth* involve categories of foods that are and are not permissible according to Or-thodox Jewish halakhah, both as written explicitly in the Torah and as inter-preted by rabbinical authorities. For example, permitted animals include only domestic and wild animals that chew their cud and have completely cloven hooves (e.g., cow, goat, sheep, deer). Animals with only one or neither of these characteristics are forbidden. All domesticated fowl are permitted, while all birds of prey are forbidden. One can eat fish that have both scales and fins (e.g., tuna, salmon, halibut) but not scavenger fish, shellfish, and other seafood.

In addition to the mere permissibility of animal or bird, *kashruth* is also de-termined by the way an animal is slaughtered. One must slaughter a kosher animal or bird (but not fish) in a ritually proper manner that involves cut-ting an animal's throat at a specific point using a specific type of knife. Com-mon methods of killing, such as stunning or shooting, render even a per-mitted animal unfit for consumption. Once a permitted animal is ritually slaughtered, its meat must be soaked, salted, drained, and rinsed of blood within a prescribed period of time. Finally, the entire slaughtering-salting-rinsing-packaging process must be supervised and approved by knowledgeable individuals who understand the extensive laws of *kashruth*. Any food that is not considered kosher is referred to as being *treyf*. Technical questions about *kashruth* pertain to prepared and packaged foods as well, since the food prohibitions extend to animal by-products and derivatives. Because the thousands of additives, preservatives, flavorings, colorings, and production agents that are part of modern food technology are sometimes derived from non-kosher sources, they must be specifically certified as kosher. Finally, the laws of *kashruth* also prohibit mixing dairy and meat products or even foods derived from dairy or meat sources.

The complexity of contemporary food production means that individuals cannot individually ascertain the *kashruth* of any one item. Instead, large national *kashruth* organizations, such as the Orthodox Union (the OU) and the Organized Kashruth Laboratories (the OK), supervise the production of national food brands. These large-scale supervisory organizations certify both that the food product contains permissible ingredients and that there was no mixture of dairy and meat ingredients. Many individual Jewish communities also maintain their own *kashruth* supervisory organizations for local products, butchers, and kosher restaurants. To convey to consumers the status of a product, certifying agencies often place a small logo or marking on the product's label.[11]

That the laws of *kashruth* have so much technical detail is mainly because of the development of modern food technology. The historical observance of *kashruth* presented far fewer problems for Jews in earlier generations. In the rural shtetls of Europe, Jewish families generally oversaw the entire production of their own food. Individuals slaughtered their own meat and poultry in the ritually proper manner or enlisted the services of the local *shohet* (ritual slaughterer). There was little concern about the *kashruth* of meat slaughtered by someone else, both because of the interpersonal familiarity of the shtetl and because the community could enforce strict religious standards. Moreover, because commercial food production was unknown, individuals generally produced their own food and could be sure of its *kashruth*.

In the urban neighborhoods of North America, the laws of *kashruth* were among the first rituals to be abandoned by immigrant Jews. Freed from the shtetl's communal pressures, immigrant Jews chose to eat what foods they wanted when they wanted and where they wanted. But even for those who chose to maintain the dietary rituals, several factors made the observance of *kashruth* difficult. For one thing, most Jewish immigrants lacked the space to raise their own animals; a tenement apartment, after all, made a poor barn-yard. As a result, the personal supervision over the slaughtering process that was common in Europe was transferred to a third party. But whereas in a small village, relying on someone else to do the slaughtering might have been acceptable, a person in a large urban community did not know everyone and did not always have immediate knowledge of a slaughterer's reliability. In ad-dition, North American Jewish communities lacked the enforcement capa-bilities that European shtetl communities had; the religious freedom of the United States and Canada meant that no body could legally demand that all slaughterers be subject to rabbinical supervision.

In the absence of communal regulation, many butchers and meat mer-chants seized the opportunity to defraud the Jewish community. Most com-mon, butchers sold lower-priced nonkosher meat as kosher meat, thus de-ceiving customers and obtaining an extra profit. "Kosher" butchers hung fake certificates attesting to the religious permissibility of the product. Some inten-tionally misled customers by using deceptive window signs. In Hebrew, the words *basar kasher* (kosher meat) are almost visually identical to the nonsense phrase *basar basar* (meat meat). A store owner who put the latter sign in a store window technically told the truth—he *was* selling meat, after all—even though, in reality, many customers misread the signs and assumed the meat sold inside was kosher.[12] No standards of supervision or certification existed for manufactured goods either. Some manufacturers placed their own un-substantiated claims for *kashruth* on the label, while others "cited personal endorsement by figures whose rabbinic status and personal qualifications may or may not have been identifiable."[13]

Standardization began to appear in the early 1920s, when the Union of Orthodox Jewish Congregations established the Orthodox Union as a joint rabbinical-lay program of *kashruth* supervision to oversee local slaughtering and meat processing as well as commercial food manufacturing. The first company to place the trademarked symbol—the letter "U" inside the letter "O," now known as the OU—on its label was the H. J. Heinz Company, which produced OU-supervised Vegetarian Beans in 1923.[14] In some cities, groups of rabbis cooperated to ensure that properly slaughtered meat and poultry were available for Jews who desired to purchase it. In the 1930s, for example, a group of Orthodox Jewish rabbis in St. Louis formed the Va'ad Hoeir (City Council) to provide a centralized *kashruth* certification service for local butchers. More common, however, was the situation in prewar Toronto, where Rabbis David Ochs, Myer Gruenwald, and Abraham Price each provided supervision for specific butchers and stores. Because each rabbi had his own community of followers who trusted only their rabbi, this fragmentation of supervision created some divisiveness and even open conflict in the larger Orthodox Jewish community. With this division, those Orthodox Jews who did not specifically follow one of these rabbis had little guidance in questions of *kashruth*. As Tom Brown, owner of a resort on Lake Simcoe an hour north of Toronto, explained, "pride and prejudice" and "petty politics" kept Toronto from creating a centralized *kashruth* authority. Why was it so difficult, Brown asked, for Toronto's rabbis "to get their house in order"? [15]

Toronto's fragmented state of *kashruth* supervision began to change in the late 1940s, when a group of Orthodox Jewish communal leaders, together with several rabbis who were not formerly involved in *kashruth* supervision, formed the Division of Orthodox Synagogues as a branch of the Canadian Jewish Congress's Central Region (later known as the Council of Orthodox Rabbis, or COR). Over the next decade, the Orthodox Division slowly worked to create a comprehensive plan for the communal supervision of *kashruth*. Rabbis Gedalia Felder and Nachman Shemen were selected as the Kashruth Council's chairman and secretary-director, respectively. With the support of the other rabbis in the Orthodox Jewish community, the Kashruth Council took control of the inspection and certification of the city's butchers, slaughterhouses, and food stores. As announced in 1958, any store that was certified "kosher" would be given a sign to hang on the premises, and any packaged food approved by the council would have a small "COR" logo placed on the label. In addition, the new council recognized the certification of those rabbis who already maintained their own separate supervision programs. [16]

Although the professionalization and expansion of *kashruth* supervision did not begin as a suburban phenomenon, it was important for the development of a suburban Orthodox Jewish community. First, these supervisory organizations helped to reinforce a developing consumerist identity among suburbanizing Orthodox Jews. When a series of incidents involving butchers who misrepresented the *kashruth* of their products occurred in the early 1960s, community *kashruth* leaders turned not to the butchers and store owners but directly to consumers. A 1961 editorial in the *Canadian Jewish News* declared that there was "a need to reeducate the Jewish public regarding the laws and obligation and importance of kashrut." [17] The following year, another editorial urged consumers to take matters into their own hands and buy meat only from "reputable" dealers who dealt with Toronto's Kashruth Council. "It is up to the housewife" to win the "battle for *kashruth*," the editorial concluded.[18]

The emergence of centralized *kashruth* programs also eased the burdens of maintaining a kosher kitchen at a time when the management of the family's food consumption was the primary responsibility of suburban middle-class women. As one analysis of postwar suburbia explained, women were "responsible for buying supplies, for the smooth functioning of complicated mechanical gadgets which assist her to put the finishing touches to processed and semiprocessed foods; and above all, for the maintenance of proper nutritional standards as laid down by dieticians."[19] Even as the changing realities of middle-class life compelled Orthodox Jewish women to enter the workforce, the responsibilities of food preparation and the religious imperatives of the kosher dietary laws remained in place.[20] Thus working Orthodox Jewish women were a ready and willing market for any developments that offered more convenient ways to obtain and prepare kosher food for their families.

For suburban, middle-class Orthodox Jewish consumers, then, the professionalization and standardization of *kashruth* meant that they could participate in the same consumerist trends as their nonkosher-consuming neighbors without abandoning their religious obligations. The COR and OU logos on food labels or in storefronts served as a religious equivalent to the Good Housekeeping Seal, communicating to consumers that a certain store or product was "approved." These instantly recognizable signs of *kashruth* meant that a consumer need not worry about a product's religious permissibility and could decide to purchase it based on other factors such as taste, nutritional value, or convenience. Furthermore, the availability of kosher television dinners and instant cake mixes gave the kosher homemaker the same flexibility as other suburban domestic managers. As one reporter explained in 1965, "The observant Jewish homemaker also wants preprocessed foods and she too can afford them." Like her non-Orthodox Jewish counterpart, an Orthodox Jewish housewife, not wanting to work over a stove and countertop all day, could now put together a meal for her family using ready-made and instant products without worrying about the permissibility of the ingredients contained inside.[21]

Her options were expanded greatly by the rapid increase in the number of kosher food products available. In 1926, for example, the Union of Orthodox Jewish Congregations placed its OU label on products made by fewer than a dozen companies. By 1956, this total had increased to almost two hundred producers and over a thousand different individual products. Only seven years later, the Orthodox Union supervised more than two thousand products made by over 430 companies.[22] By the mid-1990s, the OU label could be found on over ten thousand products and included some of the most popular and classic brand names, such as Oreo cookies and M & M candies. With this expansion, an Orthodox Jewish homemaker seeking to stock her pantry was no longer confined to the foods commonly associated with Eastern European immigrants such as chopped liver, delicatessen, smoked fish, and anything with garlic and onions.[23] Kosher consumers could even choose kosher versions of nonpermissible foods; food technologists produced soybean-based "Protose meats" that were meant to taste like ham, bacon, and other nonkosher beef products but were entirely acceptable. Again, it must be stressed that *kashruth* prohibitions are based on technical and legal categories of food. Although some might find the idea of eating fake ham contrary to the spirit of the *kashruth* laws—and some might even argue that eating such foods violates the religious principle of not imitating non-Jewish behaviors—there is nothing ritually improper about imitation foods. Fake bacon was perhaps an extreme example, but it reflected the extent to which kosher food was transformed from a minor ethnic concern to a major commercialized industry.

Changes in the experience of kosher consumption extended out of the kitchen to the experience of shopping as well. Historically, kosher food was purchased in the traditional manner of small corner grocers. Butchers would display their kosher meats and prepared foods in large refrigerator cases and assemble orders for customers individually. The few ready-to-buy products were also specially assembled for the customer. As the general corner grocer evolved to the large supermarket, the kosher store modernized as well.[24] At first, stores offered ready-to-eat take-out foods for customers wanting a break from cooking. "Why Waste Your Precious FUN TIME working over a hot stove?" asked a 1962 advertisement for Toronto's Rubenstein's Kosher Poultry Products, when Rubenstein's could provide "ALL YOUR FOOD ready prepared."[25] Later, stores such as Stroli's in suburban Toronto, which claimed to be the city's first "self-service" kosher grocery store, allowed shoppers to fill their own baskets from several aisles of kosher products.[26] Stroli's opening had followed on the heels of the opening of a kosher meat counter in the Steinberg's supermarket at the corner of Bathurst Street and Sheppard Avenue.[27] Looking like the regular nonkosher meat counter, the kosher meat counter was supervised by the COR and was closed on Saturdays and Jewish holidays. Because more grocery products bore kosher symbols, the Steinberg's kosher

*Millbrook Marketeria, 3101 Bathurst Street, 1950s. Note the sign in the lower right advertising that "Streit's Has Everything Kosher for Passover." Aaron Weisblatt personal collection.*

meat counter enabled shoppers to bypass the specialized kosher food stores altogether, if they so chose. By the late 1960s, Toronto's suburban Orthodox Jewish community had a range of kosher shopping options, with over twenty-five different kosher establishments in the Bathurst Street corridor, ranging from the large supermarket meat counters to smaller butchers and take-out storefronts.[28] Interestingly, the availability of kosher meat in regular grocery stores did not put the smaller, specialized kosher stores out of business. The market for kosher products in Toronto grew sufficiently large and diverse to support a range of store types. Many Jews simply preferred to shop in the all-Jewish environment, while others wanted to support Jewish entrepreneurs, and still others did not want to buy kosher food from a place that was open on the Sabbath (even if it was owned by non-Jews). In all probability, the presence of large and small stores that sold kosher meat and food helped Toronto's kosher consumers because it promoted competition, ensured a large range of products, and prevented any single store from having a monopoly position.

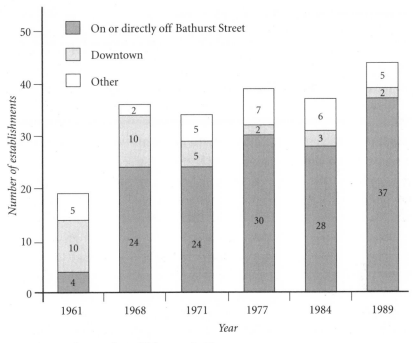

FIGURE 1. *Kosher Food Establishments in Toronto, 1961–1989*

From the professionalization and commercialization of the *kashruth* industry, it was a short step to the creation of a broader kosher lifestyle. Socioeconomic upward mobility was providing increasing amounts of disposable
income for Orthodox Jews to expand their tastes for religious consumption
beyond the basic kitchen staples. One example of this process was the growth
of "gourmet" kosher foods such as Barton's Chocolates. Similarly, the kosher
wine industry exploded in the mid-1980s with the introduction of wines that
were not of the syrupy sweet Concord grape variety. In 1984, Israel's Golan
Heights Winery marketed a kosher sauvignon blanc wine under the Yarden
label. Kosher consumers took to the Yarden wine and to the other Golan
and Gamla products issued by Golan. By the end of the decade, French, Ital-
ian, and Californian wineries had moved into the kosher wine market with
consistently high-quality wines of all types. By the early 1990s, kosher wines
were winning international wine competitions, and consumers responded.
In 1989 over 180,000 cases of kosher wines were sold in the United States; by
1994, this number had more than doubled to over 365,000 cases.[29] Like the
kosher food industry, kosher wine makers had their eyes on both Jewish and

non-Jewish consumers. Most of the new gourmet kosher wines had very non-Jewish-looking designs, with the kosher certification symbol often placed in tiny print in a corner of the label. Even the traditional sweet wines were repackaged. In a classic example of consumer-oriented marketing, Kesser Wines noted that its sweet Concord grape wine was made on "the western end of Long Island," a description that evoked far more romantic images than "Brooklyn."

For many Orthodox Jews, however, the major affirmation of material success and the key transformation of the kosher lifestyle came with the kosher restaurant and the experience of eating out. In prewar immigrant Jewish neighborhoods, restaurants often had more of an ethnic flavor than a religious one. Many "Jewish" restaurants served traditional Eastern European fare such as stuffed cabbage, delicatessen, and blintzes and provided a Jewish atmosphere for socializing. Often, the food served was not explicitly *un*kosher, but neither was it supervised by any rabbinical authority; a restaurant might have served stuffed cabbage with kosher meat while also offering bagels and cream cheese, thus violating *kashruth* prohibitions against serving dairy and meat food together. These establishments conducted their own supervision, and customers relied on the knowledge and honesty of owners not to used forbidden ingredients. Even in the urban Orthodox Jewish community, the lack of rabbinical supervision often did not hamper one's dining experience. Many Orthodox Jews simply lowered their observance levels when it came to eating in restaurants; eating cold salads, fish, or other dairy foods in a nonkosher or "Jewish" restaurant was commonplace even for otherwise strictly observant Jews.[30]

By the late 1950s, however, the changes in the kosher food experience inside the Orthodox Jewish home began to influence Orthodox Jewish eating habits outside the home. Increasingly, this community wanted religiously acceptable places to eat that also befit their newfound status as upwardly mobile consumers. In 1961, advertisements for Toronto's first kosher restaurant in the suburban neighborhoods reflected this religious consumption need. Named Sova, Hebrew for satisfaction, the "elegant" restaurant was touted as a "rendezvous of the elite," with food that was "lauded by gourmets." An Orthodox Jewish community leader expressed a similar sentiment, declaring that Sova filled the Orthodox Jewish community's "aspiration" for a "modern, deluxe, strictly kosher restaurant."[31] Over time, more kosher restaurants joined Sova and tapped into a market of religious consumption. In 1966, Eppes Essen Delicatessen opened a couple of blocks north of Sova on Bathurst Street.

The Kosher Pizza House opened a few blocks south of Sova in 1970. A few months later, the owners of the Hermes Kosher Bakery opened the Kosher Dairy Kitchen and Pastry Shop further south on Bathurst Street. The fall of 1972 saw the opening of Marky's Delicatessen as another kosher deli under COR supervision.[32] By the late 1970s, Toronto's kosher consumers had over fifteen restaurants to choose from, a total that grew to over thirty by 1989.

Together with the growing numbers of bakeries, butchers, and take-out food stores, Toronto's new kosher restaurants testified to the socioeconomic maturation of the suburban Orthodox Jewish community. As eating out had become an everyday part of suburban consumerist society, Orthodox Jews no longer found religious dietary restrictions an impediment to participating in this trend. For businessmen, kosher restaurants offered a religiously preferable alternative to eating cold salads in a nonkosher eatery. For housewives, kosher restaurants provided another option in the growing array of alternatives for domestic religious consumption. The expanding kosher restaurant market also reflected a growing sophistication and awareness among suburban Orthodox Jews of their consumer power. Even though they desired such kosher dining establishments, the suburban Orthodox Jewish community by no means acted as unthinking automatons who supported every kosher restaurant that opened. During the 1970s, for example, several kosher restaurants in Toronto opened and closed in a relatively short period of time. As reviews in the Jewish press explained, many of these failures stemmed from a poor sense of consumer relations. For example, one reviewer described the Kosher Pizza House as "not the most attractive place," "seedy" and "decrepit," with a "decor [that] is totally uninspiring." Hagalil Restaurant, a short-lived establishment that sold Israeli and Chinese food, dished "out pedestrian fare that will wilt taste buds."[33] In large part, these restaurants failed because they "tended to relax their quality control in the mistaken belief that observant Jews, as a captive group, have no other options." In reality, suburban Orthodox Jews had a very powerful consumerist option: to "stay at home and cook" rather than support unappealing restaurants simply for the sake of having kosher eateries.[34]

By the 1980s, the kosher restaurant industry had stabilized and grew at a steadier rate than it had during the decade before. A wider range of menu styles appeared, such as kosher Chinese, Moroccan, and Yemenite restaurants, and those that opened generally lasted longer than had their predecessors. Kosher pizza shops also sprouted, as Toronto joined with other Jewish communities in its affinity for permissible versions of the stereotypical North

American fast food. In fact, to many Orthodox Jews, being able to stop in at a pizza parlor and pick up a slice or two of greasy kosher pizza epitomized the kosher consumerist lifestyle. As Edward Shapiro has argued, the popularity of such religiously acceptable suburban eateries "disclosed an impulse toward cultural amalgamation as the Orthodox strove to combine the best of the Jewish and outside world." In Shapiro's estimation, "the consumption of [kosher] haute cuisine . . . was in itself a secular act."[35] As this discussion has shown, however, the exact opposite is perhaps a better interpretation: this pattern of consumption was a *religious* act. After all, what was striking about the development of the kosher lifestyle was that it was a *kosher* lifestyle. The suburban Orthodox Jewish community might have developed food habits and restaurant tastes drawn from the secular suburban world, but these habits and tastes remained adaptations nonetheless. The creation of a kosher lifestyle and broader styles of religious consumption reflected Orthodox Jews' desires not to assimilate or to shed their religious practices but to maintain their religious observances.

Having expanded its consumption activities to kosher restaurants, the suburban Orthodox Jewish community soon turned to other outlets for its newfound kosher lifestyle, including hotels, resorts, and vacation tours that provided kosher foods to patrons. Kosher hotels were already a part of Orthodox Jewish culture in some parts of North America. Outside of New York City, for example, hotels operated along the Atlantic shore and in the Catskill Mountains, serving kosher food and maintaining a generally religious atmosphere for observant Jewish guests.[36] Starting in the 1960s and 1970s and booming in the 1980s and 1990s, a newer form of kosher hotel appeared. This model involved entrepreneurs temporarily taking over nonkosher hotels and resorts and providing kosher services for a limited period of time, often over the Passover holiday. Passover was a particularly popular (and profitable) time for the kosher hotel business because of the holiday's comprehensive food restrictions.[37] Staying in a kosher hotel and receiving three meals a day for an entire week proved attractive to families—especially housewives—familiar with the extensive housecleaning and food preparation associated with the holiday. Most kosher hotels operated in Miami Beach, but others opened in Hawaii, Arizona, and even Acapulco. Kosher vacation packages also began to appear, with cruises, cross-country bus tours, and even African safaris that provided kosher food for participants.[38]

None of these developments could have happened, of course, had the Orthodox Jewish market not been both economically able and religiously interested in supporting such kosher lifestyle activities. Furthermore, the expansion of religious consumption seemed to develop a momentum of its own, as middle-class and upper-middle-class suburban Orthodox Jews developed new tastes that matched their socioeconomic standing. It was, in a sense, a confirmation of Colin Campbell's characterization of modern consumption as an "insatiability which arises out of a basic inexhaustibility of wants themselves."[39] Thus from restaurants and hotels, religious consumerism moved to other nonfood areas. Orthodox Jewish clothing styles, for example, changed. Specialized boutiques opened in many cities selling stylish hats and wigs to Orthodox Jewish women who were required by religious halakhah to cover their hair. Among certain groups of Orthodox Jewish youth, the yarmulke became a fashion statement. In centrist Orthodox Jewish circles, for example, colorful and intricately designed *kippoth* were prized for their stylish presentation. Also popular for little boys were leather yarmulkes with cartoon characters painted on. This commercialization of yarmulke fashions permitted an Orthodox Jewish boy to fulfill his obligation to cover his head while remaining connected to the secular world of pop culture.

In many communities, the development of an Orthodox Jewish market led to the creation of specialized "Yellow Pages" targeted at Orthodox Jews. In the early 1990s, the *Smart Shopper's Guide* began publishing a quarterly directory of businesses and services oriented to the Orthodox Jewish community. The guide included advertisements for kosher caterers and Jewish bands, wig and hat stores, sterling silver importers, and kosher restaurants. Many of the advertisements explicitly appealed to the consumerist tendencies of Toronto's Orthodox Jewish community. "Need to outfit your cottage?" asked an advertisement for Royal Linen, in a direct acknowledgment that Toronto's Orthodox Jews were as likely as other Canadians to own a summer vacation home. Another advertisement suggested that although Orthodox Jews have a custom of immersing new dishes and utensils in a special *mikveh* (ritual bath), they might be willing to pay someone else to perform this ritual. The owners of Dunkin' Dishes—a name that cleverly played off the prominent chain of donut stores—offered to "toivel [immerse] your dishes so you don't have to."[40] The success of publications like the *Smart Shopper's Guide* led others to undertake even larger projects such as the *Toronto Community Directory*, which was first published in 1994. The directory featured "a residential listing of the Orthodox Jewish community, as well as a listing of the many professional, commercial, and retail establishments which flourish in our midst." The 1995 directory made even more explicit its target market, explaining that the listed businesses included "only Shomer Shabbos businesses." As if to emphasize the inward focus of this marketing plan, the directory urged readers to "Support Your Community, No One Else Will." [41]

Religious consumerism also infiltrated the world of Jewish music and media. The growth of folk and other alternative forms of music received a Jewish twist in the early 1960s by Rabbi Shlomo Carlebach, who almost single-handedly created a new form of Jewish music that combined traditional *Ḥasidic* melodies with modern musical styles. Carlebach's infectious tunes proved most popular with Jewish youth, and by the 1970s Jewish teenagers began to copy Carlebach's styles. In Toronto, for example, the Shma Yisroel (Listen, Israel) band began in 1974 among a group of students at the Community Hebrew Academy. Although looking very much like a typical teenage "garage band," Shma Yisroel was as likely to play Carlebach's popular wedding song, "Od Yishama," as to bang out Led Zeppelin's "Stairway to Heaven." Carlebach-influenced music grew in popularity in the next three decades in both North America and Israel. Tapes and compact discs recorded by artists such as Mordechai Ben-David and Avraham Fried and groups such as the Miami Boys Choir took Carlebach's style and expanded and redefined it for a digital age. Recordings of such *simḥa* (lit., happiness, refers here to a celebration, often connected to the life cycle, such as a wedding) music were as professional as any secular recording, and the live shows were equally slick and well presented. In Toronto and in other cities, *simḥa* music radio shows appeared in the 1990s, replete with advertisements from kosher butchers and Jewish bookstores, providing yet another testimony to the market of Orthodox Jewish consumers.

Given the traditional Jewish emphasis on texts and learning, it was not surprising that as Orthodox Jewish consumerism expanded, publishers of sacred texts found a ready market. In 1961, Wolfe Kelman, writing in the *American Jewish Year Book*, noted that Orthodox Jewish entrepreneurs were demonstrating "great ingenuity and faith by reprinting hundreds of classic Jewish texts published in Europe in the last century. Even more surprising than the number of volumes being produced by these entrepreneurs was the large number of purchasers they attracted, suggesting that more and more American-educated Jews as well as recent arrivals cared enough to buy and study the works which had been the traditional texts and companions of the learned in Eastern Europe." [42] More important than their desire to buy books was that they had the money to do so. Perhaps the major turning point in the expansion of the Orthodox Jewish book market came in 1976 with the first publication from the Art Scroll series. Founded in Brooklyn by two Orthodox Jewish rabbis, Art Scroll was oriented to an English-speaking audience. Many centrist and left-wing Orthodox Jews criticized Art Scroll for its studious avoidance of modern scholarship and sometimes hagiographic interpretations of Jewish history. Despite these views, Art Scroll books on the Bible, the Talmud, Jewish holidays, and other topics won themselves a permanent place on Orthodox and non-Orthodox Jewish bookshelves.

Art Scroll's success also encouraged the expansion of other Torah-oriented media. Torah tapes, the Orthodox Jewish equivalent of the popular books on tape, first appeared in the late 1960s and soon became a fixture in many Orthodox Jewish homes. Initially, Torah tapes emerged from a simple desire to record and preserve *shiurim* by prominent teachers and rabbis. But as with many good ideas, this one soon became big business. Organizations such as the Orthodox Union developed tape series for purchase; the Jewish Dimensions series, for example, offered dozens of specially recorded lectures on topics from Jewish holidays to Bible study to Jewish prayer. The market for such Torah tapes was wide-ranging. One target audience was those Jews involved in the *ba'al teshuva* movement, those "returnees to Judaism" who were becoming more observant and wanted an easy "self-help" format. But another market group was the already committed Orthodox Jews whose busy professional and personal lives left them no time to attend *shiurim*. Just as secular books on tape were marketed to suburban residents who had long commutes to work, Torah tapes enabled Orthodox Jewish commuters to fulfill the obligation of Torah study while driving to work.[43]

Religious consumerism even extended to the Orthodox Jewish bedroom, in a manner of speaking. According to Orthodox Jewish halakhah, a husband and wife may not engage in sexual relations during or seven days following the wife's monthly menstrual period. At the end of the seven-day waiting period, the woman immerses herself in a *mikveh*, a ritual bath constructed according to strict religious guidelines. Only after this immersion are she and her husband permitted to each other. For centuries, the *mikveh* and the observance of the laws of *taharath mishpaḥah* (family purity) were central to the Jewish religious experience, with each community maintaining its own ritual bath for women to use. In North America, however, the observance of these laws quickly fell into disfavor with immigrant Jews. Premodern notions of female ritual "impurity" contrasted negatively with modern ideas about feminine sexuality. In addition, many urban *mikvaoth* were often set in less-than-modern physical conditions, without implementation of standards of hygiene and cleanliness. In many communities, the practice of the laws of *mikveh* was abandoned by all but a tiny minority of Jews.

For many Orthodox Jewish rabbinical and community leaders, the observance of *taharath mishpaḥah* was an essential foundation for the expansion of Orthodox Jewry, and they urged Orthodox Jewish women to maintain these laws. To make the *mikveh* experience more palatable to suburban, middle-class women, Orthodox Jewish communities began in the 1950s and 1960s to build newer facilities. In Toronto, where "people felt that the old *mikveh* was not good for the modern generation," a new *mikveh* opened in suburban North York in January 1960.[44] "Good news for Jewish women of North York and other suburban municipalities!" declared an advertisement for the new facility, located at Bathurst and Edinburgh Drive. Not only was the geographic location more convenient for women who previously had to travel downtown, but the new bathhouse was also described in popular scientific-sounding terminology—a "modern ritualarium." Eight years later, when the Orthodox Jewish community raised funds to build another facility on Sheppard Avenue, the Jewish newspaper once again emphasized the "ultramodern" nature of the new *mikveh* building. As these advertisements showed, the religious ritual of *mikveh* had become a "product" to be "marketed" to Orthodox Jewish women consumers.[45]

The commodification of the *mikveh* practice was extended in the 1970s, when the ritual was appropriated into the context of Jewish feminism. Although many women saw the ritual laws as backward and negative for women's progress, many Orthodox Jewish women saw it as a special ritual reserved for women only. Having the monthly separation from one's husband and the obligation to participate in this immersion ritual provided many Orthodox Jewish women with a source of inspiration and a source of proactive religious participation. Through their reinterpretation of the *mikveh* experience, Orthodox Jewish women became active producers of their consumption experiences, overlaying traditional observances with modern expressions of feminine spirituality and, in some cases, overt sexuality. The act of monthly immersions, then, became a conscious act that Orthodox Jewish women, as religious consumers, chose for themselves.

There were, of course, many who wondered if religious consumerism had gone too far. As early as 1961, an article in *Jewish Life* chided the Orthodox Jewish community for its commercialization of the holiday of Ḥanukkah, which was rapidly becoming the "Jewish Christmas." The proliferation of "numerous novelties, cards, display materials" as well as the "endless variety of menorahs [candelabra]—bubbling menorahs, plastic menorahs for indoor and outdoor use, decorative menorahs, musical menorahs, and so on and on" had reduced the holiday to a "businessman's dream" and denuded it of any real religious meaning.[46] Two decades later, an Orthodox Jewish rabbi questioned the value of integrating religious and modern styles when such synthesis resulted in little more than "Jewish men with yarmulkes dancing at fashionable discos."[47] In a similar vein, an article in *Tradition*, the journal of the centrist Orthodox Rabbinical Council of America, asked simply, "Is Club Med Kosher?" While it was laudable, the article's author explained, that Orthodox Jews sought to adhere strictly to the ritual laws of *kashruth* even when on vacation, it was less clear whether one should even take such vacations in the first place.[48]

Through the 1980s and 1990s, as the Orthodox Jewish world moved rightward, the debates over consumerism increased, although not to the degree of the debates in the conservative Protestant world. In the late 1980s, a controversy arose in New York City over the *kashruth* certification of the Glatt Yacht. Marketed as a kosher version of Manhattan dinner cruises, the Glatt Yacht offered fine dining and dancing on the Hudson River. For the Kof-K supervisory agency, the organization that supervised the Glatt Yacht, the dining was fine but the dancing was not. It threatened to withdraw the certification unless the boat ended the dancing; nothing, however, was said about the food that was served. Those who supported the boat argued that a *kashruth* question should be solely about the food and its permissibility. Opponents claimed that a *kashruth* agency's stamp of approval of a restaurant implies an endorsement of *all* activities in that restaurant and because the Kof-K did not approve of the mixed dancing, it had every right to withdraw certification. At stake, of course, was not the particular certification of the Glatt Yacht, which found another agency to provide supervision, but the concept of Glatt Yachts in general. Were dinner cruises, like Club Meds, kosher? Should Orthodox Jews partake of dining and dancing overlooking the Manhattan skyline? Such admonishments, however, were a case of too little, too late; religious consumption had become an integral part of the North American suburban Orthodox Jewish experience.

Ironically, as debates raged within Orthodox Jewry over the limits of kosher consumerism, the secular world had come to accept and even embrace all things kosher. By the 1990s Orthodox Jews had become a minority of consumers of kosher food products in North America. For millions of non-Jewish consumers, the designation "kosher" came to represent "quality," "healthful,"

and "good-for-you." Some consumers sought out kosher food for religious reasons. Observant Muslims, for example, bought kosher-certified food
knowing it would contain no non-*halal* ingredients. Seventh Day Adventists
relied on kosher food labeled "*pareve*" because they knew that it contained no
animal ingredients. Other nonreligious vegetarians bought kosher food for
the same reasons. Lactose-intolerant consumers also looked for the "*pareve*"
notation on foods because they could be assured that the food had no dairy
ingredients. And millions of others simply assumed that the fact that some
rabbi or organization oversaw the preparation process, it met some level of
quality or healthfulness. The reality was, of course, that kosher food in no way
implied healthy, and it is likely that Orthodox Jews became far more excited
by newly certified M & M's and Milky Way bars than they did by kosher tofu
or granola products.

The evolution of the kosher lifestyle, then, points to a major transformation in the suburban Orthodox Jewish experience. The change in *kashruth*
supervision from small-time individual rabbis to multimillion-dollar international supervisory organizations, the emergence of kosher restaurants and
vacation packages, the growth in "kosher" music and multimedia, and the
widespread secular acceptance of *kashruth* as a marketing tool all point to the
argument that the "classical sociological relationship between Orthodoxy and
social status and affluence" had been "turned on its head" in the postwar period.[49] No longer relegated to the margins of the Jewish community and the
even further margins of secular society, Orthodox Jews and their religious
practices had become mainstream. Even when most consumers were likely
unaware of the reasons for an OU on a food label, the fact that a label even had
such a marking in the first place proved that two-thousand-year-old religious
practices could mesh quite well with material consumerism of the late twentieth century. Thus Orthodox Jewish consumerism represented yet one more
way, together with the spatial and social transformations of the synagogue and
day school, that the postwar Orthodox Jewish community created a new sense
of religious traditionalism on the suburban frontier. As Chapter 6 explains,
these many trends in the synagogue, school, and home conspired to spread
postwar Orthodox Jewry not only outward from city to suburb but across the
North American continent as a whole.

*Six*

# CONTINENTAL

# CONNECTIONS

David Goldstein, a professor of political science at the University of Maryland, was presenting a paper at the American Political Science Association's annual conference in Seattle. As an Orthodox Jew and a tenured professor, David had his conference routine down pat. He knew to request a presentation time for Friday, rather than Saturday. He knew not to order any meals for the conference luncheons. And he knew to reserve a downtown hotel room for Thursday and Saturday evenings only; Friday night he would stay in Seward Park, Seattle's primary Orthodox Jewish neighborhood. Not knowing anyone in Seattle, he posted a note on an Internet bulletin board devoted to Orthodox Jewish topics. "Professor Needs Place for Shabbos," his posting read. Within fifteen minutes, David had two offers for home hospitality. After two more electronic mail exchanges, he arranged to stay with the Rubin family, who lived three blocks from one of Seattle's Orthodox Jewish synagogues.

On Friday night, when he attended Shabbat services with his host, Larry Rubin, David was asked to lead the services. Although he had never set foot in this synagogue before, he knew the correct tunes to sing and the right pace at which to pray. The next morning, at services, David was given an *aliyah* (lit., going up, refers to the honor of being called to say a blessing over the Torah). Here too, he knew when to give his Hebrew name, when to give the names of his family members for an additional blessing, and how to leave the *bimah* and walk around and shake the rabbi's hand on his way down. David was four thousand miles from his own synagogue and community, but he fit right into the one that he was visiting.

David Goldstein is fictional, but his story is not. Since the middle of the twentieth century, increasing numbers of Orthodox Jews have traveled and relocated to communities spread across North America. Their movement, whether permanent or temporary, was facilitated by what I call *experiential homogeneity* within the Orthodox Jewish world. That is, the suburbanization of Orthodox Jews in Toronto was not an isolated case but reflected roughly the same patterns that emerged at roughly the same time in dozens of metropolitan areas throughout the United States and Canada. Beginning in the 1950s, Orthodox Jews in many different cities established similar suburban neighborhoods, prayed in similar suburban Orthodox Jewish congregations, attended similar suburban Orthodox Jewish day schools, and lived similar middle-class religious consumerist lives. These standardized patterns of religious suburbanization, this experiential homogeneity, fostered communication and interaction among geographically unconnected communities and enabled Orthodox Jews to create a broad religious network that encompassed the entire North American continent. Local congregations plugged into broader continental synagogue organizations, local religious youth participated in a continental religious youth culture, and religious consumerist trends spread throughout the United States and Canada. Suburban Orthodox Jewish continentalization meant more than just a geographical expansion, however. The underlying shared suburban religious identities among Orthodox Jews enabled individuals to plug into any community and the many communities to plug into a single unified continental community.[1]

Arguing that Orthodox Jewish continentalization was a postwar phenomenon presupposes, of course, that in its presuburban phase Orthodox Jewry was not a continental community. Before 1950, even though Orthodox Jews lived in cities and towns scattered across the United States and Canada—perhaps to an even greater extent than today—there was not a shared sense of a continental community based on shared experiences.[2] An Orthodox Jewish infrastructure existed in New York City, but there were few institutions of continental scope and scale to unite the outlying religious population. For example, the Rabbinical Council of America (RCA), the Union of Orthodox Jewish Congregations of America, and the Union of Orthodox Rabbis (UOR) were continental in theory more than in practice, as their membership was "either based in New York, or served along the Baltimore-Boston corridor, in Chicago's midwest environs, or in western Pennsylvania."[3] Of the 59 charter members of the UOR in 1902, only 5 lived west of St. Louis and only 1 lived in the southern United States. Fully one-quarter lived in New York City, and twenty others were scattered in cities with over 50,000 Jews. Only five lived in cities with fewer than 5,000 Jews. By the early 1930s, the UOR's geographic diversity remained the same even though its members had increased. Almost half of the 313 members lived in New York City, and two-thirds of the membership lived along the Atlantic seaboard (Boston to Baltimore). Only 17 ministered to cities west of St. Louis, and only 4 served Jewish communities in the South.[4] Similar was the state of Orthodox Jewish education, which, before the 1940s, was confined to a handful of communities on the East Coast. Only New York had more than one day school, and Orthodox Jewish high schools were virtually unknown outside of New York. Yeshiva University, the only college that had any large-scale on-campus Orthodox Jewish community, attracted a predominantly New York enrollment.[5] The national UOJCA did establish a kashruth supervisory organization, the Orthodox Union, for the kosher food industry, but these efforts generally focused on a few products available in the New York area, not on national products.[6] Even within individual urban Orthodox Jewish communities, a lack of experiential homogeneity worked against religious cohesion. For example, urban Jewish communities tended to divide according to immigrant ethnicity. Each group maintained its own congregations and social institutions; thus, in the Kensington neighborhood of Toronto, one could find the Polish shul, the Romanian shul, and the like. These vestiges of European society meant that there was little opportunity for the development of a homogeneous North American Orthodox community. Prewar Orthodoxy was, in a sense, a religious community that was continentally undeveloped, organizationally uncoordinated, and experientially heterogeneous.

Orthodox Jewish continentalization began in earnest in the 1950s with the first waves of religious suburbanization. The experiential homogeneity found in suburbanizing Orthodox Jewish communities helped to create a continental religious community in three ways: through the development of suburban Orthodox congregations and parallel national synagogue organizations; the emergence of day schools and continental institutions of youth socialization; and the creation of a continental Orthodox consumption market.

The experience of founding new suburban Orthodox Jewish congregations was repeated in dozens of communities across North America as congregational founders in most synagogues debated similar sets of questions: should the congregation be a "social center" as well as a religious center? Which prayer *nusaḥ* (prayer liturgy style) should the synagogue adopt? What kind of *meḥitsah* should the sanctuary have? The question of synagogue *meḥitsah*s in particular fostered a continental awareness for Orthodox Jews, since members of a congregation debating the fate of its own *meḥitsah* would most likely have taken note of the court cases in New Orleans and Mt. Clemens, Michigan. They would have seen that their particular issues of local concern were in fact part of a larger, continental debate over the direction of suburban Orthodox Jewry.[7] In addition, although the planting of Orthodox Jewish synagogues in suburbia was a congregationally driven enterprise, national Orthodox Jewish synagogue organizations provided support and direction to local suburbanization experiences. Several times during the 1950s and 1960s, the Union of Orthodox Jewish Congregations of America issued statements affirming the continental importance of expanding Orthodox Judaism to new suburban neighborhoods. In 1956, for example, the UOJCA's Personnel and Budget Control Committee made explicit reference to the "New Synagogue Bureau" designed to "focus on the establishment of congregations in suburbia." The committee noted with pride that in the previous year, twelve new congregations had been established in New Jersey and Long Island alone.[8] At the UOJCA's biennial convention in 1962, the organization adopted a resolution titled "Synagogue Perpetuity," declaring that "without a House of Worship no meaningful Jewish life can develop in the newly developing suburban neighborhoods or city housing projects. We therefore urge our Regions and Local Councils to give priority in their programs to the establishment of new synagogues in such newly developing neighborhoods and housing projects within their respective areas. We further call upon our congregations to establish branch synagogues to serve the Jewish families residing in these new locations."[9] Eight years later, the convention reiterated the importance of planning the establishment of branch synagogues in the new environments at an early stage so that "the congregational fabric may be retained and the priceless communal asset of the congregational family not be lost in the population shift."[10]

Other aspects of congregational life also fostered a continental Orthodox Jewish consciousness. Synagogue lectures, for example, offered an opportunity for members of one congregation to hear speakers from another city. In 1958, Rabbi Solomon Sharfman traveled from Brooklyn to speak at the dedication of the Young Israel of Cleveland's new building. In 1961, the featured speaker at the dedication of Toronto's Shaarei Tefillah Synagogue was Rabbi Samuel Belkin, the president of New York's Yeshiva University. In a one-month period in 1962, Toronto's Orthodox Jewish congregations scheduled lecturers from, among other places, New York City, Chicago, Nashville, and Malden, Massachusetts.[11] Even the process of hiring a congregational rabbi involved a widening of geographic horizons. Clanton Park Synagogue, Shaarei Tefillah Synagogue, and several of Toronto's other suburban Orthodox Jewish congregations tended to hire nonlocal rabbis. Although the main reason for this was the larger pool of available rabbis found outside the city, hiring rabbis from another city created other opportunities for cross-geographic relationships to occur. The exposure to different rabbinical styles on the part of the congregation and different congregational styles on the part of the rabbi opened the eyes of both to the range of communities within North American Orthodoxy.

As these events fostered continental awareness at the local level, synagogue organizations also brought local communities together in a continental forum. Annual conventions added a social dimension to the continentalization process by providing an opportunity for face-to-face interaction. A participant in the 1948 UOJCA Women's Branch convention commented that the meeting allowed local delegates "to meet personally [national] presidents and officers who had only been names on letters."[12] Such yearly meetings also enabled individuals to see problems of their local community and congregation in the context of the continental religious community. At the 1951 UOJCA convention, for example, delegates sought to "grapple with the real problems that face the Orthodox community" and to ask that the *national* UOJCA "take a more active interest in *local* community activity" (emphasis added). They "demanded that the rabbinate clarify the standards that must be maintained in a traditional Jewish house of worship," such as the halakhic status of mixed pews, which was then a major problem in many suburban Orthodox Jewish congregations.[13]

Finally, national synagogue organizations also promoted continentalization by having Orthodox Jewish leaders go out and visit other communities. In particular, the Rabbinical Council of America's National Torah Tour put Orthodoxy into a continental context. By the early 1950s, it had become "increasingly evident" to the leadership of the RCA "that non-orthodox sects have taken full advantage of Orthodoxy's lackadaisical attitude toward newer communities and public relations." By putting Orthodox Jewry "on the march," the National Torah Tour would demonstrate to the Jewish public that Orthodoxy was neither dead nor unresponsive to contemporary demands.[14] The initial tour had two wings, an eastern group that went through Pennsylvania and a western group that visited communities in California. Traveling from town to town, groups of Orthodox Jewish rabbis met with community leaders and laypeople and discussed Orthodox Judaism's attitudes, views, and practices. By the late 1950s and 1960s, Torah Tours had expanded across North America. In Ontario and Quebec, for example, Orthodox rabbis from Toronto, Montreal, and even the United States made annual visits to many of the smaller communities in those provinces.[15] These visits put local Orthodox Jews in contact with religious leaders and reinforced to those leaders the extent to which a suburban-based Orthodoxy had sprouted in communities outside the traditional strongholds of the New York metropolitan area.

The second component of religious suburbanization, the development of institutions of youth socialization, also contributed to the creation of a North American Orthodox Jewish subculture. On a purely quantitative scale, the growth of Orthodox Jewish day schools in the postwar period testified to the increased continentalization of Orthodoxy. In 1940, only 35 day schools were in existence, mostly concentrated in the New York area. Ten years later, 139 schools were found in fifty-two different cities. Another decade of growth brought the total to 265 schools in ninety-five cities, and by the late 1980s, this number had increased to almost 600 schools.[16]

Beyond the sheer quantitative growth in numbers of day schools, Orthodox Jewish continentalization was accelerated by the schools' experiential homogeneity. In large part, this standardization was funneled through Torah Umesorah, the national association of Orthodox Jewish day schools. According to one study in 1958, Torah Umesorah had founded half of all the day schools outside New York City.[17] Through its centralized office in New York, Torah Umesorah established day schools in hundreds of communities, assisting with teacher placement, curriculum development, and interschool relationships. Those who went through Torah Umesorah–affiliated day schools in the postwar period not only learned about Orthodox Judaism but generally learned the same things as students in other cities. They were taught by the same types of teachers, often young rabbis or women with teachers' seminary training. Each Friday, they took home the same summary of the weekly Torah Portion, and each month they read the same *Olameinu*, Torah Umesorah's magazine for schoolchildren.[18] Obviously, there was variation among schools, and not every student who passed through a Torah Umesorah day school experienced the school in the same way. Many non-Orthodox Jewish students who attended Orthodox Jewish day schools, for example, never participated in any other aspect of the Orthodox Jewish subculture.[19] But for those

within the Orthodox Jewish subculture, the day school experience was a crucial component of the socialization into the continental world of suburban
Orthodoxy.

Day schools also facilitated continentalization by bringing together students from different places. In 1960, a group of female students at Toronto's
Eitz Chaim Day School traveled to Detroit for a day school convention, while
the boys visited the Telshe Yeshiva in Cleveland.[20] A year later, students from
the Beth Yehuda Yeshiva in Detroit spent a weekend as guests at Toronto's Ner
Israel Yeshiva.[21] Another mode of interaction came through sports. A New
York City inter-yeshiva basketball league was formed in the 1950s, playing
its championship game on the court at Madison Square Garden.[22] In later
decades, Orthodox Jewish high schools would host regional or even national
yeshiva basketball tournaments. In the 1980s and 1990s, Yeshiva University
held an annual tournament to which teams from all over North America came
for a weekend of basketball, Torah study, and socializing. In the 1980s, some
schools attempted to form a broader association among Orthodox Jewish high
schools in the Torah Education Network (TEN). For a few years, TEN held
regional *shabbatons* (weekend retreat held over the Sabbath) and published
a national newsletter to keep participating schools apprised of the activities of
others.

The positive impact of shared experiences in day schools and high schools
spilled over to other extracurricular areas of youth socialization such as youth
groups and summer camps. In 1963, Yeshiva University's Torah Leadership
Seminar, held in London, Ontario, attracted more than two hundred teenagers from twenty-five different communities, including Toronto, Detroit,
Dayton, and Buffalo.[23] In a similar manner, forty-two girls from Toronto
attended an Agudath Israel–sponsored *shabbaton* in Baltimore during the
weekend of 18 November 1966. Later that year, a boys-only *shabbaton* in Toronto attracted twenty-three Agudath Israel youth from Chicago.[24] During
the summer months, camps brought together Orthodox Jewish youth from
a wide geographical region. In 1957 at Camp Massad, just north of Toronto,
about 30 percent of the campers were non-Torontonians. Five years later this
total rose to almost 50 percent, with campers coming from as far as St. Louis,
Pittsburgh, and Lawrence, New York. The camp staff as well was a geographic
blend, with counselors from Toronto being joined by others from Brooklyn,
Buffalo, and even San Diego.[25] Similarly, the B'nei Akiva–affiliated Camp
Moshava in Peterborough, Ontario, was attended by campers from several
American states in addition to a large contingent from Toronto. When Or-

thodox Jewish youth came together in youth groups and summer camps, they were able to form relationships in large part because of a common middle-class suburban Orthodox Jewish background and the shared experiences of Orthodox Jewish day schools. Coming from similar types of communities particularly helped when youth attended *shabbatons* in other communities. Visiting a different Orthodox Jewish congregation in a different suburban community would not be so strange for out-of-town visitors because they most likely hailed from similar congregations and suburban communities.

Continental socialization continued beyond the high school years as well. At the Orthodox Jewish Yeshiva University, for example, the proportion of students from outside New York City steadily increased in the postwar period from less than 20 percent to almost 60 percent.[26] Those Orthodox Jewish college students who did not attend Yeshiva or its sister school, Stern College for Women, created religious communities in other universities. In the 1960s, Orthodox Jewish students formed kosher dining clubs and other religious organizations in many Ivy League colleges and other universities.[27] High school students looking at colleges took into account the presence or absence of groups like Yavneh or Young Israel as an indicator of Orthodox Jewish life on campus. These campus organizations provided a setting for interaction among Orthodox Jewish students, who, by and large, hailed from similar backgrounds and similar communities across North America.

The final component of Orthodox Jewish continentalization was the emergence of an Orthodox Jewish market for religious consumption and the growth of a national, standardized, kosher food industry. As discussed in Chapter 5, the postwar period saw the development of Orthodox Jewish religious consumerism, particularly in the area of kosher food. For the purposes of this chapter, however, the growth of *kashruth* has an importance beyond that of the integration of suburban consumption styles and religious observances. Rather, the expansion of *kashruth* introduced a level of continental homogeneity into the experience of keeping kosher. Whereas in the prewar period, few kosher products were available nationally, the postwar growth of *kashruth* made more products available in more places. By the mid-1960s, national brands made up more than half of the products supervised by the Orthodox Union.[28] With the availability of national kosher brands, not only could Orthodox Jewish homemakers across the United States and Canada buy the same brands as their non-Jewish neighbors, but, more important, they could buy the same brand *as one another*. A shopper in New York and one in Los Angeles might never meet, but both could purchase the same kosher products for their respective families and thus participate in the same experience of Orthodox Jewish consumption.

The development of Orthodox Jewish consumption styles also led to the expansion of kosher travel, in both business and leisure forms. For business travelers, the availability of national kosher brands eased concerns about finding permitted food on the road. Whatever city one might be in, a business traveler could usually find a supermarket that had at least some grocery products with proper *kashruth* supervision. Similarly, the appearance of kosher airline meals in the 1960s made business trips less troublesome. The expansion of *kashruth* also eased the burdens of leisure travel. A 1952 article in *Jewish Life* published one woman's account of the "coast-to-coast journey of an observant family." Despite the fears of "well-meaning friends and anxiety-ridden relatives"—"What! Motor across the United States with two small children and eat Kosher too? It just can't be done!" they said—the author and her family demonstrated that kosher travel was possible in North America. The key was the availability of kosher groceries in dozens of cities across the United States. By stocking up along the way, this author and her family could see the "long procession of hitherto story book places," such as the Grand Canyon, Las Vegas, and the Great Lakes, while maintaining their dietary restrictions.[29] In short, kosher travel fostered continentalization by enabling Orthodox Jews to visit other parts of the United States and Canada and to see that one could live a religiously observant life in many parts of North America.

Tying together the various strands of religious suburbanization into a continental package were national Orthodox Jewish publications that disseminated information about the expanding geographical scope and experiential homogeneity of suburban Orthodoxy.[30] In 1958, *Jewish Life* published an article on Spring Valley and Monsey, New York, two "out-of-the-city" suburbs that were becoming self-contained "Torahtowns."[31] Two years later, another article detailed the religious and socioeconomic successes of the suburban Orthodox Jewish community of Far Rockaway, Long Island. "America's outstanding Torah-Suburb," as the article described the community, embodied the essence of religious suburbanization, the integration of secular suburban styles with religious practices and observances. On one hand, Far Rockaway was "part and parcel of the American milieu," with "the omnipresent evils of suburbia—keeping up with the Joneses, idle gossip, and divisive politics." On the other hand, this middle-class and upper-middle-class community devoted its "spare energies to building a Torah community and all its components—*yeshivoth, mikvaoth, shuls.*"[32] This description of a community dually immersed in suburban ways of life and dedicated to building a religious sub-culture undoubtedly would have been recognized by the thousands of Ortho-dox Jewish suburbanites reading *Jewish Life*, thus reinforcing the continental connections among them.

National publications also expanded the geographic horizons of Orthodox Jews by publishing articles about religious Jewish communities outside of the New York core. Through the 1950s and 1960s, *Jewish Life* printed articles on Orthodox Jewish communities in the American Southwest, Canada, and Los Angeles.[33] Similarly, each issue of the *Young Israel Viewpoint* contained a sec-tion titled "Rustlings in Our Branches," with notes and news from member congregations across North America.[34] In presenting these "out-of-town" perspectives, these magazines gently (and not so gently) nudged their readers to recognize the geographic diversity of their religious community. As early as 1948, a *Jewish Life* article sought to dispel the notion that "out-of-town" of-fered nothing for Orthodox Jews. Titled "The Jew in the Present-Day South," the article was written by Samuel Rubinstein, a rabbi who had moved from New York to Charleston, South Carolina, six years earlier. Rubinstein admit-ted that when he had migrated southward his "first and most important ques-tion" was simply, "What are the Jewish people in the South like?" Writing as a former New Yorker, the author knew that his mostly New York–based readers would have had similar questions, and he described his feelings in terms his readers would undoubtedly recognize: "Taking a trip to the South was an un-accustomed experience. A subway ride from Brooklyn to the Bronx once in a long while was a sufficiently trying and tiring experience. New Jersey, Con-necticut, perhaps Massachusetts, was the furthest I dreamed my vacation would take me. Now, here I was, on my way to a strange land."[35]

Despite those initial fears, six years of living in Dixie had erased any doubts. "Rest assured," Rubinstein wrote, "the Jews of the South are very much the same as their kinsmen of the north." Not only that, but "traditional Judaism in the South compares favorably with that of any other section of the U.S.A." because many positive features of Orthodox Jewish life existed in the South: the availability of Jewish education, the interest in practical observances such as Sabbath, *kashruth*, and family purity laws, and support for Israel and Zion-ism. By the end of the article, the author completed his transformation from New York insider to "out-of-towner," as he criticized those in northeastern communities for ignoring the religious needs of the South. In Rubinstein's words, supposedly "national" Orthodox Jewish organizations needed to dem-onstrate that "their interests apply countrywide as well as [to] New York City.

They must bring home to American Jewry that their purpose is to serve Judaism everywhere—East, West, North, or South, in the large or the small communities."[36]

A decade and a half after Rubinstein's article, many of these continental problems had not disappeared. In a 1963 article in the *Jewish Observer*, Atlanta-based Rabbi Emanuel Feldman castigated New Yorkers for their "vast, provincial insularity." As he explained, "For New York Jews, there are only two cities in the United States: New York is one; the other is that vast area stretching from the Atlantic to the Pacific, from Maine to Texas, known as 'out of town.'" Because New York City abounded with kosher stores and yeshivoth, "New York Orthodoxy takes all of this luxury for granted. It also takes for granted that outside of New York City no Jews and no Judaism exist."[37] In the same magazine one month later, Rabbi Meir Belsky, the director of a day school in Memphis, discussed the virtues of life in an "American shtetl." The vitality of his community and other Orthodox Jewish communities in the South, Midwest, and West proved that "*Yiddishkeit* [Jewish ways of life] does not drown as it crosses the Hudson."[38] Such geographically far-flung articles served two important purposes. For those in the "provinces," reading about themselves reinforced their connection to the larger religious community along the East Coast. For those in the religious core, seeing that Orthodoxy was not confined solely to a few big cities on the Atlantic seaboard went a long way toward developing a continental identity.

By the 1990s, what had been novel three decades before had become commonplace.[39] Suburban Orthodox Jewish communities could be found in almost every metropolitan region in the United States and Canada. Although the New York–New Jersey–Connecticut region remained by far the single largest concentration of Orthodox Jews, the continental expansion of Orthodox Jewry could not be denied. One could look in many places for evidence of the suburban continentalization. As of September 1997, Yeshiva University reported knowing the addresses of 32,000 alumni. Of these, more than 18,000 lived in the New York area (including the five boroughs of New York City, Nassau and Suffolk Counties on Long Island, and Westchester and Rockland Counties north of the city). The rest, however, were spread across the United States and Canada in almost every major metropolitan area. Almost 900 lived in Florida and 1,300 lived in California. Other areas of concentration included Illinois (359), Michigan (154), Missouri (112), Georgia (132), Ohio (302), Texas (256), and Washington (134). Almost 400 individuals lived in Canada.[40] Many of these alumni likely received the Orthodox Union's directory of Passover foods, a publication detailing products supervised by the OU. In the 1999 directory, a list of times for candlelighting at the commencement of the Passover holiday (Orthodox Jews light candles at the commencement of the Sabbath or a holiday at a prescribed eighteen minutes before sunset) included the usual centers of Orthodox Jewish life such as Baltimore, Chicago, New York, and Toronto, as well as less prominent communities such as Atlanta, Dallas, Denver, Milwaukee, Phoenix, San Francisco, Seattle, and Winnipeg. More important, three places in the list suggested the extent to which a suburbanized Orthodox Jewish community had become taken for granted. Instead of Boston, Detroit, Cleveland, or Washington, the list showed candlelighting times for their respective suburbs, Brookline, Oak Park, Cleveland Heights, and Silver Spring.[41]

The Internet offers yet another hint at the extent to which Orthodox Jewry had continentalized. In October 1999, the Kosher Restaurant Database, a compilation of kosher facilities around the world, listed more than nine hundred establishments in over seventy different metropolitan areas in the United States and Canada.[42] Elsewhere on the Web, the Orthodox Union's own Web site provided names, contact information, and links to synagogues in forty different states and provinces (see Maps 8 and 9).[43] These electronic resources not only testified to the geographic spread of Orthodox Jews but also contributed to that growth. With this easily accessible information, Orthodox Jewish travelers could track down places to eat and pray while on the road, and those who were considering relocation could better assess the Orthodox Jewish facilities in their prospective destinations.

As much as the continentalization of American Orthodox Jewry emerged out of internal developments, it did not happen in a social vacuum. In the postwar period, one could find many examples—both secular and religious—where experiential homogeneity was tying together spatially and otherwise unconnected individuals and groups. In the secular realm, suburbanization and consumer commodification bred a sense of experiential homogeneity among many North American metropolitan regions; more people in more places were living their lives in the same "metropolitan" culture. Architectural styles might have differed—mission and stucco ranches in southern California, aluminum-sided Cape Cod Colonials in the East—but a basic residential model with cul-de-sacs and two-car garages prevailed in geographically dispersed areas. Other economic institutions such as malls and office parks became cultural and commercial links among suburban communities. These common features created a continental metropolitan homogeneity that eased the strain of relocation for the millions of North American families who

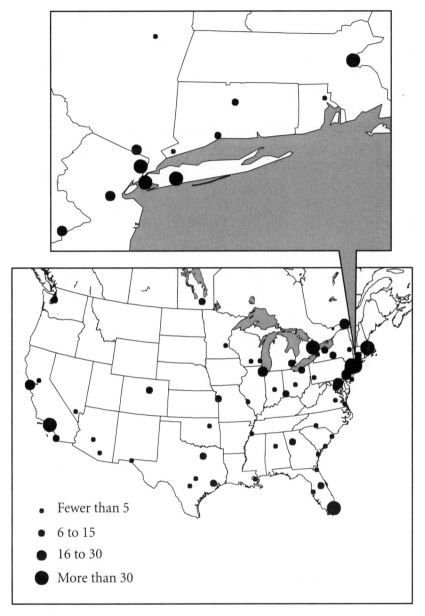

MAP 8. *Kosher Facilities by Metropolitan Area, 1999. Source: Shamash, "Kosher Restaurant Database." Note: Because the database contains only listings submitted by users, it is far from comprehensive. Some cities have listings for kosher caterers, bakeries, and grocery stores, as well as restaurants, while other cities have only restaurants listed. Despite these inconsistencies, the map shows that at least some form of kosher food is available in almost every major metropolitan area in the United States and Canada.*

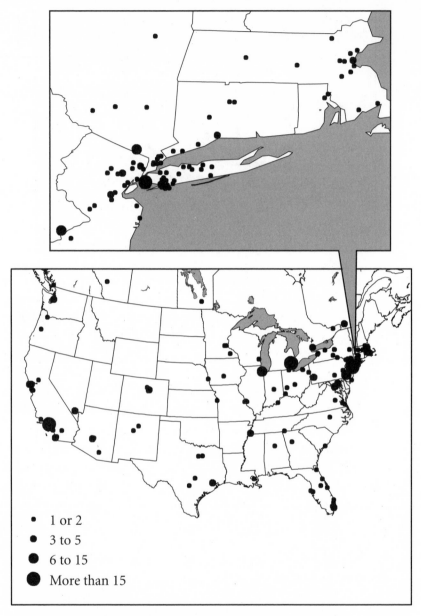

MAP 9. *Orthodox Jewish Synagogues by Metropolitan Area, 1999. Source: Orthodox Union, "Worldwide Orthodox Synagogue Network." Note: The Orthodox Union synagogue listings are not comprehensive. Nevertheless, what is listed is representative of the continental distribution of Orthodox Jewish communities.*

Legend:
• 1 or 2
• 3 to 5
● 6 to 15
● More than 15

moved annually; they knew that each new city contained dozens of suburban neighborhoods with housing stock, schools, commercial establishments, and neighbors similar to the ones left behind.

North American society also saw a trend toward religious homogeneity. The ecumenical efforts of mainline Protestant churches, for example, represented this desire to create a common religious experience across all regions of North America.[44] Other actions, such as the Catholic Church's reforms of the Second Vatican Council, resulted in the elimination of differentiating religious practices. Now, Catholics were no longer made distinct by their Latin Mass or their abstinence from meat on Fridays; they began to look more like other religious groups. Religious homogeneity also set in through the geographic mobility of various groups. The growth of formerly regional denominations, such as Southern Baptists and Latter-day Saints, into continental religions meant that these religious communities could be found in almost every major metropolitan region; it became easy, for example, to be a Southern Baptist who moved to a new city knowing that the new place already had established Southern Baptist congregations.[45] Finally, the expansion of Christian media such as gospel rock music and Christian television, together with the development of other Christian institutions such as national systems of Christian schools and Bible camps, led to a degree of Christian continentalization, since geographically unconnected Christians could increasingly share in standardized and homogeneous sets of experiences.[46]

These trends toward suburban continentalization and homogenization did not mean that Orthodox Jewish suburban continentalization was simply a Jewish version of larger cultural developments. Yes, Orthodox Jews suburbanized and continentalized like the rest of North American society, but how they did so and what it meant for the Orthodox Jewish community are the important points. In fact, the Orthodox Jewish experience in suburbia reflects a convergence between religion, place, and community unlike that of any other religious or social group. As the final chapter will discuss, this convergence offers a hopeful model for those who are searching for community in our modern metropolis.

# Seven

## SQUARE PEGS INTO ROUND HOLES: RELIGION, PLACE, AND COMMUNITY IN THE LATE TWENTIETH CENTURY

In its broadest sense, this book has studied how a religious group—Orthodox Jews—experienced large-scale changes to secular society—suburbanization. It has done so through a variety of analyses of the development of sacred suburban space, the formation of new suburban congregations, the growth of institutions of youth socialization, the expansion of kosher consumerism, and the continentalization of the suburban Orthodox Jewish community. Throughout these stories, it has become clear that the suburban Orthodox Jewish community is *suburban*, *Orthodox Jewish*, and a *community*. This statement is not meant humorously, but rather as a way to hone in on the central analytical point of this book. Each of the components of that phrase—"suburban," "Orthodox Jewish," and "community"—has its own meaning and relevance to the overall understanding of the story told in the preceding pages. This final chapter explores these meanings and discusses what it means to have a religiously based community that is thriving in the late twentieth-century metropolis.

## The *Suburban* Orthodox Jewish Community

At the beginning of the twentieth century, whatever sense of an Orthodox Jewish community that existed in North America was a lower-class, immigrant phenomenon concentrated in a handful of large East Coast cities. Ten decades later, a community of middle-class and upper-middle-class Orthodox Jews based in individual suburban localities is linked across dozens of major metropolitan areas in the United States and Canada. As this book has made clear, this transformation from "urban" to "suburban" was comprehensive, involving physical and geographical migrations as well as social and economic mobility. In many ways, the integration of Orthodox Jewry into the suburban environment and lifestyle is almost taken for granted. Note, for example, the way Stanley Chyet includes Orthodoxy in his broad description of the contemporary American Jewish landscape:

Not atypical is the American Jew of East European antecedents who lives in a comfortable suburban enclave and who—even in the hazardous 1990s—draws on his or her university training to earn a good, maybe even an enviable, living in a managerial or "middle management" position with a massive corporation or with a government agency, or as the owner of a medium-sized business enterprise or as a professional (whether physician, psychiatrist, dentist, pharmacist, lawyer, accountant, educator, journalist, social worker, or computer specialist). This American Jew whose lifestyle is so decidedly middle class will usually support self-described liberal political candidates and be often willing to affiliate with a non-Orthodox *or "Modern Orthodox"* synagogue. [emphasis added] [1]

Yet despite this almost "natural" association of Orthodox Jewry and suburbia in the late twentieth century, a romantic image of the urban Orthodox Jew persists in the minds of many who study North American Jewry. This persistence has many sources, although a main reason is the continuing visibility of urban-based *Ḥasidic* and *ḥaredi* neighborhoods in New York City that continue to look like "authentic" Orthodox Jewish places. Outsiders see the densely settled, ghettolike, urban environment, filled with people who look like Orthodox Jews "should" in their black coats, hats, and beards. Furthermore, because of the density at which these urban neighborhoods are often built, the religious landscape is highly visible to anyone looking for evidence of traditionalist religion.

The world of suburban Orthodox Jewry is more hidden. The neighborhoods of Orthodox Jewish suburbia spread out in a low-density sprawl with little pedestrian activity on the streets. Even if there were pedestrian activity, the visibility would still be minimal because most Orthodox Jewish families who live in suburbia generally do not wear traditionalist clothing other than the yarmulke. As discussed in Chapter 1, although the commercial religious infrastructure in Orthodox Jewish neighborhoods often clusters in distinct nodes, these nodes are mixed in with many other secular commercial establishments. A shopping strip center that has a Jewish bookstore, a kosher pizza shop, and a kosher bakery might also have a hairdresser, a pet store, a drugstore, and several other nonreligiously oriented stores that do not serve an exclusively Jewish clientele. In short, while the contents of suburban Orthodox Jewish neighborhoods might be similar to those of urban Orthodox Jewish neighborhoods, the two religious landscapes are very different. As a result, one can easily overlook the existence of suburban Orthodox Jewish neighborhoods if one is not attuned to their religious geography.

The fact that suburban Orthodox Jews do not always look like one might expect them to also creates some level of suspicion *within* the Orthodox Jewish community that observant Judaism and the suburban middle-class lifestyle do not—or should not—mesh. This line of thinking suggests that Orthodox Jewish suburbanites have somehow compromised their "authentic" religion in return for materialistic comforts, in contrast to those who have not "sold out" to the material lifestyle and have retained religious legitimacy. In Toronto in the late 1990s, for example, the term "905ers" became a quasi-derogatory code phrase for Orthodox Jews living north of Steeles Avenue in the suburb of Thornhill (905 is the area code for Thornhill and suburbs north of Steeles, as opposed to 416 for the city of Toronto south of Steeles). For the more *ḥaredi* Orthodox Jews in Toronto, most of whom lived in the Bathurst-Lawrence neighborhoods at the southern end of North York, 905ers represented all that was bad about Orthodox Jewish suburbanization—they were observant Jews whose lives were closely aligned with material consumerism. The northerners were contrasted with the Bathurst-Lawrence crowd, who were presumably less tainted by materialism. The entire debate had an element of absurdity, since geography had nothing to do with levels of material comfort or obsession with consumerism. If anything, the cost of living was as high if not higher in the Bathurst-Lawrence area than in Thornhill, and one might have argued that Orthodox Jewish wealth and material comfort were actually concentrated in the southern end of Bathurst Street. But between the absence of external trappings of Orthodoxy (few black hats or black coats) and the presence of material objects (typified by owning a television), suburban Orthodox Jews left themselves open to criticism.

The tension between 905ers and others in Toronto's Orthodox Jewish community was even more ludicrous because those within the *ḥaredi* Orthodox Jewish community had also bought into the suburban way of life. Although developed much earlier than Thornhill, the Bathurst-Lawrence neighborhood was built up in the 1950s and looks like many postwar neighborhoods in Toronto. Other places, such as Rockland County, New York, are also full of *ḥaredi* and *Ḥasidic* Jews who are living some form of the suburban life. Although these Jews might claim to shun the materialist aspects of suburbia (and it is not clear that they succeed in doing so), they nevertheless become part of suburbia simply by choosing to live in those environments. Their homes are often indistinguishable from other non-*ḥaredi* homes, with well-manicured lawns and often two automobiles in the garage. Their neighborhoods are the low-density subdivisions typical of suburbia and oriented to the automobile rather than to public transportation or to pedestrians. Thus, even for *ḥaredi* Jews, the walk to synagogue on the Sabbath and holidays takes them through an automobile-oriented environment, a suburban reality that would not exist were they to live in an urban neighborhood.

It is clear from the story told in this book that Orthodox Judaism is not only alive and well at the end of the twentieth century but that it was already alive and well half a century earlier. Even as the dominant sociological observations of the immediate postwar period claimed that Orthodox Judaism was a fossil from an earlier urban period and had no future in the suburbs of North American cities, the Orthodox Jewish community was proving those observations wrong.[2] In Toronto, Boston, Chicago, and elsewhere across the continent, where people like Marshall Sklare and Albert Gordon were busy studying and writing about the suburban Jewish communities with virtually no mention of Orthodoxy, Orthodox Jews were busy in those same suburban places setting up their own suburban religious infrastructures, infrastructures that have not only lasted but have thrived and expanded at the end of the twentieth century.

## The Suburban *Orthodox Jewish* Community

While the story of Orthodox Jewish suburbanization is important in terms of the urban-suburban issue, it is also important because it is a story about a traditionalist religious community. The idea that such groups can successfully integrate into the modern suburban environment and lifestyle without sacrificing religious content or practice runs directly counter to most historical notions about North American religion. Just half a century ago, observers of religion in the United States and Canada predicted either full-blown secularization and assimilation or the adherence to mainstream, liberal denominations. Will Herberg, for example, argued in the 1950s that while everyone seemed to claim some religious attachment, the content of these attachments was becoming less and less distinctive.[3] Other scholars who wrote about postwar suburbia noted that people were building more ecumenical and less theologically distinct churches in their new communities. In Park Forest, Illinois, home to William Whyte for a couple of years in the 1950s, a new United Protestant Church was to serve as the community church, which would replace denominational differences with religious unity.[4]

More recently, scholarly and lay interest in the growth of "spirituality" has continued to testify to a decline of religious traditionalism in the contemporary metropolitan environment.[5] "I'm spiritual but not religious in a traditional sense," the popular claim goes. In this conceptualization, traditionalist religious structures are deemed too bureaucratic, restrictive, conformist, or antagonistic to modern sensibilities. Because of its individualist nature, the content of "spirituality" is as varied as those who claim its affiliation. Anything from walks in the forest to listening to classical music to personal "quiet time" can count as spiritual worship. Spirituality's sacred writings include a growing literature on personal fulfillment and growth and on nature and ecology. In an era of do-it-yourself home building stores and brew-your-own-beer pubs, such individualized religions fit well with the spirit of the times.

If one were to judge contemporary religion solely on the growth of alternative faiths, then there would be ample justification for negatively assessing the future of traditionalist religion. But other facts tell a different story. Many people, for example, are finding their spiritual home not in built-from-scratch models of religion but in more tried-and-true settings. Conservative and fundamentalist Protestant churches are among the fastest-growing congregations in North America, and their denominations have seen growth rates of several hundred percent over the past few decades.[6] Such churches run the gamut from small prayer groupings of a few dozen people to full-service "megachurches" with thousands of members.[7] Whatever the size, the message is the same: preservation of traditional family values and an emphasis on some degree of personal piety. Moreover, the emphasis is not solely on the individual but on the individual in a community. Such a community reinforces one's per-

sonal commitment and acts as a peer influence on behavior. In addition, this
continued strength of traditionalism is happening at all socioeconomic strata
of metropolitan society, including the middle class and upper middle class of
metropolitan suburbs. Suburban consumerism, then, is no barrier to traditionalist religion.

The Orthodox Jewish community fits snugly into this broader religious
trend. While "unaffiliated" continues to grow as the largest group in the Jewish community and Reform and Conservative Judaism have far more members, Orthodoxy continues to be North America's fastest-growing group
of affiliated Jews. This growth is due largely to higher birthrates within Orthodoxy, but it is also testament to a retention rate far above that of any other
Jewish denomination.[8] No longer does the Jewish affiliation stream go from
Orthodox grandparents to Conservative parents to Reform children. Instead,
Orthodox Jewish families have successfully regenerated themselves over the
past half-century. More important, as the postwar period progressed, Orthodox Jewish institutions flourished to an extent never before seen in North
America, a development that was directly connected to the material success of
those who used those institutions. Whether it was synagogues, day schools, or
kosher food facilities, the Orthodox Jewish community's newfound socioeconomic standing enabled it to build, support, and patronize an extensive religious infrastructure. Moreover, the growing affluence of the suburban Orthodox Jewish community proved attractive for producers of religious consumer
goods. By the 1990s, for example, one could safely speak about a "kosher market" in the food industry, a term that was unimaginable fifty years earlier. In
short, suburban consumerism and religious traditionalism have jointly blossomed within the suburban Orthodox Jewish community over the past fifty
years.

## The Suburban Orthodox Jewish *Community*

Beyond the issues of suburban Orthodox Jews or even of traditionalist religion in suburbia, the story told in the preceding chapters has one final essential lesson: that "community" has an important place in the contemporary
metropolis. As I explained in the introduction to this book, many observers
consider the twentieth-century metropolis to be a communityless and placeless society, where changes in transportation and communication technologies seem to have rendered place-bound communities irrelevant to an individual's life. This is most obvious in the popularized imagery of the Internet,

where individuals can "travel" across the globe without leaving their desks and form virtual "communities." But even in terms of actual physical travel, a person can go where he or she wants to go in the sprawling city, thanks to relatively affordable automobile travel and relatively accessible roads and superhighways. The idea of living in a single neighborhood, with schools, stores, and jobs all in close proximity, is long forgotten. As Robert Fishman has argued, the spatial logic of the city is such that each person creates his or her own city with one's own home rather than the traditional "downtown" at its center. It is a "city à la carte," Fishman explains, where a person picks different parts of the metropolis to incorporate into one's daily paths.[9] All of this suggests that it matters little where one lives, since one's ties are primarily external to the locality.

Taking this idea of the nonspatially bound city, others have investigated whether this notion extends to those groups for whom the local neighborhood has historically had particular importance, such as ethnic groups. Here too, they discovered that place-specificity has decreased. In the western suburbs of Toronto, the Portuguese community is spread across several suburban neighborhoods. Even though they do cluster, or at least migrate in a relatively linear pattern similar to that of the Jewish community, the Portuguese have little to do with their immediately local places. There is little inherently "Portuguese" about their neighborhoods.[10] In Indianapolis, the growing Mexican community has almost no connection to a single space in the city. The city has no barrio of Mexicans, who prefer instead to move into white, working-class neighborhoods spread across the southern and western sides of the city.[11]

As attractive as the image of the placeless metropolis is, the point should not be taken too far. It cannot be said, after all, that there is *no* spatial logic in the city. True, people "select" their city from a range of opportunities across the metropolis, but these choices are not entirely random. People still arrange their lives based on factors such as transportation flow, proximity of one facility to another, and social homogeneity. In Indianapolis, for example, someone living on the north side of the city almost always confines his or her life to that same north side and probably only a "pie wedge" of that north side. Downtown Indianapolis, at the center of Marion County, is often the farthest south this individual will travel in his or her normal routine; the south side is almost entirely a "foreign" place.[12] Similar are the northern suburbs of Toronto, or the western suburbs of Chicago, or the metropolitan peripheries of most North American cities, where a person will most likely maintain a stable assortment of places in a reasonably fixed space in which to live his or her life.

Only in extreme circumstances will someone drive very far from home to accomplish a particular task, even though it is possible to do so with relative ease on the interstate highway. The point is, then, that place does matter, even if it is in a modified form from several decades ago.

This idea that place still matters becomes even more evident when applied to the question of religion. Again, much fanfare has been given to "megachurches" that attract metropolitan-wide populations. But putting these popular exceptions aside—and it is likely that even these cases do not draw from the region evenly but from selected "wedges" of the metropolis—most congregations are tied in some way to specific portions of the city. When a congregation picks a site to locate itself, it consciously chooses one place over another. When individuals or families attend a certain church, they consciously choose to attend one church over another. These choices, made by both congregations and individuals, are influenced by place. It is, after all, not coincidental that we continue to refer to churches, synagogues, and mosques as *places* of worship.[13]

The continuing importance of place in religion is perhaps no more evident than in the Orthodox Jewish community. Orthodox Jews do not randomly choose where they will live but make deliberate choices about locating within walking distance of a synagogue. When they do move to areas without a synagogue, they almost always do so with the intention of forming a new synagogue in that area. The history of Orthodox Jewish suburbanization makes this point clearly, as Orthodox Jews who moved to new suburban neighborhoods sought to organize a congregation as soon as possible. Moreover, once a congregation was founded in a neighborhood, those who moved to the area chose their places of residence nearby. But "place" to Orthodox Jews means more than just a geographical neighborhood. Place also means the experience of having many families living within walking distance of one another and engaging in the same rituals and practices according to the same calendar. On the Sabbath, when the rest of society is out running errands or staying at home to do housework, one finds Orthodox Jews visiting each other's homes or walking leisurely around their neighborhood. The contrast is even more striking when a Jewish holiday occurs on a weekday. Then, when the rest of metropolitan society is involved with the daily patterns of dispersal and placelessness, Orthodox Jews turn their neighborhood—their *place*—into a "walking village."

Just as the suburban Orthodox Jewish community offers an alternative to suburban placelessness, it also presents a competing vision of social relations in the form of the "caring community." One of the strongest criticisms of twentieth-century metropolitan society is that it lacks institutional bases for social support, or what social commentators call "social capital." [14] The dispersed geographic nature of suburban life and its fragmented social networks do not foster the building of relationships among individuals and families. Although he did not use this language specifically, David Riesman's early critique of postwar society described much the same thing: a place where relationships are built superficially around issues of status and achievement rather than meaningfully around personal bonds or shared identities. [15] Social capital is exactly what the Orthodox Jewish community provides—almost instantaneously. Someone moving to a new neighborhood and joining an Orthodox Jewish synagogue finds more than a community. He or she finds a range of formal and informal social services and social networks. Members of the synagogue share tips about child care, often send their children to the same school, and pass through life cycle stages together. In many communities, when a women gives birth, members of the synagogue will provide meals for the family for a week or two. The weekly Sabbath provides time for social interaction among families who invite one another for meals. The holiday of Purim, usually celebrated in mid-March, is marked by the exchange of gifts of food between friends and neighbors. [16] The celebration of rites of passage, such as the eight-day-old boy's *brit milah* (ritual circumcision, also known as a *bris*), the bar mitzvah and bat mitzvah of a thirteen-year-old boy or twelve-year-old girl, or the period of shivah (lit., seven, referring to the seven days of mourning), all occur in the context of the larger community. Communalism is so important that certain rituals, such as the wedding celebration, can occur only in a public setting; for example, ten men are required to say the *sheva berakhot* (seven blessings recited at a meal attended by a bride and groom in the first seven days of their marriage). The mourner's prayer, the kaddish, can be recited only at a prayer service with a minyan. In short, suburban Orthodox Jewish communities offer places of assuredness and comfort in a geographic and social environment not typically associated with such values.

For all the positive characteristics of the caring community within the Orthodox Jewish world, one cannot overlook the fact that it can lead both to conformity on one hand and to a sense of exclusiveness and insulation on another. In an analysis of food exchanges during the holiday of Purim among Orthodox Jews in the pseudonymous community of Forest Park, New Jersey, the anthropologist Maurie Sacks noted the "establishment of multiple links between households so that individuals encounter each other in many roles:

neighbor, friend, fellow worshipper, coworker on committees, carpooler, parent of children's friends, etc." While such linkages promote community, they also "minimize privacy for each household, and create a tight-knit community normatively associated with the Orthodox life-style." One simply has fewer opportunities to diverge from Orthodox Jewish behavior when it seems that everyone else is watching.[17]

In addition to keeping a tight rein on the in-group, the existence of a tight-knit caring community can also keep people out. I do not refer to exclusion based on religious orientation. Problems between Orthodox and non-Orthodox Jewish groups and within the world of Orthodox Judaism have already been the fodder for countless discussions over the past few decades and, as of the end of the century, are not close to being resolved.[18] Rather, the exclusion referred to here is based on social issues. The strong emphasis on family in Orthodox Jewish circles often means that single people, whether never married, divorced, or widowed, do not always fit into the family-oriented institutions of the synagogue and day school.[19] Positions of synagogue leadership tend not to go to single people, and an unmarried rabbi is a rarity across the continent. Sabbath meal invitations too often go out to other families rather than to singles who would otherwise eat alone. Because they are often renters rather than homeowners in a neighborhood and are more likely to be transient than homeowners, singles do not face the same issues of mortgage payments, gardening, and home repairs that is the stuff of casual conversation and community development. Moreover, because they do not have children, Orthodox Jewish singles (and childless couples for that matter) lack the same day school concerns that other families have. But even families who have children can face problems, especially when those children do not fit the traditionalist Jewish ideal. A family whose children have learning disabilities, for example, might find other families feeling ambivalent about their own children being friends. Although almost never articulated, there is often an underlying attitude that external defects or flaws or other problems are an indication of spiritual defects, and thus associating with a person who has such external problems is to be avoided.[20] Such families often have difficulty having their children mainstreamed into Jewish day schools because those schools are usually geared to high academic achievement and are often unequipped to provide services for children with special needs.

It would be entirely wrong for any reader to deduce from these comments that, because flaws exist in this highly socialized, tight-knit community, the solution is to do away with "Orthodoxy" and promote some sort of religious moderation, pluralism, or reform instead. Such an attitude assumes that other, less traditional forms of Judaism are more successful at social inclusion (not necessarily true) or that the problem lies with the religion rather than with the people practicing the religion (also not necessarily true). It would also be wrong to conclude that the entire Orthodox Jewish community is guilty of the characteristics mentioned here. In some communities, special day schools cater specifically to children with special needs, and the goal of such schools is to mainstream these children into regular Jewish day schools. The National Conference of Synagogue Youth's Our Way and Yachad (Together) programs target deaf and developmentally challenged Orthodox Jews, respectively. Chai (Life) Lifeline, a national organization for families of children with cancer and other diseases, provides a network of support services, including a summer camp and a Make-a-Wish-style program to take children to Israel and elsewhere.

One can conclude, however, that attitudes toward conformity and exclusions are symptomatic of the suburban world in which the Orthodox Jewish community is immersed. In many aspects, suburban society encourages homogeneity and exclusiveness.[21] Gated neighborhoods filled with socially and racially isolated populations make suburbia exclusive. The consumerist homogeneity of the shopping mall makes suburbia conformist. Despite the appearance of racial minorities and higher-density, lower-income housing in suburban areas, the ideal suburban family remains white and middle-class, with academically successful and properly socialized children. That the Orthodox Jewish community relegates to its margins those who do not fit the traditional family mold is in large part an extension of this secular desire for homogeneity and, one might even argue, an outright uncomfortableness with nonconformity. But even though it should not surprise that Orthodox Jews reflect this attitude, given that they reflect much else in suburban society, one could also reasonably expect that traditional Judaism's religious orientation to charity and helping those in need would work to overcome these secular tendencies to social exclusion.

For both good and bad, then, the Orthodox Jewish community has become enmeshed in suburban society and, in so doing, directly challenges many of the popular notions about religion, place, and community in the twentieth-century metropolis. The Orthodox Jewish community maintains a strong traditionalist orientation yet is equally integrated into the consumerist, materialist culture of the modern metropolis. The Orthodox Jewish community maintains strong religiously rooted connections to the places in which it lives—connections that have particular importance on the Sabbath—yet religion in no way limits the connections to the spatially dispersed metropolis during the other six days of the week. And Orthodox Jews form a community that extends far beyond membership in particular congregations. Shared religious practices and behaviors bring individuals and families together in schools and yeshivoth, youth groups and summer camps, kosher bakeries, butchers, and restaurants, and many other Orthodox Jewish institutions and organizations. These shared experiences at the neighborhood level feed into shared identities at the metropolitan and national levels to create a continentally connected but locally rooted religious community.

For all these changes over the past half-century, an observer will surely ask about the sustainability of growth within the suburban Orthodox Jewish world. That Orthodoxy seems to have higher birthrates and retention rates than do other forms of Judaism is well documented. From these data alone, one can safely assume that the numbers of Orthodox Jews will continue to increase, both absolutely and in proportion to other Jewish denominations. Simple demographic expansion, however, does not necessarily equate with communal expansion. One potential problem lies in the economics of Orthodox Jewish communities, which might seem odd for a group so closely associated with upward mobility and consumerist affluence. In the early years of Orthodox Jewish suburbanization, the majority of the financial supporters of Orthodox Jewish institutions had their roots in business, for example, the nationally prominent philanthropists in the Orthodox Jewish community: the Schottensteins in Columbus, Ohio, the Stones in Cleveland, the Reichmanns in Toronto, the Feuersteins in Boston. All made their fortunes as businessmen and industrialists, and all contributed mightily to the institutional and communal structures of Orthodox Jewry during the second half of the twentieth century. At the local level, the less prominent but equally essential supporters of synagogues and schools tended to concentrate in business. In contrast to this first generation of suburban Orthodox Jews, many of those who came of age from the 1960s forward became professionals, lawyers and doctors especially. There are many sociological reasons for this trend, such as the opening of professional schools to Jews since the 1960s. But for the purposes of this discussion, the relevant point is that doctors and lawyers amass a different kind of wealth than do real estate developers and corporate industrialists. The former is a wealth that allows for comfortable and even luxurious living but does not usually allow for million-dollar gifts to building campaigns. Only in the past few years, as high-tech industries have boomed, have Orthodox Jews re-entered the business world in large numbers. It remains to be seen, however, whether this younger generation will garner the same kinds of wealth that their grandparents' generation did.[22]

This economic trend will directly affect levels of financial support for Orthodox Jewish institutions. For the ongoing maintenance of synagogues and schools, these levels of affluence will suffice. But who will build the next generation of synagogues? Who will provide the large capital gifts to build a new day school or a new *mikveh*? It is a question that, I suspect, few in the Orthodox Jewish community have thought about because enough first-generation business-derived money remains. One possibility is that newly built synagogues will be smaller, with fewer educational wings and auxiliary spaces than earlier models of Orthodox Jewish synagogues. Or perhaps we will see the increased reuse or conversion of existing buildings into synagogues. In any case, the shape of the suburban Orthodox Jewish community over the next half-century will reflect in large part the shape of its affluence.[23]

Throughout this book, the story of Orthodox Jewish suburbanization has been used to tell the larger story of religion in suburbia. Doing so raises the inevitable question about the uniqueness of the Orthodox Jewish case. There are, after all, few examples of other groups for whom religious restrictions interact with the suburban way of life as intensely as they do for Orthodox Jews. Most religions do not have as extensive a list of obligatory religious behaviors as do Orthodox Jews, and none has the spatial constraints of the Sabbath. But this uniqueness hardly renders this story irrelevant. When looking to make comparisons with other religious groups, researchers should see the suburban Orthodox Jewish community as an "ideal type," to borrow a term from the sociologist Max Weber. As this ideal type—a representation of an idea that is perhaps never actualized but still serves as a reference model—the suburban Orthodox Jewish community becomes a standard of how a traditionalist religious community operates in the contemporary metropolis against which other comparisons can be made. The story of Orthodox Jewish suburbanization offers an example of how shared religious experiences lead to shared religious identities, experiences and identities that are rooted not in occasional religion but in daily ubiquitous religion. Religion matters not only on the Sabbath but every day because it directs where people send their children to school and where they buy their food. Orthodox Jewish observance renders meaningless the problems of geographic mobility because a stranger in a new city can always plug into an existing community, with a built-in familiarity with what the local religious institutions will be like. In short, here is a community for whom questions of anomie and placelessness rarely emerge.

Does this mean that everyone must become an Orthodox Jew? Obviously not. But the story told above provides a compelling argument for the possibilities of religion—and traditionalist religion specifically—for bringing people together. Religion that is lived and made a part of the everyday—religion of the daily, and not just the weekend—binds a community through shared experiences and shared identities. For those with an applied interest in suburban religion, it is important to understand that religion need not be reduced to a "feel good" lifestyle that places few obligations on adherents. Traditionalist faith groups, as represented by Orthodox Jews, have a role in the suburban landscape, building communities and reducing contemporary metropolitan placelessness. For those who have an academic interest in cities and in the religion of those cities, the existence of such a religiously bound community makes clear that long-held assumptions about the twentieth-century metropolis must be rethought. Suburban society need not be seen as an empty space, void of meaningful social relations. Rather, in the right conditions, it can be a place where community thrives and strong social networks connect strangers and friends across neighborhoods, cities, and even continents.

# GLOSSARY

Except where noted, terms listed are designated Hebrew (H) or Yiddish (Y). Definitions include both literal translation (lit.) and common meaning.

*Adon Olam* (H) hymn sung at conclusion of Sabbath evening and morning services.

*agunah* (plural, *agunoth*) (H) women whose husbands refuse to grant religious divorces, thus prohibiting them from remarrying.

*Aish Hatorah* lit., Fire of Torah. Refers to an international organization dedicated to outreach into the unaffiliated Jewish community.

*aliyah* (H) lit., going up. Refers to the honor of being called to say a blessing over the Torah. In an entirely different context, it refers to the act of moving permanently moving from the diaspora to Israel.

*aron kodesh* (H) Holy Ark. Structure at the front of the sanctuary containing Torah scrolls.

*ba'al teshuva* (H) lit., a repentant person. Refers to a formerly nonobservant Jew who takes on more religious observances.

*Bais Ya'acov* (H) lit., House of Jacob. Name of international network of girls-only Orthodox Jewish schools.

*bar mitzvah* (also, *bat mitzvah*) (H) lit., son (or daughter) of the commandment. Refers to a boy's thirteenth birthday or a girl's twelfth birthday, which marks the beginning of their obligations to observe Jewish law. In modern times, many uninformed people use these terms to refer to the party associated with a child turning twelve or thirteen rather than to the religious obligations.

*basar basar* (H) lit., meat meat. In Hebrew, these words are visually similar to *basar kasher* and were used by unscrupulous butchers to fool customers into thinking the butcher sold kosher meat.

*basar kasher* (H) lit., kosher meat. See *basar basar*.

*bimah* (H) prayer stand, usually in the center of the sanctuary in Orthodox Jewish congregations but at the front of the sanctuary in Conservative and Reform congregations.

*brit milah* (also, *bris*) (H) ritual circumcision.

*capote* (Y) black coat worn by Ḥasidic Jewish men.

*chasid* (H) see Ḥasid.

*chai* (H) life.

*daven* (Y) to pray.

*divrei torah* (H) lit., words of Torah. Refers to short sermons on a scriptural or religious legal topic.

*eruv* (H) lit., fence. Enclosure created by wires, strings, and natural landmarks to transform public space into "private space" for purposes of carrying objects on the Sabbath.

*esheth ḥayil* (H) lit., a woman of valor. The first two words of Proverbs 31:10, which begin a popular poem about the value and beauty of women, commonly recited at the Shabbat meal on Friday nights.

*hakarath hatov* (H) acknowledgment of good, appreciation.

*halakhah* (H) Jewish religious law.

*ḥalal* (Arabic) Islamic religious dietary laws, similar to laws of *kashruth*.

*Ḥanukkah* (also *Chanukah*) (H) eight-day holiday celebrating victory of Jews over Syrian rulers in second century B.C.E. Begins on twenty-fifth day of Hebrew month of *Kislev*, which usually occurs in mid-December. Primarily observed by lighting candles in a *ḥanukkiah*, a special candelabra for the holiday.

*ḥaredi* (H) lit., fearful. Refers to communities of ultra-Orthodox Jews in Israel and the diaspora who limit contacts with secular culture.

*Ḥasid* (H) lit., pious Jews. Refers to Orthodox Jews who follow the traditions of specific rabbis or communities, such as the Lubavitch or Satmar *Ḥasidim*. Often distinguished by traditional clothing (see *capote* and *streimel*).

*ḥeder* (H) lit., room. Refers to afternoon Hebrew schools common in Eastern European towns and American immigrant neighborhoods.

*ḥerem* (H) excommunication.

*hiddur mitzvah* (H) enhancement of a *mitzvah*. Refers to the use of luxurious materials in ritual objects (such as a silver wine goblet or candlesticks) to emphasize the importance of the ritual action.

*ḥumra* (Aramaic) religious stringency.

*Judenrein* (German) free of Jews. Used by German Nazis to refer to an area that had been "cleansed" of Jews.

*Kaddish* (Aramaic) prayer recited by mourners during the eleven months following the death of an immediate relative.

*kasher* (Y) to make an object or food ritually permissible for use.

*kashruth* (H) Jewish religious dietary laws.

*kehillah* (H) central communal organization, common in preemancipation European Jewish communities.

*kiddush* (H) blessing over wine recited on the Sabbath in evening and morning. Also refers to light refreshments (wine, cake, and other foods) served after Sabbath morning services.

*kikhel* (Y) dry egg cookie, commonly served at Sabbath morning *kiddush*.

*kippah* (plural, *kippoth*) (H) skullcap. Also known in Yiddish as *yarmulke*.

*kiruv* (H) lit., bringing closer. Refers to outreach efforts aimed at nonobservant Jews.

*kol toov* (H) all that is good.

*landsmanschaft* (Y) ethnically based mutual benefit/synagogue organization.

*landsmanschaften* (Y) plural of *landsmanschaft*.

*matana* (H) gift.

*megillah* (H) scroll. Usually refers to one of the five scrolls included in the Bible (Esther, Song of Songs, Lamentations, Ecclesiastes, and Ruth).

*meḥitsah* (H) barrier separating men and women in an Orthodox Jewish sanctuary.

*melamed* (Y) teacher.

*menorah* (H) candelabra used on the holiday of Ḥanukkah.

*middos tovos* (H) good moral characteristics.

*mikveh* (plural, *mikvaoth*) (H) ritual baths used by women following monthly menstrual period. In addition, someone who converts to Judaism must immerse him or herself in a *mikveh* as part of the conversion process.

*minyan* (H) quorum of ten men necessary for Orthodox Jewish worship services. Conservative and Reform law permits the inclusion of women in a *minyan*.

*mishpocha* (H) family.

*mitzvah* (plural, *mitzvoth*) (H) religious commandment.

*mitzvoth maasiyoth* (H) religious commandments.

*nusaḥ* (H) prayer liturgy style. Most common styles are *nusaḥ ashkenaz* (Germanic–Eastern European) and *nusaḥ sefard* (based on Ḥasidic liturgies).

*Olameinu* (H) Our World. Torah Umesorah's magazine for schoolchildren.

*oneg* (H) party. Usually used in reference to Sabbath evening or afternoon gathering.

*pareve* (Y) lit., neutral. Refers to kosher food that is considered neither dairy nor meat.

*Ribono Shel Olam* (H) Master of the Universe.

*Rosh Yeshiva* (H) head of the academy.

*Shabbat* (H) Sabbath. Interchangeable with *Shabbos*.

*shabbaton* (H) weekend retreat held over Sabbath.

*Shabbos* (Y) Sabbath.

*Shavuoth* (H) Jewish holiday, falling in late spring, celebrating God's giving the Torah to the Israelites on Mount Sinai. The holiday is marked by staying up all night studying Jewish texts.

*sheitel* (Y) wig.

*sheva berakhot* (H) lit., seven blessings. Refers to the seven blessings recited at a Jewish wedding and at meals attended by a bride and groom during the first seven days of their marriage.

*shiur* (plural, *shiurim*) (H) class or lecture on Jewish texts.

*shiva* (H) lit., seven. Refers to seven-day period of mourning following the death of an immediate relative. Traditionally, mourners remain in the house of mourning for the entire week (except on the Sabbath, when mourning is prohibited), where they are visited by friends and well-wishers who pay their condolences.

*Shma Yisroel* (H) Listen Israel. Refers to the first two words of the famous Jewish declaration of faith (Listen, Israel, the Lord our God, the Lord is one).

*shnoddering* (Y) practice of selling synagogue honors via auction. Common in early twentieth-century immigrant congregations but generally abandoned over time. Derived from Hebrew phrase *sheh nadar*, or "who pledged."

*shoḥet* (H) ritual slaughterer.

*shomer shabbos, shomer shabboth* (H) Sabbath observant.

*shteiblakh* (Y) plural of *shteibel*.

*shteibel* (Y) small, informally organized congregation, usually meeting in a house or other nonsynagogue structure. A Jewish analogue to the Christian "storefront" church.

*shtetl* (Y) self-contained, often rural Jewish village in Eastern Europe.

*shul* (Y) synagogue.

*simḥa* (H) lit., happiness. Refers to a celebration, often connected to the life cycle, such as a *bris*, a bar or bat mitzvah, or a wedding.

*streimel* (Y) large black hat worn by *Ḥasidic* Jewish men.

*Sukkoth* (H) Jewish thanksgiving festival, falling in midautumn. The holiday is marked by the erection of temporary booths or huts, in which one eats and sometimes sleeps. Another ritual is the taking of the four species—a palm branch known as a *lulav*, a lemony fruit called an *ethrog*, willow leaves, and myrtle leaves—and reciting blessings over them in synagogue.

*taharath mishpaḥah* (H) lit., family purity. Refers to Jewish laws that regulate sexual relations between husbands and wives.

*Talmud Torah* (H) see *ḥeder*.

*toivel* (H) to immerse, usually in a *mikveh*.

*Torah* (H) lit., teachings. Refers to the first five books of the Bible, the Five Books of Moses.

*Torah Im Derekh Erets* (H) Torah with the ways of the world. Slogan used by Rabbi Samson Raphael Hirsch in nineteenth-century Germany to refer to his theories of religious synthesis with secular society.

*Torah Umesorah* (H) lit., Torah and Tradition. Refers to national organization dedicated to founding and supporting Orthodox Jewish day schools.

*treyf* (Y) unkosher.

*tsniuth* (H) modesty.

*Va'ad HaRabbonim* (H) council of rabbis.

*Va'ad Hoeir* (H) lit., city council. Refers to organizations responsible for local religious activities such as *kashruth* supervision.

*Yachad* (H) together. Refers to national organization for developmentally challenged Orthodox Jewish youth.

*yarmulke* (Y) skullcap. Also known in Hebrew as *kippah*.

*yeshiva* (plural, *yeshivoth*) (H) Academy where Jewish texts are studied in depth.

*Yiddishkeit* (Y) Jewish ways of life.

*Yigdal* (H) hymn sung by some congregations at end of Sabbath services on Friday evening.

*yiras shomayim* (H) fear of heaven.

*Yomtov* (H) Jewish holidays.

# NOTES

## NOTE ON SOURCES

The bulk of this research was conducted from 1994 to 1997. At that time, the Municipality of Metropolitan Toronto consisted of the city of Toronto and five surrounding suburban municipalities (East York borough, York Township, and the cities of Etobicoke, Scarborough, and North York). Under the metropolitan form of government, each municipality had its own local government and its own public institutions, such as libraries. In January 1998, an act of the Ontario provincial government abolished Metro Toronto and its constituent municipalities and replaced it with a single city of Toronto, with a single mayor and a single government. While this reorganization had considerable ramifications for the entire Toronto region, it had a particular impact on this book. Specifically, several of the institutions in which I did research no longer existed in the same form as they did only a few years earlier. For example, the North York Public Library was blended into the Toronto Public Library. The North York Planning Department, Assessor's Office, and City Clerk's office all disappeared as well. Although such places have ceased to exist, I have cited them with the names that applied at the time of my research. Readers wishing to follow up on any of the source materials should contact the relevant office of the city of Toronto and ask about tracking down the specific records for North York.

## ABBREVIATIONS

*Archives*

| IHS | Indiana Historical Society, Indianapolis |
|---|---|
| OJA | Ontario Jewish Archives, Toronto |
| CC/VUA, | |
|     LCHFC | United Church of Canada/Victoria University Archives, Local Church History Files Collection, University of Toronto |
| YUA | Yeshiva University Archives |

*Newspapers*

| | |
|---|---|
| *CJN* | *Canadian Jewish News* |
| *Enterprise* | *North York Enterprise* |
| *JS* | *Jewish Standard* |

*Other*

| | |
|---|---|
| DBS | Dominion Bureau of Statistics, Canada |
| SCJE | Study Committee on Jewish Education, Toronto |
| SEPP | Sol Edell Personal Papers, Toronto |

CHAPTER ONE

1. Edell interview.
2. Silverberg interview.
3. Weisblatt interview.
4. Wertheimer, "Orthodox Moment," 18.
5. Wirth, "The City."
6. Fishman, "Megalopolis Unbound." See also Vance, *Continuing City*.
7. See Leven, "Distance, Space, and the Organisation of Urban Life." There are, of course, exceptions to the metropolitan choice argument. Various lower-income groups and racial or ethnic groups, most notably, often have far more restricted access to jobs and neighborhoods than upper-income whites. Criticism of suburbia for such restrictions is clearly valid. Nevertheless, the present discussion is neither about universal suburban access nor about whether suburbs are good or bad for urban populations. Instead, the focus is on suburbia as its own environment. For those with access, however few or many they might be, suburbia is a choice-laden environment.
8. Riesman, *Lonely Crowd*.
9. Janowitz, *Community Press in an Urban Setting*.
10. Rybczynski, *Waiting for the Weekend*, 18.
11. See Zerubavel, *Hidden Rhythms*, and O'Malley, *Keeping Watch*.
12. Leo, "Sabbath Observed."
13. In 1950, Conservative Judaism's Rabbinical Assembly voted to permit the use of automobiles on the Sabbath for the sole purpose of attending synagogue services. Recognizing that most suburban worshipers lived too far from their synagogue to walk, Conservative rabbis decided that allowing them to drive to services (and violate the prohibition on driving) was better than forcing them to stay home (and not attend services). In reality, the rabbinical edict had little effect because most Con-

servative Jews at that time had already begun to drive on Saturday, to services and elsewhere. See a reprint of responsa on the various aspects of travel and Sabbath observance in Waxman, ed., *Tradition and Change*, 351–407.

14. Waxman, "Sabbath as Dialectic," 42.

15. For a treatment on Latter-day Saints, see Shipps, *Mormonism*. For the story of Southern Baptists, see Ammerman, *Southern Baptists Observed*. For an analysis of an Islamic community in a nonsuburban setting, see Waugh, "Reducing the Distance." See also *New York Times*, 2, 3, 4, 7 May 1993.

16. Gross, "Young Orthodox Jews Blend Word and World."

17. Although there are no exact census counts of Orthodox Jews—let alone a count of all Jews—most surveys generally show Orthodox Jews to constitute somewhere around 5 to 10 percent of the North American Jewish population, an estimate equivalent to three to five hundred thousand people. Of course, these percentages vary greatly by region and city. Cities on the Atlantic seaboard, for example, historically have had a much larger Orthodox Jewish presence than have newer communities in the South and West. In Toronto, the community studied in this book, recent demographic studies placed the Orthodox Jewish population at roughly 10 percent of the Jewish community, or between ten and twelve thousand people. See Brodbar-Nemzer, *Greater Toronto Jewish Community Study*, 12.

18. Liebman, "Orthodox Judaism Today," 19.

19. Heilman and Cohen, *Cosmopolitans and Parochials*.

20. This discussion of Orthodox Jewish suburbanization will focus predominantly on the Ashkenazic (Eastern European) community and not on the Sephardic (Spanish-Oriental) population. In North American Jewish history, there have been two major waves of Sephardic immigration. In the seventeenth and eighteenth centuries, Sephardic Jews constituted the majority of Jewish immigrants to this continent. They formed small, tightly knit communities that followed the European *kehillah* communal structure. With the influx of Ashkenazic Jews in the nineteenth and early twentieth centuries, however, Sephardic-Americans became a minority of the Jewish community. Only in the post–World War II period did a second Sephardic Jewish immigration occur, this time from various North African and Middle Eastern countries. In the United States and Canada, they often established their own communal structures that were separate from the existing Ashkenazic-oriented institutions. For example, the Syrian Jewish community built several institutions in Brooklyn, and French-speaking North African Jews developed a comprehensive religious infrastructure in Montreal. To be sure, Sephardic Jews have attained as much material success and socioeconomic integration into North American middle-class suburban society as Ashkenazic Jews. Their integration into the mainstream of Jewish community structures, however, has lagged behind that of their numerically dominant Ashkenazic brethren. Thus while the discussions and conclusions of this book do not explicitly include the Sephardic community, neither should it be assumed that this community is entirely untouched by the process of religious suburbanization.

21. Ellenson, "German Jewish Orthodoxy." For Hirsch's influence in America, see Lowenstein, *Frankfurt on the Hudson.* See also Ellenson, *Rabbi Esriel Hildesheimer.*

22. Heilman and Cohen, *Cosmopolitans and Parochials,* 17.

23. Cohen, *American Modernity and Jewish Identity,* 30.

24. For a history of Yeshiva University, see Gurock, *Men and Women of Yeshiva.*

25. See three essays in Wertheimer, *The Uses of Tradition*: Michael K. Silber, "The Emergence of Ultra-Orthodoxy: The Invention of a Tradition," 23–84; Lawrence Kaplan, "The Hazon Ish: Ḥaredi Critic of Traditional Orthodoxy," 145–73; and Menachem Friedman, "The Lost *Kiddush* Cup: Changes in Ashkenazic ḥaredi Culture—A Tradition in Crisis," 175–86.

26. See El-Or, *Educated and Ignorant.*

27. See Bianco, *Reichmanns,* 327–29, 473–86. See also Dewar, "Mysterious Reichmanns."

28. For an excellent documentary analysis of Ḥasidic Jewry, see Rudavsky and Daum, *Life Apart.*

29. For a discussion of one such isolated suburban ḥaredi community, see William Shaffir, "Separation from the Mainstream in Canada: The Hassidic Community of Tash," in Brym, Shaffir, and Weinfeld, *Jews of Canada,* 126–41.

30. For a discussion of the historical differences between centrist and right-wing Orthodox Jewish rabbis and their gradual convergence over the past few decades, see Gurock, "Resisters and Accommodators."

31. Soloveitchik, "Rupture and Reconstruction."

32. See Gurock, "Resisters and Accommodators," 154–55.

33. *New York Jewish Week,* 5, 19, 26 February 1999.

34. Wuthnow, *Restructuring American Religion.*

35. See Soloveitchik, "Migration, Acculturation, and the New Role of Texts in the Ḥaredi World."

36. In the Orthodox Jewish community, such debates between the right and the center wings escalated in the 1980s and 1990s. Lamm's *Torah Umadda* provided a defense of the centrist Orthodox position that championed the integration of religious and secular ideas. Not surprisingly, Lamm's book sparked much harsh criticism from the more right-wing Orthodox Jewish community, which interpreted Lamm as giving equal weight to nonreligious ideas and values. See, for example, Rosenblum, "'Torah Umadda,'" and Perlow, "Clash between Modernity and Eternity." For a response to these critiques and a defense of Lamm, see Schiller, "*Torah Umadda* and *The Jewish Observer* Critique."

37. Over the course of the postwar period, the term "Modern Orthodox" has fallen increasingly out of vogue in the Orthodox world, mostly because it evoked an Orthodox Judaism that was too accommodating toward modernity and not religiously strict enough. The current preferred usage seems to be "Centrist Orthodoxy," which is a conscious attempt to contrast with the ḥaredi "right wing." Whatever the term, the values of this group of Orthodox Jews have remained relatively constant: to encourage contact with the secular world but within a religious frame-

work. For a longer discussion on the changing dynamics within Orthodoxy, see Wertheimer, *People Divided*, 114–36.

38. Liebman, "Orthodoxy in American Jewish Life," 22.

39. See Liebman, "Studying Orthodox Judaism"; Heilman, *Synagogue Life*; Heilman, *Defenders of the Faith*; Heilman, *People of the Book*; Heilman and Cohen, *Cosmopolitans and Parochials*; Joselit, *New York's Jewish Jews*; Helmreich, *World of the Yeshiva*; Mayer, *From Suburb to Shtetl*.

40. Soloveitchik, "Rupture and Reconstruction," 74–75.

41. Wunsch, "Suburban Cliche," 655. Although Wunsch was not writing specifically about religion, his comments accurately describe the ways most urban historians have depicted metropolitan religion and metropolitan society in general. Among the guilty parties in this regard are Jackson, *Crabgrass Frontier*; Fishman, *Bourgeois Utopias*; Miller, *Suburb*; Palen, *Suburbs*; Kelly, *Suburbia Re-Examined*. In many cases, historians have engaged in entire debates about suburbia without even considering religion. See the following essays: Sharpe and Wallock, "Bold New City or Built-Up 'Burb?'"; Sharpe and Wallock, "Response"; Bruegmann, "Twenty-Three Percent Solution"; Fishman, "Urbanity and Suburbanity"; Marsh, "(Ms)Reading the Suburbs"; Thomas, "Forces of Urban Heterogeneity Can Triumph."

Those who have confronted the question of urban and metropolitan religion head-on include Winston, "Babylon by the Hudson"; McGreevy, *Parish Boundaries*; Lewis, "Going Downtown"; Lewis, *Protestant Experience in Gary, Indiana*; Kane, *Separatism and Subcultures*; Wind and Lewis, eds., *American Congregations, Volume 1* and *Volume 2*; Hunter and Rice, "Unlikely Alliances"; Conzen, "Forum"; and Hudnut-Beumler, *Looking for God in the Suburbs*. Sociological studies of the same topic include Ammerman, *Congregation and Community*; Warner, *New Wine in Old Wineskins*; Silk, *Spiritual Politics*; Roof and McKinney, *Generation of Seekers*; Demerath and Williams, *Bridging of Faiths*; and Balmer, *Mine Eyes Have Seen the Glory* (book).

42. See Linteau, "Canadian Suburbanization in a North American Context." See also Lipset, *Continental Divide*, and Goldberg and Mercer, *Myth of the North American City*.

43. For a history of Canadian Jewry, see Tulchinsky, *Taking Root*. See also Weinfeld, "Canadian Jews and Canadian Pluralism"; and Brym, Shaffir, and Weinfeld, *Jews of Canada*. For a demographic snapshot of the prewar Canadian Jewish community, see Rosenberg, *Canada's Jews*. For a history of the Jews of Toronto in the same era, see Speisman, *Jews of Toronto*. See also Frager, *Sweatshop Strife*.

44. Weinfeld, "Canadian Jews and Canadian Pluralism," 94.

45. Jackson, *Crabgrass Frontier*, 238–41.

46. Strong-Boag, "Home Dreams," 492.

47. See Teixiera, "Ethnicity, Housing Search, and the Role of the Real Estate Agent"; and Hill, *Canadian Urban Trends*, 98–99.

48. *Globe and Mail*, 18, 20 July 1995.

49. Kong, "Geography and Religion," 367.

50. See Bianco, *Reichmanns*.

CHAPTER TWO

1. *CJN*, 18 March 1960.

2. Jakobovits interview.

3. Eliade, *The Sacred and the Profane*. See also a discussion of sacred space in Park, *Sacred Worlds*, 245–85. See also Scott and Simpson-Housley, *Sacred Places and Profane Spaces*.

4. For a similar analysis of the religious landscape of suburban Los Angeles, see Weightman, "Changing Religious Landscapes in Los Angeles."

5. Geographers R. H. Jackson and R. Henrie describe sacred space as any "portion of the earth's surface which is recognized by individuals or groups as worthy of devotion, loyalty, or esteem.... Sacred space does not exist naturally, but is assigned sanctity as man defines, limits, and characterizes it through his culture, experience, and goals" ("Perception of Sacred Space").

6. For a brief description of Teaneck, see Korn, "Modern Orthodox Community." For a discussion of Orthodox Jewish suburbanization in Boston, see Gamm, "In Search of Suburbs."

7. For a complete history of Jewish Toronto in the prewar period, see Speisman, *Jews of Toronto*. See also Hayman, *Toronto Jewry*.

8. Rosenberg, *Canada's Jews*, 308.

9. For a history of Toronto's garment industry, see Frager, *Sweatshop Strife*, and Hiebert, "Jewish Immigrants and the Garment Industry of Toronto."

10. Rosenberg, *Canada's Jews*, 308.

11. *JS*, June 1949.

12. Forest Hill became famous as the fictionalized community in the 1956 sociological study of Crestwood Heights. See Seeley, Sim, and Loosley, *Crestwood Heights*. For a more recent review of this still important study, see Schoenfeld, "Re-reading an American Classic."

13. Rosenberg, *Study of the Changes in the Geographic Distribution of the Jewish Population*.

14. DBS, *Ninth Census of Canada*, Table 1.

15. The story of Toronto's kosher food industry is complicated. Not until 1958 did a central supervisory organization for kosher food emerge out of the Canadian Jewish Congress's Orthodox Division. Before that, the community had a disorganized system of individual rabbinical supervision. Personality conflicts and economic competition drove the market, and, more often than not, it was easier for a butcher simply to post a sign claiming his meat or poultry was "kosher" rather than to submit to rabbinical supervision that would actually certify the food's kosher status. The community's attempt to form a *kehillah* (central communal organization) in the 1920s included a try at kosher food regulation. This failed miserably when the

various butchers and slaughterers protested the costs of supervision. Even after the 1958 supervisory system was in place, deceit in advertising and selling continued into the early 1970s. For a concise history of the legal controversies over kosher supervision in North America, see Stern, "Kosher Food and the Law."

16. Hart, *Pioneering in North York*. See also Reitman, "North York."

17. There is virtually no historiographical work on twentieth-century religion in Toronto or Ontario. Nevertheless, the common perception (and most likely the accurate one as well) is that the religious patterns set in the nineteenth century held true for the first half of the twentieth century also. Only with the postwar immigration from Europe, the Caribbean, Asia, and the Middle East did the Anglo-Protestant hegemony decline. See Westfall, *Two Worlds*, and Grant, *Profusion of Spires*.

18. DBS, *Eighth Census of Canada*, Table 38.

19. Much of the information in this section is from Hart, *Pioneering in North York*.

20. For a contemporary discussion of the housing shortage in Toronto and Canada, see Carver, *Houses for Canadians*.

21. *Enterprise*, 6 January 1949, 12 January 1950.

22. For a brief history of Don Mills, see *Globe and Mail*, 29 May 1993.

23. *Enterprise*, 2 March 1950; *Asbury and West United Church Herald*, 12 October 1950, UCC / VUA, LCFHC, Toronto, Ontario—Asbury and West United Church.

24. Northways, Metro Toronto Aerial Photographs.

25. The North York–York Township boundary is actually a few blocks north of Eglinton along Hillhurst Boulevard. But because there is little qualitative difference between the neighborhoods on either side of the border and because Eglinton is a major east-west road, I have used Eglinton as the boundary of the corridor rather than Hillhurst.

26. The population figures are only estimates from the 1940 and 1970s population censuses, derived from the sum of the population of those census tracts that abutted Bathurst Street. In larger tracts that extended beyond the immediate vicinity of Bathurst, I included only a percentage of the tract population in the estimate. DBS, *Eighth Census of Canada*, Table 38; and Statistics Canada, *1971 Census of Canada*, Table 1.

27. *Enterprise*, 6 April, 16 November 1950, 15 March 1951.

28. Deacon, Arnett, and Murray, *Bathurst Street, Forest Hill to Don River*.

29. *Enterprise*, 28 February 1952.

30. Deacon, Arnett, and Murray, *Bathurst Street, Forest Hill to Don River*.

31. DBS, *Ninth Census of Canada*, Table 1.

32. *CJN*, 4 December 1964; Grossman interview.

33. The following chapter provides a more detailed history of Toronto's suburban Orthodox Jewish congregations.

34. Rubinstein interview. For a personal history of one Hungarian immigrant family who achieved much success in Toronto, see Mandelbaum, ed., *Family Chronicles*.

35. Bianco, *Reichmanns*.

36. Data taken from Clanton Park Synagogue, Membership Lists (1957–58, 1960–61), SEPP; and City of North York, Property Assessment Rolls (1957–60).

37. DBS, *Ninth Census of Canada*, Table 1; DBS, *1961 Census of Canada*, Table 1.

38. City of North York, Property Assessment Rolls (1955–65).

39. Statistics Canada, *1971 Census of Canada*, Table 1.

40. *CJN*, 3 September 1981, 13 August 1987.

41. Lipsitz, ed., *Ontario Jewish Resource Directory*.

42. The journalist Joel Garreau, in his analysis of contemporary suburban "edge cities," makes the same point regarding the design of shopping malls. He explains that a rule of thumb among mall developers is to keep shoppers from seeing how far it really is between stores. If shoppers realized the distances they actually walked in a mall, they would get in their cars and drive to the other end of the mall rather than walk. The developers' fear, of course, is that once in their car, shoppers might leave the mall altogether. See Garreau, *Edge City*.

43. *CJN*, 4 October 1979.

44. *CJN*, 22 June 1961.

45. Levine and Harmon, *Death of an American Jewish Community*; Diamond, "Urban Ministry and Changing Perceptions of the Metropolis." For an Orthodox Jewish perspective on white flight and black-Jewish relations, see Cohen, "Changing Neighborhoods" and "The Orthodox Synagogue," and Goldstein, "Exploitation in the Ghetto."

46. See Gamm, *Urban Exodus*.

47. *CJN*, 20 January 1961.

48. See Gad, Peddie, and Punter, "Ethnic Difference in the Residential Search Process"; Richmond, *Ethnic Residential Segregation in Metropolitan Toronto*; Breton, Isajiw, Kalbach, and Reitz, *Ethnic Identity and Equality*.

49. North York Planning Department, *South Bathurst Street Study*.

50. In the town of Beachwood, Ohio, a suburb of Cleveland, a proposal to build a new synagogue was met with harsh opposition. See Schack, "Zoning Boards, Synagogues, and Bias." These anti-Jewish opinions did not ever dissipate, and in the 1990s, several zoning battles still simmered in the Cleveland suburbs. In Airmont, New York, in the early 1990s, the United States government filed a lawsuit against the town for passing zoning laws that made it all but impossible to establish local synagogues. See *CJN*, 27 February 1992.

51. *Asbury and West United Church Herald*, 12 April 1958; *Toronto Telegram*, n.d. (prob. early 1960s), UCC/VUA, LCFHC, Toronto, Ontario—Asbury and West United Church.

52. *Toronto Telegram*, 10 August 1968, UCC/VUA, LCHFC, Toronto, Ontario—Wilson Heights United Church.

53. *CJN*, 18 November 1966.

54. Wells, *Report of the Royal Commission*.

55. Ibid.

56. See Bradley et al., *Churches and Church Membership in the United States, 1990*.

57. Klaff, "Urban Ecology of Jewish Populations," 61.

58. Shaarei Shomayim Synagogue, Board of Governors Minutes, 7 April 1957, OJA.

59. Ibid., 30 January 1958.

60. *JS*, 1 May 1963; *CJN*, 26 April 1963, 11 September 1964, 9 September 1966.

61. For a fuller discussion on the reasons for the inflated costs of suburban housing throughout Canada in the mid-1970s, see Lorimer, *Developers*.

62. Zaionz interview; *CJN*, 27 August, 24 September 1971, 5 October 1973, 7 March 1975, 28 August 1980, 15 January 1981, 28 October 1982.

63. *CJN*, 5 February, 17 September 1981.

64. Kehillat Shaarei Torah, *A Tribute to Dr. Joel David Cooper* (ca. 1985), OJA; Gerry Urbach to congregational membership, ca. 1986, OJA.

65. Lynch, *Image of the City*.

66. Kehillat Shaarei Torah, *Nachas of the North East Hebrew Congregation* (September 1981), OJA.

67. *Windsor-Heights Herald*, 21 November 1997.

68. Ibid.; *New York Times*, 22 February 1993. See also Trillin, "Drawing the Line."

69. In an entirely different context, this halakhic reasoning echoes the complaints often voiced about urban expressways. So often over the past half-century, an urban expressway would be bulldozed through an inner city neighborhood, leaving one area cut off from another and generally destroying the fabric of neighborhood life. Even when transportation officials built bridges over the highway, the road clearly acted as a barrier and impediment to neighborhood interaction. As if to confirm this situation, the halakhic perspective similarly interprets a highway as a "fence" and permits it as an *eruv*.

70. See Weiss, "Eruv."

71. *CJN*, 4 March 1966, 22 November 1974, 8 October 1981.

72. Bianco, *Reichmanns*, 475–76. See also *CJN*, 27 August 1987.

CHAPTER THREE

1. *CJN*, 6 September 1974.

2. See Luchetti, *Under God's Spell*. For an example of an itinerant preacher's life, see Gaustad, ed., *Documentary History of Religion in America to the Civil War*, 388–89.

3. See Finke and Stark, *Churching of America*.

4. Ahlstrom, *Religious History of the American People*, 164.

5. See the pioneer metaphor invoked repeatedly in Garreau, *Edge City*.

6. Northways, Metro Toronto Aerial Photographs.

7. Godfrey interview; Rubinstein interview; Silverberg interview; Neuberger interview. See also Strong-Boag, "Home Dreams," 493.

8. *Enterprise*, 7 September 1950.

9. The remaining congregants eventually established Beth Joseph, a small con-

gregation that later affiliated with the Lubavitch Ḥasidic Orthodox community. Beth Joseph was involved in a congregational merger in the mid-1960s.

10. Clanton Park Synagogue, *Clanton Park Synagogue Bulletin*, April 1955, SEPP.

11. Sol Edell to E. L. Sanderson, Engineering Department, Township of North York, 15 April 1995, SEPP.

12. Mandlebaum, ed., *Family Chronicles*, 314.

13. Edell interview.

14. Torrance, "Report of Toronto Home Missions Council," UCC/VUA.

15. Hay, "Report of the Synod of Toronto," *Acts and Proceedings of the 77th General Assembly of the Presbyterian Church in Canada*, Presbyterian Church in Canada Archives.

16. Hay, "Report of the Synod of Toronto," *Acts and Proceedings of the 79th General Assembly of the Presbyterian Church in Canada*, ibid.

17. See Looby, *Flowering of a Community*.

18. Thatcher, *Study of the Position of the Church in an Expanding Community*.

19. Ibid. See also R. M. Warne, "On Choosing a Church Site," UCC/VUA.

20. In Herbert Gans's study of Levittown, New Jersey, he reported that one-third of the new suburban residents had relocated from urban neighborhoods (*Levittowners*, 32).

21. Clanton Park Synagogue totals were calculated by matching names listed in the synagogue's 1957 membership list to entries in *Might's Toronto City Directory* for the same year. Information for Palm Drive residents was obtained by matching North York Property Assessment Rolls to city directories.

22. Again, in comparison to Herbert Gans's Levittowners, 53 percent of that suburban population had never previously owned a house (*Levittowners*, 32).

23. Edell interview.

24. Clanton Park Membership List, 1957–58, SEPP; City of North York, 1957 for 1958 Property Assessment Rolls.

25. Rubinstein interview. See also Mandlebaum, ed., *Family Chronicles*.

26. Krumbein and Spetner, "Genesis of a Washington Synagogue," 54.

27. Duckat, "Careers for the Sabbath Observant."

28. Even in the late 1990s, Sabbath-observant Jews still sometimes faced difficulties in balancing work and religion. For a personal account of this negotiation, see Borsuk, "Old Fashioned Jew, Old Fashioned Reporter."

29. Data found in the property assessment records for Subdivision Plan 4883, City of North York, 1957 for 1958 Property Assessment Rolls and 1958 for 1959 Property Assessment Rolls.

30. *CJN*, 8 January 1960.

31. Gasner interview. Similar perceptions about women's work were expressed in Silverberg interview and Rubinstein interview.

32. Kaufman, "Far Rockaway—Torah-Suburb by-the-Sea."

33. Krumbein and Spetner, "Genesis of a Washington Synagogue."

34. Gersh, "New Suburbanites of the 50's," 221. See also Glazer, *American Judaism*; Glazer, "Jewish Revival in America: II"; Gans, "American Jewry."

35. *JS*, 15 September 1957.

36. These four issues have been discussed by other scholars in relation to the general transformation of the North American synagogue with little consideration for suburbanization or Orthodoxy. See, for example, Sarna, "Evolution of the American Synagogue," and Jick, *Americanization of the Synagogue*. Even though these trends might have appeared in other types of Jewish synagogues earlier than the 1950s, I believe that the presence of these pioneering issues in Orthodox synagogues in the 1950s can be rightfully linked to the broader suburbanization of this religious community and the larger experience of combining suburban middle-class styles with religious traditionalism.

37. For a discussion of the growth of Jewish "centers," see Kaufman, *Shul with a Pool*. See also Moore, *At Home in America*.

38. Herberg, *Protestant, Catholic, Jew*. Many Christian observers, however, did not look kindly upon the increased emphasis on churches' social functions. For example, Gibson Winter lamented the "suburban captivity of the churches," a reference to congregational tendencies to concentrate on church socials rather than social justice. See Winter, *Suburban Captivity of the Churches*. For a more recent analysis of 1950s religious critiques of suburban religion, see Hudnut-Beumler, *Looking for God in the Suburbs*, 109–74.

39. Shoulson, "Synagogues and Centers," 63.

40. Shaarei Tefillah Synagogue, *Shaarei Tefillah Synagogue Bulletin*, December 1961, OJA; Clanton Park Synagogue, "Shul Activities from Dedications 61—to Anniversary 1962," mimeograph, n.d., SEPP.

41. William Whyte's research in Park Forest, Illinois, found that the pastor of the suburb's United Protestant Church drew "heavily on young business talent for leadership." The church's finance committee chairman, for example, was an advertising executive. See Whyte, *Organization Man*, 371.

42. Neuberger interview.

43. *CJN*, 10 September 1960, 17 March 1961.

44. According to traditional halakhah, women are obligated in prayer but do not participate in the public functions of religious services. The inclusion of women in a minyan and their participation in services differentiates Reform and Conservative congregations from Orthodox ones.

45. For nineteenth-century examples of women's "domestic" involvement in the public sphere, see Ryan, *Cradle of the Middle Class*, and Stansell, *Sex and Class in New York*. For discussions of the same phenomenon in the twentieth century, see Seeley, Sim, and Loosley, *Crestwood Heights*.

46. The exact origins of the kiddush, with its traditional foods of liquor, fish, and *kikhel* (dry egg cookie) is unclear. It has roots in Jewish tradition, where a drink of wine or heavier alcohol was customary after morning prayers. At the same time, the kiddush bears a strong resemblance to the church coffee hours held Sunday mornings following services. Further historical (and gastronomic) research will likely find the answer.

47. See Isaacs, "National Gathering of Sisterhoods."

48. For an early discussion of the women's movement in the Orthodox Jewish community, see Greenberg, *On Women and Judaism*.

49. See Weiss, *Women at Prayer*; Solomon, "Hard to Be a Feminist Orthodox Jew"; Weinberg, "Orthodox Feminists Must Be Heard."

50. See Auman and Herring, *Prenuptial Agreement*. The issue of women's "rights" in Orthodox Judaism is far from agreed upon among women, let alone among male rabbinical authorities. Many women, in both centrist and *ḥaredi* circles, find few faults with the religious division of labor and want little to do with the empowering activities of Orthdox Jewish feminists.

51. Clanton Park Synagogue, "Shul Activities from Dedication 61—to Anniversary 1962," mimeograph, n.d., SEPA.

52. Krumbein and Spetner, "Genesis of a Washington Synagogue," 56.

53. *CJN*, 15 December 1961.

54. Much folklore surrounds the problems of noise and talking in contemporary Orthodox Jewish congregations. Rare indeed is the synagogue where one hears only the sounds of praying congregants. For a discussion of this problem, see Samuel Heilman's ethnographic study of an Orthodox Jewish congregation in Boston, *Synagogue Life*.

55. Shoulson, "Let Us Look to Our Own," 48.

56. Clanton Park Synagogue, "High Holiday Schedule of Services," September 1957, SEPP.

57. Gordon, "Through a Journalist's Eyes," 32.

58. Sussman, "Suburbanization of American Judaism," 31.

59. *CJN*, 21 September 1960.

60. Grossman interview.

61. The quotation, taken from Cohen's 1983 book of American Jewry, is part of a larger discussion of Orthodox Judaism's relationship to modernity. The full quotation is, "At the same time as Orthodoxy certainly defined the essential 'kernel' of Judaism, so too did it define a 'husk' to be abandoned. In contrast with traditional Judaism, modern Orthodoxy understood aspects of the liturgy (e.g., the vernacular sermon, use of professionally trained choirs) and of the public sphere (dress, secular education, etc.) as discretionary, that is, beyond the purview of the mandatory *halacha* (religious law). In these areas, even the faithful Jew could westernize. In short, where Modern Orthodox rabbis have seen the *halacha* as silent, they allowed modernity to fill the normative void created by the retreat of traditional law and custom. Modern Orthodoxy facilitated integration by relaxing controls over many areas of life which were formerly regulated by custom and social sanction. As a result of changing and differing interpretations of the discretionary zone, Orthodoxy embraced more diversity than many of its doctrinaire adherents or uninformed outside observers perceive" (*American Modernity and Jewish Identity*, 30).

62. See Max, "Mixed Pews."

63. Sarna, "Debate Over Mixed Seating in the American Synagogue."

64. Today, no member congregation of the Union of Orthodox Jewish Congregations of America lacks a *meḥitsah*. For a compilation of primary documents on the *meḥitsah* debates, see Litvin, *Sanctity of the Synagogue*.

65. Tannenbaum, "Religion," 60.

66. See Bernstein, *Orthodox Union Story*, 162–67.

67. Tannenbaum, "Religion."

68. Bienenfeld interview.

69. *CJN*, 29 June 1962.

70. E. G. Faludi and Associates, *Proposed Residential Development*, 14.

71. DBS, *1961 Census of Canada*, Table 1.

72. City of North York, *1963 for 1964 Property Assessment Rolls*.

73. A small Orthodox Jewish congregation was formed in the Bathurst Manor neighborhood in the late 1950s, where Congregation Shaare Emunah was founded as a breakaway minyan from the Conservative Beth Emeth Congregation. Shaare Emunah remained a small congregation for most of the 1960s and eventually was incorporated into Congregation Beth Jacob, which moved to Bathurst Manor from Kensington. In part because of its somewhat isolated location in the Manor and in part because of its small size, Shaare Emunah/Beth Jacob did not have the impact that other congregations had on Orthodox Jewish suburbanization. As such, its story is secondary to the analytical framework of this chapter.

74. Wenner interview; Lane interview.

75. *CJN*, 14 September 1966.

76. *CJN*, 11 June 1965; Wenner interview; Lane interview; Jakobovits interview.

77. Wenner interview; Jakobovits interview; Zaionz interview; Lane interview.

78. Wenner interview.

79. In its actual construction, the balcony represented the use of modern technology to create a traditional setting. In the first phase of sanctuary construction, financial constraints prohibited the installation of the balcony. To save money later, however, the engineer embedded three large steel beams into the structure from which a balcony could later be "hung." The result, after the congregation raised enough capital to install the upstairs addition, was a balcony that did not need supporting pillars and thus provided an obstruction-free view from above or below (Wenner interview).

80. B'nai Torah Congregation, *B'nai Torah Bulletin*, December 1976, OJA; B'nai Torah Congregation, Board of Directors Minutes, 10 July 1986, B'nai Torah Congregation Archives.

81. See, for example, Kelley, *Why Conservative Churches Are Growing*.

82. For discussions of how the centrist Orthodox Jewish community reacted to this "turn to the right," see Schick, "New Style of American Orthodoxy"; Lamm, "Voice of Torah in the Battle of Ideas"; and Hochbaum, "Middle-of-the-Road Orthodoxy."

83. *CJN*, 29 June, 5 January 1962, 2 December 1966, 2 February 1968.

84. *JS*, 5 June 1970; *CJN*, 14 April 1972; Council of North York Congregations, Minutes, 11 July 1955, SEPP.

85. Somerville and Macfarlane, *History of Vaughan Township Churches*.

86. *CJN*, 5 February 1981.

87. *CJN*, 22 June 1989, 3 September 1981.

88. See Finke and Stark, *Churching of America*.

CHAPTER FOUR

1. Stolper, "What Does Jewish Youth Really Want?"

2. Seeley, Sim, and Loosley, *Crestwood Heights.*

3. Babylonian Talmud, *Tractate Kiddushin,* 29a.

4. Moses Maimonides, *Mishneh Torah, Hilkhot De'ot* 4:23.

5. For an extensive discussion of this mimetic culture, see Soloveitchik, "Rupture and Reconstruction."

6. Shapiro, *Time for Healing,* 183.

7. Wertheimer, *People Divided,* 130. Despite Wertheimer's comment, few studies of Orthodox Jewish education have looked at the role of class or geography in shaping the day school experience. Neither Alvin Schiff in *The Jewish Day School in America* nor Doniel Zvi Kramer in *The Day Schools and Torah Umesorah,* for example, included an explicit consideration of Orthodox Jewish suburbanization in their histories of the North American Jewish day school. Other books and articles that discuss Orthodox Jewish education without an explicitly suburban analysis include Kaminetsky, *Hebrew Day School Education;* Inbar, "Hebrew Day Schools"; Helmreich, *World of the Yeshiva;* Joselit, *New York's Jewish Jews,* 123–46; Dahlen, "Our Lives Revolve around the Holidays"; Himmelfarb and DellaPergola, *Jewish Education Worldwide;* Gleicher, "Origins and Early Years of Chicago's Hebrew Theological College"; and Gurock, *Men and Women of Yeshiva.* In this last book, Gurock does note the role of Yeshiva University's students in working to export Orthodoxy to newly developing suburban neighborhoods. His main focus, however, is on the institutional history of Yeshiva, which, being an urban campus, had little to say directly about the state of education among the broader suburban Orthodox Jewish community. Finally, for a complete listing of works on Jewish education, see Drachler, *Bibliography of Jewish Education in the United States.*

8. See Kanarfogel, *Jewish Education and Society in the High Middle Ages.*

9. For a historical discussion of Talmud Torahs, see Kaufman, *Shul with a Pool.*

10. Toronto Board of Jewish Education, *Home and School* 4 (April 1957), OJA. The full quotation is taken from a survey by the American Jewish Congress of day school students who wanted "as full integration into American life as those attending public school."

11. Moore, *At Home in America.*

12. Hirsch, "What Shall I Tell My Teacher?"

13. Ibid.

14. For a complete history and analysis of Torah Umesorah, see Kramer, *Day Schools and Torah Umesorah.*

15. The data from the 1950s and 1960s come from Schiff, *Jewish Day School in America,* 49. The data for the 1980s are taken from Walter I. Ackerman, "Strangers to Tradition: Idea and Constraint in American Jewish Education," in Himmelfarb and DellaPergola, *Jewish Education Worldwide,* 71–116.

16. Schiff, *Jewish Day School in America,* 50–54; H. F. Epstein Hebrew Academy, *Fiftieth Anniversary Commemorative Journal; Jewish Action* 16 (October 1962), Benjamin Koenigsberg Papers, Folder 9/5, YUA.

17. *Enterprise*, 9 December 1954.

18. There is little evidence of controversy over the closing of the downtown branches in the early 1960s. By this point, Kensington had already lost the bulk of families with school-age children to the new neighborhoods of North York. Only a generally older population remained downtown.

19. Toronto Board of Jewish Education, *Home and School* 3 (September 1955), OJA.

20. Quoted in Kramer, *Day Schools and Torah Umesorah*, 11.

21. See Weissman, "Bais Yaakov."

22. The exact issue involved in the founding of Maimonides School is the subject of much debate within the Orthodox Jewish community. Some believe that Rabbi Soloveitchik created a coeducational school only by default because it was difficult enough to convince community leaders to have any sort of Jewish parochial school; to propose two separate schools would have been ludicrous. Others claim that Rabbi Soloveitchik supported coed schools from the beginning. At the heart of the debate is the extent to which the attitudes and behaviors of mid-century "Modern Orthodox" Jewry, which are usually judged as lax by contemporary religious standards, can find legitimation through the actions of a rabbinic luminary such as Rabbi Soloveitchik. For a more complete discussion of this issue, see Farber, "Community, Schooling, and Leadership."

23. For a discussion of these programs, see Kramer, *Day Schools and Torah Umesorah*, 50–114.

24. Ribalow, "My Child Goes to Jewish Parochial School," 66.

25. Kaminetsky, "Orthodox Unity and the Day Schools," 49.

26. *CJN*, 12 October 1960.

27. Kaminetsky, "Yeshiva Ketanah," 35.

28. Kramer, *Day Schools and Torah Umesorah*, 67.

29. Kaminetsky, "Ways to Religious Growth in the Home"; Kaminetsky, "Parents Too Grow through Day Schools."

30. Kaminetsky, "Ways to Religious Growth in the Home," 4.

31. Horowitz, "Education Begins at Home."

32. *CJN*, 15 January 1960.

33. *CJN*, 15 December 1961.

34. See various advertisements and articles on these camps in *JS*, 1 December and 15 March 1958; and *CJN*, 8 January, 1 March 1960, and 7 February 1964.

35. See Stuart Schoenfeld, "Jewish Education and Jewish Continuity." See also Jerome Kutnick, "Jewish Education in Canada," in Himmelfarb and DellaPergola, *Jewish Education Worldwide*, 135–69.

36. Letter from Frank Newman to S. P. Goldberg, 4 November 1964, Box 53, Folder 10, IHS.

37. Kramer, *Day Schools and Torah Umesorah*, 134.

38. See Plotinsky, "Hebrew Academy of Indianapolis." Also see Endelman, *Jewish Community of Indianapolis*; Jewish Federation of Greater Indianapolis, *Federation News*.

39. Ribalow, "My Child Goes to Jewish Parochial School."

40. Hertzberg, "Religion," 114.

41. Robert Gordis, "A Strategy for Jewish Survival Today," *Congress Bi-Weekly* 38 (17 September 1971): 8, quoted in Kramer, *Day Schools and Torah Umesorah*, 166.

42. *CJN*, 13 April 1962; SCJE, *Study on Jewish Education*, 2:14–18.

43. SCJE, *Study on Jewish Education*, 2:10–14.

44. Ibid., 24–26.

45. Ibid., 3, 7.

46. *CJN*, 14 April 1967.

47. Schiff, *Jewish Day School in America*, 72; Frost, "Jewish Education in the United States: Three Comments," in Himmelfarb and DellaPergola, *Jewish Education Worldwide*, 117–22.

48. Hechinger and Hechinger, *Teen-Age Tyranny*. See also the chapters on the 1960s in Katz, *Home Fires*.

49. For a discussion of 1960s religion, see Hudnut-Beumler, *Looking for God in the Suburbs*, 175–207.

50. Stolper, "What Does Jewish Youth Really Want?"

51. SCJE, *Study on Jewish Education*, 3:9–11. For a brief discussion of the opening of Beth Jacob, see Bianco, *Reichmanns*, 329.

52. *CJN*, 22 April, 26 August 1966, 27 August 1965, 29 July 1966.

53. *CJN*, 2 December 1966, 27 June 1969; *Jewish Western Bulletin*, 30 April 1971, Benjamin Koenigsberg Papers, Box 25/3, YUA; *CJN*, 23 July 1971.

54. The information on abuse of drugs among Ḥasidic Jewish youth is taken from a 1968 conference report by the Commission on Synagogue Relations of the New York Federation of Jewish Philanthropies and was cited in an article in *CJN*, 12 August 1968. For a longer discussion of Jewish drug problems, see several articles in Rosenthal, ed., *Jewish Family in a Changing World*, including Stanley Einstein, "The Use and Misuse of Alcohol and Other Drugs," 86–121; Meyer H. Diskind, "The Jewish Drug Addict—A Challenge to the Community," 122–35; Richard I. Schachet, "The Rabbi and the Addict," 136–44; Adolph E. Wasser, "On the Prevention of Drug Addiction," 145–48; and Arnold Mendelson, "On the Prevention of Addiction—A Family Agency View," 149–56.

55. See Gurock, *Men and Women of Yeshiva*, 224–25.

56. Bienenfeld interview.

57. Heilman, *Portrait of American Jews*, 83.

58. As early as 1948, the Orthodox Jewish–affiliated *Jewish Life* published by Philip Isaacs examined the problems faced by observant students in secular college settings. See Isaacs, "The Jewish Home versus Campus Temptations."

59. Oppenheim, "Orthodoxy on the Campus," 47.

60. For other discussions of the Orthodox Jewish college experience, see Lerner, "College Dilemma"; Pelcovitz, "Challenge of College"; Seidman, "On Choosing a College Away from Home"; and Leiman, "Campus Problem and Jewish Education."

61. The estimate comes from my father, Rabbi Jim Diamond, who has headed various university Hillel Houses since 1968. For a recent listing of campus kosher food facilities, see Cernea, ed., *Hillel Guide to Jewish Life on Campus*.

62. For the history of Orthodox Jews at an Ivy League university, see Sanua, "Stages in the Development of Jewish Life at Princeton University."

63. Eisen, "Interim Report of the Special Committee in the Curriculum and Structure of the Community Hebrew Academy," 21 February 1972, in Community Hebrew Academy of Toronto, *Board of Directors Manual.*

64. Ibid., 9.

65. *CJN,* 1 June 1973.

66. SCJE, *Study of Jewish Education,* 3:11–12.

67. Other than a rather humorous topology of yarmulke wearers (Powell, "Jews at a Glance (Kipahology)"), little has been written about the traditional Jewish head covering. See Brasch, "Why Jews Cover the Head," and Greenberg, *On Women and Judaism.* Given the many levels of social and symbolic meaning, a fuller anthropological, sociological, and historical analysis of the yarmulke would be a welcome addition to the literature on twentieth-century Orthodox Judaism.

68. For an early discussion about head coverings, see Weiss, "Why Wear a Yarmulka?"

69. *CJN,* 18 August 1967, 5 January 1968.

70. Shapiro, *Time for Healing,* 182.

71. Cohen, "Impact of Jewish Education on Religious Identification and Practice." See also Sigal, August, and Beltempo, "Impact of Jewish Education on Jewish Identification in a Group of Adolescents."

72. Cohen, "Impact of Jewish Education on Religious Identification and Practice," 325. Cohen's argument supports a similar argument made by Andrew Greeley that Catholic schools have the highest measurable impact on the development and maintenance of religious attitudes among students from religious Catholic homes. See Greeley and Rossi, *Education of Catholic Americans.*

73. Friedman, *Faithful Youth.*

## CHAPTER FIVE

1. Freedman, "Orthodox Sweets for Heterodox New York."

2. Ibid., 478.

3. Gans, "American Jewry," 428.

4. Heinze, *Adapting to Abundance,* 5.

5. The more common, and more recent, explanation for breaking a glass is as a remembrance of the destruction of the Temple in Jerusalem by the Romans in 70 c.e. That the original explanation has been generally forgotten is evidenced by the absence of material restraint at many contemporary weddings. For a discussion of breaking the glass, see Lamm, *Jewish Way in Love and Marriage,* 228–31.

6. See Part 3 of Balmer, *Mine Eyes Have Seen the Glory* (videorecording).

7. Schmidt, *Consumer Rites;* McDannell, *Material Christianity;* Nissenbaum, *Battle for Christmas.*

8. Van Esterik, "Celebrating Ethnicity." See also Sack, "Food and Eating in American Religious Cultures."

9. Anderson and Alleyne, "Ethnicity, Food Preferences and Habits of Consumption."

10. James Donner, "The Food Revolution and Kashruth," *Jewish Affairs*, November 1965, Benjamin Koenigsberg Papers, Folder 10/1, YUA. For other studies of Jewish materialism, see Heinze, *Adapting to Abundance*, and Joselit, *Wonders of America*. Both examine the emergence of consumerism in immigrant Jewish society in the first half of the twentieth century. Joselit also includes a discussion of consumption in her work on New York's Orthodox Jewish community in the 1920s and 1930s, although she does not push her analysis into the postwar, suburban phase of Orthodox Jewish growth. See Joselit, *New York's Jewish Jews*.

11. For further explanations of the laws of *kashruth*, see Lipschutz, *Kashruth*.

12. For a history of *kashruth* supervision problems, see Gastwirt, *Fraud, Corruption, and Holiness*.

13. Bernstein, *Orthodox Union Story*, 92.

14. Union of Orthodox Jewish Congregations of America, Department of Public Relations, "Heinz to Be Honored for Being First Company to Debut Kosher Symbol," press release, 25 May 1999.

15. *JS*, 1 May 1952.

16. *JS*, 1 March 1958; *CJN*, 19 April 1989. For similar stories on the development of other community *kashruth* programs, see Engelberg, "Kashruth Is a Community Program," and Miller, "They Did It in Worcester."

17. *CJN*, 28 April 1961.

18. *CJN*, 28 September 1962.

19. Seeley, Sim, and Loosley, *Crestwood Heights*, 45.

20. Even as early as the mid-1950s, Orthodox Jewish magazines recognized the trend toward women entering the workforce. See Duckat, "New Careers for Jewish Women."

21. James Donner, "The Food Revolution and Kashruth," *Jewish Affairs*, November 1965, 18, in Benjamin Koenigsberg Papers, Folder 10/1, YUA. Interestingly, the first instant cake mixes, which included dried eggs in the recipe and required cooks only to add water, did not meet with automatic success. Researchers found that housewives felt that they were not actually "cooking" if they added no fresh ingredients on their own. As a result, food technicians reformulated the recipes to allow cooks to add eggs. This minor alteration worked wonders, as consumers quickly made the instant cake mixes a staple of their pantries. See Schremp, *Kitchen Culture*, 55.

22. Press release, Union of Orthodox Jewish Congregations of America, December 1963, Benjamin Koenigsberg Papers, Folder 9/5, YUA.

23. For an extensive discussion of the Jewish affinity for spicy foods, and Chinese foods specifically, see Tuchman and Levine, "New York Jews and Chinese Food."

24. For a discussion of the impact of supermarket chains on local and ethnic grocery stores in the 1920s and 1930s, see Cohen, *Making a New Deal*, 106–20.

25. *CJN*, 27 June 1962.

26. *CJN*, 23 February 1968.

27. *CJN*, 22 September 1967.

28. Kashruth Council of Toronto, *Kashruth Directory* (1968), OJA.

29. Goldberg, "Slaves No More to Sweet Wine"; Ben-Joseph, "Renaissance."

30. Cynthia Gasner of Toronto recalled the practice of eating "milky *treyf*," referring to the fact that although there was nothing dietarily impermissible about the dairy food, it was ultimately still considered unkosher because the food was not prepared under *kashruth* supervision (Gasner interview).

31. *CJN*, 10 March, 17 March, 28 July 1961.

32. *CJN*, 28 January 1966, 11 December 1970, 5 February 1971, 6 October 1972.

33. *CJN*, 11, 18, 25 July 1975.

34. *CJN*, 24 January 1980.

35. Shapiro, *Time for Healing*, 182.

36. For a history of kosher resorts and summer "bungalow" colonies, see Kanfer, *Summer World*.

37. On Passover, one is forbidden to eat any form of leavened food that contains flour, grain, or grain by-product, a restriction that eliminates most foods eaten during the year. Instead, one must eat only specially supervised "Kosher for Passover" food. In addition, because one must not even see or own forbidden leavened food products during the week of Passover, traditionally observant Jews clean their entire house to remove even crumbs that are hidden from sight. Kitchens are scoured and *kashered* (made kosher) for Passover, and special Passover dishes and utensils are used during the week. With all the cleaning and other preparations that precede Passover, it is not difficult to understand the popularity of Passover hotel packages.

38. See an early advertisement for a kosher vacation tour to Puerto Rico by a company called Orthodox Tours, in *CJN*, 5 August 1966.

39. Campbell, *Romantic Ethic and the Spirit of Modern Consumerism*, 37.

40. *Smart Shopper's Guide*, June 1996, 9; September–October 1996, 55.

41. *Toronto Community Directory, 5754; Toronto Orthodox Jewish Community Directory, 5755.*

42. Kelman, "Religion," 138.

43. For an early review of Torah tapes and other religious media, see "New Casks for Old Wine."

44. Mandlebaum, ed., *Family Chronicles*, 314.

45. *CJN*, 15 January 1960, 6 September 1968.

46. Tuchman, "Chanukah—or Jewish Christmas?" For a broader critique of all branches of North American Jewry, see also Loewy, "Vulgarization of the American Jewish Community."

47. Berkowitz, "Challenge to Modern Orthodoxy," 104.

48. Singer, "Is Club Med Kosher?" A response to Singer's article with a larger discussion of leisure in Orthodox Judaism is found in Carmy, "Rejoinder." For two critiques of the place of moral values in the world of observant Judaism, see Hofmann, "Are We Teaching Our Values," and Levitz, "Crisis in Orthodoxy." Berger,

"Holy Hypocrites," provides more recent analysis of cases of moral corruption within Orthodoxy.

49. Shapiro, *Time for Healing*, 184–85.

## CHAPTER SIX

1. Some sources that discuss the continental dimensions to the North American Jewish community are Sheshkin, "Jewish Metropolitan Homelands," and Moore, *To the Golden Cities*.

2. For a discussion of the difficulties of small-town Orthodox Jewish life, see Schloff, "Overcoming Geography." See also Katz and Lehr, "Jewish Pioneer Agricultural Settlements in Western Canada."

3. Gurock, *Men and Women of Yeshiva*, 95.

4. Gurock, "Resisters and Accommodators," 173–74, n. 66. For the story of one such rabbi serving a non–New York community, see Rakeffet-Rothkoff, *Silver Era*.

5. Data on the percentages of New York and non–New York enrollment are taken from Jeffrey Gurock's survey of approximately 9,500 students who attended Yeshiva University from 1928 to the mid-1980s. Although the survey is not entirely inclusive (representing about three-quarters of the entire student population), there is little evidence that the averages would be greatly different with the entire data set. See a discussion of these data in Gurock, *Men and Women of Yeshiva*, 257–58, n. 5. The data tabulations can be found in the Yeshiva University Archives, Yeshiva University, New York.

6. In 1926, only about "half a dozen" items were supervised by the Orthodox Union. See the *OU News Reporter* 1 (May 1956), Benjamin Koenigsberg Papers, Folder 9/3, YUA.

7. Many of the documents published in Litvin, *Sanctity of the Synagogue*, came from national sources.

8. Minutes, Personnel and Budget Control Committee, UOJCA, 8 May 1956, Benjamin Koenigsberg Papers, Folder 9/3, YUA.

9. Resolutions adopted by UOJCA 64th National Biennial Convention, 25 November 1962, Benjamin Koenigsberg Papers, Folder 9/5, YUA.

10. Resolutions of 70th National Biennial Convention, 27 November–1 December 1968, Washington, D.C., Benjamin Koenigsberg Papers, Folder 9/5, YUA.

11. "Progress in the Mid-West"; Shaarei Tefillah Congregation, *Dedication Weekend Program* (1962), Records Group MG-3 A34, OJA; *CJN*, 9, 16, 23 February 1962.

12. Isaacs, "National Gathering of Sisterhoods."

13. Gordon, "Decision for Action."

14. Tabak, "National Torah Tour."

15. *CJN*, 3 March 1961, 8 February 1963.

16. Schiff, *Jewish Day School in America*, 49; Soloveitchik, "Rupture and Reconstruction," 91.

17. Brafman, "Yeshiva Problem."

18. Kramer, *Day Schools and Torah Umesorah*.

19. Particularly among non-Orthodox Jewish students, the Orthodox Jewish day school could be seen as stifling and downright antagonistic to their religious differences. In an anonymous response to a survey of alumni of the Epstein Hebrew Academy of St. Louis, one former student recalled "the insults and put-downs from the many ultra-Orthodox teachers and students towards me and other students, because we were not from Orthodox families with lots of money and we did not attend the only 'acceptable' synagogue" (H. F. Epstein Hebrew Academy, *Fiftieth Anniversary Alumni Survey*, Respondent No. 4).

20. *CJN*, 13 May 1960.

21. *CJN*, 20 January 1961.

22. See Hoenig, "Great Victory."

23. *CJN*, 3 January 1964.

24. *CJN*, 13 January 1967.

25. Camp Massad Camper Lists, 1957, 1962, Records Group 42-B, OJA.

26. The averages used here were obtained from the printed summaries of Gurock's Yeshiva University student survey, *Men and Women of Yeshiva*.

27. See Sanua, "Stages in the Development of Jewish Life at Princeton University."

28. Press release, Orthodox Jewish Congregations of America, December 1965, Benjamin Koenigsberg Papers, folder 10/1, YUA.

29. Abramson, "Traveling Kosher."

30. The role of print media in linking unconnected people is dealt with extensively by Benedict Anderson in *Imagined Communities*.

31. Sigelschiffer, "Torahtown Is on Its Way."

32. Kaufman, "Far Rockaway—Torah-Suburb by-the-Sea."

33. Weisfeld, "Jewry in the Southwest"; Givon, "By the Waters of Malibu"; Biberfeld, "Report from the North."

34. See Gooen, "Rustling Out West."

35. Rubinstein, "The Jew in the Present-Day South."

36. Ibid.

37. Feldman, "Case for 'Out-of-Town.'"

38. Belsky, "American 'Shtetl' Emerges."

39. To be sure, a chasm between New East Coast Orthodox Jews (primarily New Yorkers) and "out-of-towners" remained well into the 1990s. A September 1999 column by Rafael Grossman, rabbi of Memphis's Baron Hirsch Synagogue, commented on Hillary Rodham Clinton's candidacy for the Senate from New York by observing that "New York's Jewish voters give themselves more importance than they deserve" because "Israel's future will not be determined by the winner of the 2000 Senatorial election." Most New Yorkers, and "most especially" New York Jews, Grossman argued, have a provincialism that can blind them to the realities of Jewish life "out of town" (Grossman, "To the Wonderful Jews of New York").

40. "It's All in the Demographics."

41. Orthodox Union, *Jewish Action Special Kashrut Supplement*, 10.

42. Shamash, "Kosher Restaurant Database."

43. Orthodox Union, "Worldwide Orthodox Synagogue Network."

44. For a discussion of ecumenism and suburbanization, see Finke and Stark, *Churching of America*, 225–36.

45. Zelinsky, "Approach to the Religious Geography of the United States."

46. Balmer, *Mine Eyes Have Seen the Glory* (book).


CHAPTER SEVEN

1. Chyet, "American Jews," 337.

2. Sklare, *Conservative Judaism*; Gordon, *Jews in Suburbia*; Glazer, *American Judaism*.

3. Herberg, *Protestant, Catholic, Jew*.

4. Whyte, *Organization Man*.

5. See Bellah et al., *Habits of the Heart*; Roof and McKinney, *Generation of Seekers*; Roof, *Spiritual Marketplace*.

6. See the religious affiliation data collected in Johnson, Picard, and Quinn, *Churches and Church Membership in the United States*, and Bradley et al., *Churches and Church Membership in the United States 1990*.

7. Miller, *Reinventing American Protestantism*; Wuthnow, "*I Come Away Stronger*"; Wuthnow, *Sharing the Journey*.

8. For a discussion of the retention of youth among Orthodox Jewish families, see Friedman, *Faithful Youth*.

9. Fishman, "Megalopolis Unbound."

10. Teixiera, "Ethnicity, Housing Search, and the Role of the Real Estate Agent"; Texiera and Murdie, "Role of Ethnic Real Estate Agents in the Residential Relocation Process"; Goldenberg and Haines, "Social Networks and Institutional Completeness."

11. Guthrie, Brier, and Moore, *Indianapolis Hispanic Community*.

12. Diamond, "Places of Worship"; Diamond, "Uptown, Downtown, Northside, Southside."

13. For a further discussion of religion and metropolitan mobility, see Diamond, "Religious Mobility."

14. Coleman, *Foundations of Social Theory*; Putnam, "Bowling Alone"; Ammerman, "Bowling Together"; Greeley, "Coleman Revisited."

15. Riesman, *Lonely Crowd*.

16. For an analysis of how this gift exchange helps to construct community, see Sacks, "Computing Community at Purim."

17. Ibid., 277.

18. See Wertheimer, *People Divided*, and Wertheimer, "Orthodox Moment."

19. Comments about the lack of understanding for the situation of unmarried Jews were made in a lecture by Krohn, "Rebuilding the Bais Hamikdash."

20. See a comment by the medieval Torah commentator Rashi (Rabbi Shlomo Yitshaki) on the phrase "I am God, who heals you" in Exodus 15:26: "But according

to its literal sense the meaning is: For I am the Lord who healeth thee and teacheth thee the Law and Commandments in order that thou mayest be saved from them (these diseases)—like a physician who says to a man: Do not eat this thing lest it will bring you into danger from this disease. So, too, it states, (Proverbs 3:8) 'It (obedience to God) will be wholesome to thy body' (implying that disease will not fall upon thee)" (Silbermann, *Chumash*).

21. See Diamond, "Middle Class in Suburbs."

22. In 1999, Chicago-based photographer Yves Mozelsio presented a provocative exhibit focusing on the occupations of Orthodox Jews. Combining black-and-white portraits and narrative text, Mozelsio's exhibit explored the ways Orthodox Jews use their traditionalist religion to mediate their work experiences. One should note that a majority of Mozelsio's subjects worked in "secular" occupations ranging from biochemist and prison officer to musician and artist. A minority worked as "professional Jews" in synagogues, day schools, or kosher food establishments. See Mozelsio, "Fruits of Our Labor."

23. There may, however, be a silver lining in this economic change, in that it might hasten the democraticization of some Orthodox Jewish communities. Too often, a community can become overly reliant on a single family or a handful of families for support, giving the benefactors a disproportionate and potentially harmful amount of influence and a seemingly permanent hold on positions of leadership. If communities are forced to spread the financial responsibilities around, greater numbers of people will have opportunities to contribute to community development and leadership.

# BIBLIOGRAPHY

PRIMARY SOURCES

*Newspapers*

*Canadian Jewish News.* 1960–97.
*Jewish Standard.* 1948–73.
*New York Times*, 22 February 1993.
*North York Enterprise.* 1947–60.
*Windsor-Heights Herald*, 21 November 1997.


*Interviews*

Unless otherwise indicated, all interviews were conducted by the author.
Jeffrey Bienenfeld. St. Louis, Missouri, 24 April 1995
Sol Edell. North York, Ontario, 2 December 1994
Cynthia Gasner. North York, Ontario, 9 November 1994
Joseph Godfrey. North York, Ontario, 29 December 1994
Irving Grossman. Interview by Sheldon Levitt. 5 January 1978. MSR No. JEW-4756-GRO, Form 1688, Multicultural Historical Society of Ontario, Toronto.
Shaya Izenberg. St. Louis, Missouri, 25 April 1995
Shlomo Jakobovits. North York, Ontario, 25 January 1995
Joseph Kelman. Interview by Sheldon Levitt. 15 December 1977 and 12 January 1978. MSR No. JEW-4758-KEL, Form 1685, Multicultural Historical Society of Ontario, Toronto.
Mark, Ruth, and David Lane. North York, Ontario, 7 November 1994
Max Neuberger. North York, Ontario, 12 December 1994
Bill and Judith Rubinstein. North York, Ontario, 11 December 1994
Lillian Silverberg. North York, Ontario, 7 December 1994
Aaron Weisblatt. North York, Ontario, 6 November 1994
Marvin Wenner. North York, Ontario, 20 October 1994
Bernie and Hedda Zaionz. Thornhill, Ontario, 14 May 1995

*Archival Sources*

Indianapolis
  Indiana Historical Society
    Jewish Welfare Federation Collection, Records Group M463.
New York
  Yeshiva University Archives
    Benjamin Koenigsberg Papers.
St. Louis
  St. Louis Jewish Community Archives
Toronto
  B'nai Torah Congregation
  Sol Edell Personal Papers
  Metropolitan Toronto Archives
    Northways. Metro Toronto Aerial Photographs (1947–56), Series 1993.056.
  Ontario Jewish Archives
    Records Group MG-3 A31 (Synagogue Records). Shaarei Shomayim
    Synagogue—Toronto, Ontario.
    Records Group MG-3 A33 (Synagogue Records). B'nai Torah
    Congregation—Toronto, Ontario.
    Records Group MG-3 A34 (Synagogue Records). Shaarei Tefillah
    Synagogue—Toronto, Ontario.
    Records Group MG-3 A51 (Synagogue Records). Kehillat Shaarei Torah
    (North East Hebrew Congregation)—Toronto, Ontario.
    Records Group MG-3 A71 (Synagogue Records). File 89-303.
    Records Group MG-8-R. Canadian Jewish Congress–Central Region box,
    Kashruth Directories file.
    Records Group 42-A/B. Toronto Board of Jewish Education.
  Presbyterian Church in Canada Archives
    *Acts and Proceedings of the 77th General Assembly of the Presbyterian Church
    in Canada.* June 1951.
    *Acts and Proceedings of the 79th General Assembly of the Presbyterian Church
    in Canada.* June 1953.
    *Presbyterian Record.* 1950–60.
  United Church of Canada/Victoria University Archives
    Local Church History Files Collection.
      Armour Heights United Church records.
      Asbury and West United Church records.
      Wilson Heights United Church records.
    Torrance, J. C. "Report of Toronto Home Missions Council." *United Church
    of Canada Yearbook* (Toronto, 1949), 129–30.
    Warne, R. M. "On Choosing a Church Site." United Church of Canada
    Board of Home Missions fonds, Church Extension Correspondence, 1959,
    Acc. 83.050c-box 276-file 2.

*Government Sources*

Dominion Bureau of Statistics. *Eighth Census of Canada, Population by Local Subdivisions, 1941.* Vol. 2. Ottawa, 1944.

———. *Ninth Census of Canada, Population and Housing Characteristics by Census Tracts, Toronto, 1951.* Ottawa, 1953.

———. *1961 Census of Canada, Population and Housing Characteristics by Census Tracts, Toronto.* Ottawa, 1963.

———. *1971 Census of Canada, Population and Housing Characteristics by Census Tracts, Toronto.* Ottawa, 1973.

City of North York. Property Assessment Rolls. 1954–75. City Clerk's Department, North York City Hall, North York.

North York Planning Department. Municipal Numbering Sheets. North York, 1985–88.

———. *South Bathurst Street Study.* North York, 1988.

Statistics Canada. *1971 Census of Canada: Population and Housing Characteristics by Census Tracts.* Ottawa, 1974.

———. *1981 Census of Canada: Census Subdivisions of 5000 Population and Over, Selected Social and Economic Characteristics.* Ottawa, 1983.

———. *1991 Census Profiles CD-ROM.* Ottawa, 1993.

*Other*

Babylonian Talmud, *Tractate Kiddushin.*

Brodbar-Nemzer, Jay. *Greater Toronto Jewish Community Study: A First Look.* Toronto: Toronto Jewish Congress and the Jewish Federation of Greater Toronto, 1991.

Cernea, Ruth Fredman, ed. *The Hillel Guide to Jewish Life of Campus.* New York: Random House, 1997.

Community Hebrew Academy of Toronto. *Board of Directors Manual.* Toronto, 1989.

David, J., and G. Walker. "Changes in a Former Jewish Area in Toronto." Unpublished research paper, Toronto, n.d. [prob. 1961]. Albert J. Latner Jewish Public Library Reference Room, Toronto.

Deacon, Arnett, and Murray Deacon. *Bathurst Street, Forest Hill to Don River: A Study.* Toronto, 1957. Metro Toronto Urban Affairs Library, Toronto.

E. G. Faludi and Associates. *Proposed Residential Development, Parts of Lots 22 and 23, Con. 2, WYS, Township of North York.* Toronto, 1961.

H. F. Epstein Hebrew Academy. *Fiftieth Anniversary Alumni Survey.* St. Louis, 1992.

———. *Fiftieth Anniversary Commemorative Journal.* St. Louis, 1992.

Friedman, Nathalie. *Faithful Youth: A Study of the National Conference of Synagogue Youth.* New York: National Conference of Synagogue Youth, 1998.

"It's All in the Demographics." *Yeshiva University Review* 4 (Fall 1997): 24.

Jewish Federation of Greater Indianapolis. *Federation News*. March 1998.

Krohn, Paysach. "Rebuilding the Bais Hamikdash Word by Word: The Tisha B'Av '98 Event." Audiotape. Monsey, N.Y.: Chofetz Chaim Heritage Foundation, 1998.

Lipsitz, Edmund, ed. *Ontario Jewish Resource Directory*. Toronto: Canadian Jewish Congress, 1989.

Looby, A. R. *Flowering of a Community: Story of St. Eugene's Church, North York Township*. North York: St. Eugene's Chapel, 1991.

Maimonides, Moses. *Mishneh Torah, Hilkhot De'ot*.

*Metropolitan Toronto City Directory*. 1950–75. Toronto: Might Directories.

Mozelsio, Yves. "Fruits of Our Labor: Orthodox Jews and Their Work." Exhibition at the Spertus Museum of Judaica, Chicago, Spring 1999.

Orthodox Union. *Jewish Action Special Kashrut Supplement: Passover Directory 1999*. New York: Orthodox Union, 1999.

———. "Worldwide Orthodox Synagogue Network." <http://www.ou.org/network/shulslist.htma>. 31 October 1999.

Rasky, Frank, and Cynthia Gasner. *Continuing from Strength to Strength: The People and Events That Shaped the Development of Associated Hebrew Schools of Toronto and the Jewish Community of Ontario, 1907–1987*. Toronto: Associated Hebrew Schools, 1987.

Rosenberg, Louis. *A Study of the Changes in the Geographic Distribution of the Jewish Population in the Metropolitan Area of Toronto, 1851–1951*. Canadian Jewish Population Studies, Jewish Community Series No. 2. Montreal: Bureau of Social and Economic Research, Canadian Jewish Congress, 1954.

Shamash: The Jewish Internet Consortium. "Kosher Restaurant Database." <http://shamash.org/kosher>. 8 October 1999.

Silbermann, A. M. *Chumash with Rashi's Commentary*. Jerusalem: Silbermann Family, 1934.

*Smart Shopper's Guide*. Toronto, June 1996.

Study Committee on Jewish Education. *Study on Jewish Education*. Toronto: United Jewish Welfare Fund, 1975.

Thatcher, K. A. *A Study of the Position of the Church in an Expanding Community*. North York: North York Planning Board, 1962.

*Toronto Jewish Orthodox Community Directory, 5755*. Toronto: Persomet Publishing, 1995.

*Toronto Community Directory, 5754*. Toronto: Persomet Publishing, 1994.

Torczyner, James L., Shari L. Brotman, and Jay Brodbar. *Rapid Growth and Transformation: Demographic Challenges Facing the Jewish Community of Greater Toronto*. Toronto: McGill Consortium for Ethnicity and Strategic Social Planning, 1995.

Wells, Dalton C. *Report of the Royal Commission of Inquiry Reporting the Arrest and Detention of Rabbi Norbert Leiner by the Metropolitan Toronto Police Force*. Toronto, 1962.

SECONDARY SOURCES

Abramson, Lillian S. "Traveling Kosher." *Jewish Life* 19 (July–August 1952): 50–54.

Ahlstrom, Sidney E. *A Religious History of the American People*. New Haven: Yale University Press, 1972.

Allen, James B., and Glen M. Leonard. *The Story of Latter-day Saints*. Salt Lake City: Deseret Book Co., 1976.

Ammerman, Nancy. "Bowling Together: Congregations and the American Civic Order." University Lecture in Religion, Arizona State University, 1996.

———. *Congregation and Community*. New Brunswick, N.J.: Rutgers University Press, 1997.

———. *Southern Baptists Observed: Multiple Perspectives on a Changing Denomination*. Knoxville: University of Tennessee Press, 1993.

Anderson, Benedict. *Imagined Communities: Reflections on the Origin and Spread of Nationalism*. London: Verso, 1991.

Anderson, Grace M., and J. M. Alleyne. "Ethnicity, Food Preferences and Habits of Consumption as Factors in Social Interaction." *Canadian Ethnic Studies* 11 (1979): 83–87.

Auman, Kenneth, and Basil Herring. *The Prenuptial Agreement: Halakhic, Legal, and Pastoral Considerations*. New York: Jason Aronson and the Orthodox Caucus, 1995.

Balmer, Randall. *Mine Eyes Have Seen the Glory: A Journey into the Evangelical Subculture*. Videorecording. Chicago: WTTW/Chicago and Isis Production, 1992.

———. *Mine Eyes Have Seen the Glory: A Journey into the Evangelical Subculture in America*. New York: Oxford University Press, 1989.

Bellah, Robert N., Richard Masden, William M. Sullivan, Ann Swindler, and Steven M. Tipton. *Habits of the Heart: Individualism and Commitment in American Life*. New York: Harper & Row, 1985.

Belsky, Meir. "The American 'Shtetl' Emerges." *Jewish Observer*, November 1963, 11, 20.

Ben-Joseph, Michael. "Renaissance: The Revival of Israel's Wine Industry." *Jerusalem Report*, 2 August 1999, 27–36.

Berger, Bennett. *Working-Class Suburb: A Study of Auto Workers in Suburbia*. Berkeley: University of California Press, 1960.

Berger, Peter L. *The Sacred Canopy: Elements of a Sociological Theory of Religion*. Garden City, N.Y.: Doubleday, 1967.

Berkowitz, Joshua. "The Challenge to Modern Orthodoxy." *Tradition* 33 (Winter 1984): 101–6.

Bernstein, Saul. *The Orthodox Union Story: A Centenary Portrayal*. Northvale, N.J.: Jason Aronson, 1997.

Bianco, Anthony. *The Reichmanns: Family, Faith, Fortune, and the Empire of Olympia and York*. New York: Times Business, 1997.

Biberfeld, Henry. "Report from the North." *Jewish Life* 31 (September–October 1963): 18–24.

Binford, Henry. *The First Suburbs: Residential Communities on the Boston Periphery, 1815–1860.* Chicago: University of Chicago Press, 1985.

Borsuk, Alan J. "Old Fashioned Jew, Old Fashioned Reporter." *Nieman Reports* 51 (Fall 1997): 15–17.

Bourne, L. S., R. D. MacKinnon, and J. W. Simmons, eds. *The Form of Cities in Central Canada: Selected Papers.* Toronto: University of Toronto Department of Geography, 1973.

Bradley, Martin B., Norman M. Green, Dale E. Jones, Mac Lynn, and Lou Macneil. *Churches and Church Membership in the United States, 1990: An Enumeration by Region, State, and County Based on Data Reported by 133 Church Groupings.* Atlanta: Glenmary Research Center, 1992.

Brafman, Morris. "The Yeshiva Problem: A New Approach." *Jewish Life* 26 (October 1958): 28–33.

Brasch, R. "Why Jews Cover the Head." *Commentary* 17 (January 1954): 37–40.

Breton, Raymond, Wsevold W. Isajiw, Warren E. Kalbach, and Jeffrey G. Reitz. *Ethnic Identity and Equality: Varieties of Experience in a Canadian City.* Toronto: University of Toronto Press, 1990.

Bruegmann, Robert. "The Twenty-Three Percent Solution." *American Quarterly* 46 (March 1994): 31–34.

Brym, Robert J., William Shaffir, and Morton Weinfeld. *The Jews of Canada.* Toronto: Oxford University Press, 1993.

Bulman, Nathan. "Revitalizing the Synagogue for the Next Generation." *Jewish Life* 30 (January–February 1963): 14–17.

Campbell, Colin. *The Romantic Ethic and the Spirit of Modern Consumerism.* London: Basil Blackwell, 1987.

Carmy, Shalom. "Rejoinder: Synthesis and the Unification of Human Existence." *Tradition* 21 (Fall 1985): 37–51.

Carver, Humphrey. *Houses for Canadians: A Study of Housing Problems in the Toronto Area.* Toronto: University of Toronto Press, 1948.

Chyet, Stanley F. "American Jews: Notes on the Idea of a Community." *American Jewish History* 81 (Spring–Summer 1995): 331–39.

Cohen, Jack Simcha. "Changing Neighborhoods: The Drive to the Sea." *Jewish Life* 1 (Winter 1976): 29–33.

———. "The Orthodox Synagogue: Challenges of the Inner City and Suburbia." *Jewish Life* 2 (Fall–Winter 1977–78): 67–72.

Cohen, Lizabeth. *Making a New Deal: Industrial Workers in Chicago, 1919–1939.* Cambridge: Cambridge University Press, 1990.

Cohen, Steven M. *American Modernity and Jewish Identity.* New York: Tavistock, 1983.

———. "The Impact of Jewish Education on Religious Identification and Practice." *Jewish Social Studies* 36 (July–October 1974): 316–26.

Coleman, J. S. *Foundations of Social Theory*. Cambridge, Mass.: Belknap Press of Harvard University Press, 1990.

Colton, Timothy L. *Big Daddy: Frederick G. Gardiner and the Building of Metropolitan Toronto*. Toronto: University of Toronto Press, 1980.

Conzen, Kathleen Neils. "Forum: The Place of Religion in Urban and Community Studies." *Religion and American Culture* 6 (Summer 1996): 108–14.

Craven, Paul, and Barry Wellman. "The Network City." *Sociological Inquiry* 43 (1973): 57–88.

Dahlen, Anna. "Our Lives Revolve around the Holidays: Holidays in the Transmission of Jewish Ethnicity." In *Encounters with American Cultures*, edited by Philip L. Kilbride, Jane C. Goodale, and Elizabeth R. Ameisen, 225–39. Tuscaloosa: University of Alabama Press, 1990.

Danzger, M. Herbert. "The Meaning of Keeping Kosher: Views of the Newly Orthodox." *Judaism* 39 (Fall 1990): 461–69.

Demerath, Nicholas J. III, and Rhys Williams. *A Bridging of Faiths: Religion and Politics in a New England City*. Princeton: Princeton University Press, 1992.

Dewar, Elaine. "The Mysterious Reichmanns: The Untold Story." *Toronto Life*, November 1987, 61–186.

Diamond, Etan. "Middle Class in Suburbs." *Encyclopedia of Urban America*, edited by Neil Larry Shumsky, 463–65. New York: ABC-Clio, 1998.

———. "Places of Worship: The Historical Geography of Religion in a Midwestern City, 1930–1960." *Pennsylvania Geographer* 35 (Fall 1997): 45–69.

———. "Religious Mobility in the 20th Century." *Research Notes from the Project on Religion and Urban Culture* 1 (November 1999).

———. "Uptown, Downtown, Northside, Southside: Religious Regions in Indianapolis." Paper presented at the annual meeting of the American Society of Church History, Washington, D.C., January 1999.

———. "Urban Ministry and Changing Perceptions of the Metropolis." Paper presented at the annual meeting of the Organization of American Historians, Indianapolis, April 1998.

Drachler, Norman, ed. *A Bibliography of Jewish Education in the United States*. Detroit: Wayne State University Press, 1996.

Duckat, Walter. "Careers for the Sabbath Observant." *Jewish Life* 20 (September–October 1952): 16–21.

———. "New Careers for Jewish Women." *Jewish Life* 21 (November–December 1953): 20–25.

Ebner, Michael. *Creating Chicago's North Shore: A Suburban History*. Chicago: University of Chicago Press, 1988.

Edwards, Harry. *Fairfax*. New York: Copley Press West, 1976.

Eliade, Mircea. *The Sacred and the Profane: The Nature of Religion*. New York: Harcourt, Brace and World, 1959.

Ellenson, David. "German Jewish Orthodoxy: Tradition in the Context of Culture." In *The Uses of Tradition: Jewish Continuity in the Modern Era*, ed.

Jack Wertheimer, 5–22. New York: Jewish Theological Seminary of America, 1992.

———. *Rabbi Esriel Hildesheimer and the Creation of a Modern Jewish Orthodoxy*. Tuscaloosa: University of Alabama Press, 1990.

El-Or, Tamar. *Educated and Ignorant: Ultraorthodox Jewish Women and Their World*. Boulder, Col.: Lynne Reinner, 1994.

Endelman, Judith E. *The Jewish Community of Indianapolis, 1849 to the Present*. Bloomington: Indiana University Press, 1984.

Engelberg, Louis. "Kashruth Is a Community Program." *Jewish Life* 16 (June 1949): 34–37.

Farber, Seth. "Community, Schooling, and Leadership: Rabbi Joseph Soloveitchik's Maimonides School and the Development of Boston's Orthodox Jewish Community." Ph.D. diss., Hebrew University of Jerusalem, in progress.

Feldman, Emanuel. "The Case for 'Out-of-Town.'" *Jewish Observer*, September 1963, 13–14, 20.

Finke, Roger, and Rodney Stark. *The Churching of America, 1776–1990: Winners and Losers in Our Religious Economy*. New Brunswick, N.J.: Rutgers University Press, 1992.

Fischer, Claude S. *To Dwell among Friends: Personal Networks in Town and City*. Chicago: University of Chicago Press, 1982.

Fishman, Robert. *Bourgeois Utopias: The Rise and Fall of American Suburbia*. New York: Basic Books, 1987.

———. "Megalopolis Unbound: America's New City." *Wilson Quarterly* 16 (Winter 1990): 24–45.

———. "Urbanity and Suburbanity: Rethinking the 'Burbs." *American Quarterly* 46 (March 1994): 35–39.

Frager, Ruth A. *Sweatshop Strife: Class, Ethnicity, and Gender in the Jewish Labour Movement, 1900–1939*. Toronto: University of Toronto Press, 1992.

Freedman, Morris. "Orthodox Sweets for Heterodox New York: The Story of Barton's." *Commentary* 13 (May 1952): 472–80.

Gad, G., R. Peddie, and J. Punter. "Ethnic Difference in the Residential Search Process." In *The Form of Cities in Central Canada: Selected Papers*, edited by L. S. Bourne, R. D. MacKinnon, and J. W. Simmons, 168–80. Toronto: University of Toronto Department of Geography, 1973.

Gamm, Gerald. "In Search of Suburbs: Boston's Jewish Districts, 1843–1994." In *The Jews of Boston: Essays on the Occasion of the Centenary (1895–1995) of the Combined Jewish Philanthropies of Greater Boston*, edited by Jonathan D. Sarna and Ellen Smith, 127–64. Boston: Combined Jewish Philanthropies of Greater Boston, 1995.

———. *Urban Exodus: Why the Jews Left Boston and the Catholics Stayed*. Cambridge, Mass.: Harvard University Press, 1999.

Gans, Herbert J. "American Jewry: Present and Future." *Commentary* 21 (May 1956): 422–30.

———. "The Future of American Jewry: Part II." *Commentary* 21 (June 1956): 555–63.

———. *The Levittowners: Ways of Life and Politics in a New Suburban Community.* New York: Pantheon Books, 1967.

Garreau, Joel. *Edge City: Life on the New Frontier.* New York: Doubleday, 1991.

Gastwirt, Harold P. *Fraud, Corruption, and Holiness: The Controversy over the Supervision of Jewish Dietary Practices in New York, 1881–1940.* Port Washington, N.Y.: National University Publications, 1974.

Gaustad, Edwin S., ed. *A Documentary History of Religion in America to the Civil War.* Grand Rapids, Mich.: William B. Eerdmans, 1982.

Gersh, Harry. "The New Suburbanites of the 50's." *Commentary* 17 (March 1954): 209–21.

Givon, S. "By the Waters of Malibu." *Jewish Life* 18 (September–October 1950): 70–76.

Glazer, Nathan. *American Judaism.* Chicago: University of Chicago Press, 1957.

———. "The Jewish Revival in America: I." *Commentary* 20 (December 1955): 493–99.

———. "The Jewish Revival in America: II." *Commentary* 21 (January 1956): 17–24.

Gleicher, David. "The Origins and Early Years of Chicago's Hebrew Theological College." *Tradition* 27 (1993): 56–68.

Goldberg, Howard G. "Slaves No More to Sweet Wine." *Jerusalem Report*, 20 April 1995, 56–57.

Goldberg, Michael A., and John Mercer. *The Myth of the North American City: Continentalism Challenged.* Vancouver: University of British Columbia Press, 1986.

Goldenberg, Sheldon, and Valerie A. Haines. "Social Networks and Institutional Completeness: From Territory to Ties." *Canadian Journal of Sociology* 17 (1992): 301–13.

Goldstein, Herbert. "The Popular Image of the Scientist: Real of Imaginary?" *Jewish Life* 30 (January–February 1963): 9–11.

Goldstein, Simeon H. F. "Exploitation in the Ghetto: Reality or Myth." *Jewish Life* 38 (November–December 1970): 8–16.

Gooen, Martin. "Rustling Out West." *Young Israel Viewpoint*, March–April 1958, 52–54.

Gordon, Albert I. *Jews in Suburbia.* Boston: Beacon Press, 1959.

Gordon, Irwin. "Decision for Action." *Jewish Life* 19 (January–February 1952): 12–13.

Gordon, Nissan. "Through a Journalist's Eyes." *Jewish Life* 22 (November–December 1954): 31–34.

Goren, Arthur A. *New York Jews and the Quest for Community: The Kehillah Experiment, 1908–1922.* New York: Columbia University Press, 1970.

Grant, John Webster. *A Profusion of Spires: Religion in Nineteenth-Century Ontario.* Toronto: University of Toronto Press, 1988.

Greeley, Andrew. "Coleman Revisited: Religious Structures as a Source of Social Capital." *American Behavioral Scientist* 40 (March–April 1997): 587–94.

Greeley, Andrew, and Peter H. Rossi. *The Education of Catholic Americans.* Chicago: Aldine, 1966.

Greenberg, Blu. *On Women and Judaism: A View from Tradition.* Philadelphia: Jewish Publication Society of America, 1981.

Grossman, Rafael G. "To the Wonderful Jews of New York: We're Not All 'Out of Town.'" <http://www.ou.org/torah/grossman/1999/090499.htm>. 4 September 1999.

Gurock, Jeffrey S. *The Men and Women of Yeshiva: Higher Education, Orthodoxy, and American Judaism.* New York: Columbia University Press, 1988.

———. "Resisters and Accommodators: Varieties of Orthodox Rabbis in America, 1886–1983." *American Jewish Archives* 35 (November 1983): 100–187.

Guthrie, Charles, Dan Brier, and Mary Moore. *The Indianapolis Hispanic Community.* Indianapolis: University of Indianapolis Press, 1995.

———. "Religious Behavior in the Indianapolis Hispanic Community." Indianapolis: Polis Center, 1996.

Harris, Chauncy D., and Edward L. Ullman. "The Nature of Cities." *Annals, American Academy of Political and Social Science* 242 (1945): 7–17.

Hart, Patricia W. *Pioneering in North York: A History of the Borough.* Toronto: General Publishing Company, 1968.

Hayman, Julius. *Toronto Jewry: An Historical Sketch.* Toronto: Canadian Jewish Congress, 1957.

Hechinger, Grace, and Fred M. Hechinger. *Teen-Age Tyranny.* New York: William Morrow, 1963.

Heilman, Samuel C. *Defenders of the Faith: Inside Ultra-Orthodox Jewry.* New York: Schocken Books, 1992.

———. *The People of the Book: Drama, Fellowship, and Religion.* Chicago: University of Chicago Press, 1983.

———. *Portrait of American Jews: The Last Half of the 20th Century.* Seattle: University of Washington Press, 1995.

———. *Synagogue Life: A Study in Symbolic Interaction.* Chicago: University of Chicago Press, 1976.

Heilman, Samuel C., and Steven M. Cohen. *Cosmopolitans and Parochials: Modern Orthodox Jews in America.* Chicago: University of Chicago Press, 1989.

Heinze, Andrew R. *Adapting to Abundance: Jewish Immigrants, Mass Consumption, and the Search for American Identity.* New York: Columbia University Press, 1990.

Helmreich, William C. *The World of the Yeshiva: An Intimate Portrait of Orthodox Jewry.* New York: Free Press, 1982.

Herberg, Will. *Protestant, Catholic, Jew: An Essay in American Religious Sociology.* Garden City, N.Y.: Anchor Books, 1955.

Hertzberg, Arthur. "Religion." *American Jewish Year Book* 59 (1958): 113–23.

Hiebert, Daniel. "Jewish Immigrants and the Garment Industry of Toronto, 1901–1931: A Study of Ethnic and Class Relations." *Annals of the Association of American Geographers* 83 (June 1993): 243–71.

Hill, Frederick I. *Canadian Urban Trends: Metropolitan Perspective, Volume 2.* Toronto: Copp Clark, 1976.

Himmelfarb, Harold S., and Sergio DellaPergola. *Jewish Education Worldwide: Cross-Cultural Perspectives.* Lanham, Md.: University Press of America, 1989.

Hirsch, Barnet. "What Shall I Tell My Teacher?" *Jewish Life* 15 (February 1948): 42–47.

Hochbaum, Jerry. "Middle-of-the-Road Orthodoxy: An Alternative to Left and Right Radicalism." *Jewish Life* 35 (July–August 1968): 27–29.

Hoenig, D. Bernard. "Great Victory: Yeshivoth Produce Scholar-Athletes." *Jewish Life* 20 (May–June 1953): 29–32.

Horowitz, Irma. "Education Begins at Home." *Jewish Life* 19 (May–June 1952): 54–59.

Hudnut-Beumler, James. *Looking for God in the Suburbs: The Religion of the American Dream and Its Critics, 1945–1965.* New Brunswick, N.J.: Rutgers University Press, 1994.

Hunter, James Davison, and John Steadman Rice. "Unlikely Alliances: Changing Contours of American Religious Faith." In *America at Century's End*, edited by Alan Wolfe, 318–31. Berkeley: University of California Press, 1991.

Inbar, Efraim. "The Hebrew Day Schools—The Orthodox Communal Challenge." *Journal of Ethnic Studies* 7 (Spring 1979): 13–29.

Isaacs, Elizabeth K. "A National Gathering of Sisterhoods." *Jewish Life* 15 (June 1948): 35–38.

Isaacs, Philip. "The Jewish Home versus Campus Temptations." *Jewish Life* 16 (October 1948): 42–47.

Jackson, Kenneth T. *Crabgrass Frontier: The Suburbanization of the United States.* New York: Oxford University Press, 1985.

Jackson, R. H., and R. Henrie. "Perception of Sacred Space." *Journal of Cultural Geography* 3 (1983): 94–107.

Janowitz, Morris. *The Community Press in an Urban Setting: The Social Elements of Urbanism.* Chicago: University of Chicago Press, 1967.

Jick, Leon A. *The Americanization of the Synagogue, 1820–1870.* Hanover, N.H.: University Press of New England [for] Brandeis University Press, 1976.

Johnson, Benton. "On Dropping the Subject: Presbyterians and Sabbath Observance in the Twentieth Century." In *The Presbyterian Predicament: Six Perspectives*, edited by Milton J. Coalter, John M. Mulder, and Louis B. Weeks, 90–108. Louisville: Westminster/John Knox Press, 1990.

Johnson, Douglas W., Paul R. Picard, and Bernard Quinn. *Churches and Church Membership in the United States: An Enumeration by Region, State, and County.* Atlanta: Glenmary Research Center, 1974.

Joselit, Jenna Weissman. *New York's Jewish Jews: The Orthodox Community in the Interwar Years*. Bloomington: Indiana University Press, 1990.

———. *The Wonders of America: Reinventing Jewish Culture, 1880–1950*. New York: Hill and Wang, 1994.

Kallen, Evelyn. *Spanning the Generations: A Study in Jewish Identity*. Toronto: Longman Canada, 1977.

Kaminetsky, Joseph. "Orthodox Unity and the Day Schools." *Jewish Life* 18 (September–October 1950): 47–52.

———. "Parents Too Grow through Day Schools." *Jewish Life* 19 (March–April 1952): 25–28.

———. "Ways to Religious Growth in the Home." *Jewish Parents Magazine*, Fall 1949, 4–5, 18.

———. "The Yeshiva Ketanah." *Jewish Life* 15 (April 1948): 29–35.

———., ed. *Hebrew Day School Education: An Overview*. New York: Torah Umesorah, the National Society for Hebrew Day Schools, 1970.

Kanarfogel, Ephraim. *Jewish Education and Society in the High Middle Ages*. Detroit: Wayne State University Press, 1992.

Kane, Paula. *Separatism and Subcultures: Boston Catholicism, 1900–1920*. Chapel Hill: University of North Carolina Press, 1994.

Kanfer, Stephan. *A Summer World: The Attempt to Build a Jewish Eden in the Catskills, from the Days of the Ghetto to the Rise and Decline of the Borscht Belt*. New York: Farrar, Straus, and Giroux, 1989.

Kaplan, Harold. *Urban Political Systems: A Functional Analysis of Metro Toronto*. New York: Columbia University Press, 1967.

Katz, Donald. *Home Fires: An Intimate Portrait of One Middle-Class Family in Postwar America*. New York: Harper Collins, 1992.

Katz, Yossi, and John C. Lehr. "Jewish Pioneer Agricultural Settlements in Western Canada." *Journal of Cultural Geography* 14 (Fall–Winter 1993): 49–67.

Kaufman, David. *A Shul with a Pool: The "Synagogue-Center" in American Jewish History*. Hanover, N.H.: University Press of New England, 1999.

Kaufman, Michael. "Far Rockaway—Torah-Suburb by-the-Sea." *Jewish Life* 27 (August 1960): 20–33.

Kelley, Dean M. *Why Conservative Churches Are Growing: A Study in the Sociology of Religion*. New York: Harper & Row, 1972.

Kelly, Barbara M., ed. *Suburbia Re-Examined*. New York: Greenwood Press, 1989.

Kelman, Wolfe. "Religion." *American Jewish Year Book* 62 (1961): 129–44.

Klaff, Vivian. "The Urban Ecology of Jewish Populations: A Comparative Analysis." *Contemporary Jewry* 8 (1987): 59–69.

Kling, Rob, Spencer Olin, and Mark Poster, eds. *Postsuburban California: The Transformation of Orange County since World War II*. Berkeley: University of California Press, 1991.

Kloetzli, Walter. *The Church and the Urban Challenge*. Philadelphia: Muhlenberg Press, 1961.

Kong, Lily. "Geography and Religion: Trends and Prospects." *Progress in Human Geography* 14 (1990): 355–71.

Korn, Lila. "A Modern Orthodox Community: Teaneck Sets the Standard." *Emunah Magazine*, Spring–Summer 1999, 26–29.

Kramer, Doniel Zvi. *The Day Schools and Torah Umesorah: The Seeding of Traditional Judaism in America.* New York: Yeshiva University Press, 1984.

Kramer, Judith R., and Seymour Leventman. *Children of the Gilded Ghetto: Conflict Resolutions of Three Generations of American Jews.* New Haven: Yale University Press, 1961.

Krumbein, Aaron, and Lee M. Spetner. "Genesis of a Washington Synagogue." *Jewish Life* 27 (October 1959): 54–57.

Labaree, David F. *The Making of an American High School: The Credentials Market and the Central High School of Philadelphia, 1838–1939.* New Haven: Yale University Press, 1988.

Lamm, Maurice. *The Jewish Way in Love and Marriage.* New York: Jonathan David Publishers, 1991.

———. *Torah Umadda: The Encounter of Religious Learning and Wordly Knowledge in the Jewish Tradition.* Northvale, N.J.: Jason Aronson, 1990.

———. "The Voice of Torah in the Battle of Ideas." *Jewish Life* 34 (March–April 1967): 23–31.

Lee, Robert, ed. *The Church and the Exploding Metropolis.* Richmond: John Knox Press, 1965.

Leiman, Shnayer Z. "The Campus Problem and Jewish Education." *Jewish Life* 35 (March–April 1968): 22–28.

Leo, Jerome. "A Sabbath Observed." *America* 18 (2 January 1999): 13.

Lerner, Isaac. "The College Dilemma." *Jewish Life* 29 (February 1962): 54–56.

Leven, Charles L. "Distance, Space, and the Organisation of Urban Life." *Urban Studies* 28 (1991): 319–25.

Levine, Hillel, and Lawrence Harmon. *The Death of an American Jewish Community: A Tragedy of Good Intentions.* New York: Free Press, 1992.

Lewis, James W. "Going Downtown: Historical Resources for Urban Ministry." *Word and World* 14 (Fall 1994): 402–8.

———. *The Protestant Experience in Gary, Indiana, 1905–1975: At Home in the City.* Knoxville: University of Tennessee Press, 1992.

Liebman, Charles S. "Orthodox Judaism Today." *Midstream* 25 (August/ September 1979): 19–26.

———. "Orthodoxy in American Jewish Life." *American Jewish Year Book* 66 (1965): 21–97.

———. "Studying Orthodox Judaism in the United States: A Review Essay." *American Jewish History* 80 (1990): 415–25.

Linteau, Paul-Andre. "Canadian Suburbanization in a North American Context: Does the Border Make a Difference?" *Journal of Urban History* 13 (May 1987): 252–74.

Lippy, Charles H. *Being Religious, American Style: A History of Popular Religiosity in the United States*. Westport, Conn.: Greenwood Press, 1994.

Lipschutz, Yacov. *Kashruth: A Comprehensive Background and Reference Guide to the Principles of Kashruth*. New York: Mesorah, 1988.

Lipset, Seymour Martin. *Continental Divide: The Values and Institutions of the United States and Canada*. New York: Routledge, 1990.

Litvin, Baruch. *The Sanctity of the Synagogue*. New York: Spero Foundation, 1962.

Loewy, Harry. "The Vulguraization of the American Jewish Community." *Jewish Life* 32 (May–June 1965): 38–41.

Lorimer, James. *The Developers*. Toronto: James Lorimer and Company, 1978.

Lowenstein, Steven M. *Frankfurt on the Hudson: The German-Jewish Community of Washington Heights, 1933–1983, Its Structure and Culture*. Detroit: Wayne State University Press, 1988.

Luchetti, Cathy. *Under God's Spell: Frontier Evangelists, 1772–1915*. New York: Harcourt Brace Jovanovich, 1989.

Luzbetak, Louis J., ed. *The Church in the Changing City*. Techny, Ill.: Divine Word Publications, 1966.

Lynch, Kevin. *The Image of the City*. Cambridge, Mass.: MIT Press, 1960.

Lynd, Robert S., and Helen Merrell Lynd. *Middletown: A Study in Modern American Culture*. New York: Harcourt, Brace, 1929.

Mandelbaum, Mordecai, ed. *Family Chronicles: Sandy Hofstedter and Aranka Hofstedter*. Toronto: N.p., 1992.

Marsh, Margaret. "(Ms)Reading the Suburbs." *American Quarterly* 46 (March 1994): 40–48.

———. *Suburban Lives*. New Brunswick, N.J.: Rutgers University Press, 1990.

Marshall, David B. *Secularizing the Faith: Canadian Protestant Clergy and the Crisis of Belief, 1850–1940*. Toronto: University of Toronto Press, 1992.

Mayer, Egon. *From Suburb to Shtetl: The Jews of Boro Park*. Philadelphia: Temple University Press, 1979.

Max, Morris. "Mixed Pews." *Jewish Life* 17 (October 1949): 16–24.

McDannell, Colleen. *Material Christianity*. New Haven: Yale University Press, 1995.

McGreevy, John. *Parish Boundaries: The Catholic Encounter with Race in the Twentieth Century*. Chicago: University of Chicago Press, 1996.

Meyer, Michael. *Response to Modernity: A History of the Reform Movement in Judaism*. New York: Oxford University Press, 1988.

Miller, Arnold J. "They Did It in Worcester." *Jewish Life* 18 (September–October 1950): 27–33.

Miller, Donald E. *Reinventing American Protestantism: Christianity in the New Millennium*. Berkeley: University of California Press, 1997.

Miller, Zane L. *Suburb: Neighborhood and Community in Forest Park, Ohio, 1935–1976*. Knoxville: University of Tennessee Press, 1981.

Moore, Deborah Dash. *At Home in America: Second Generation New York Jews*. New York: Columbia University Press, 1981.

————. *To the Golden Cities: Pursuing the American Jewish Dream in Miami and L.A.* New York: Free Press, 1994.

"New Casks for Old Wine: Teaching Traditional Values in Novel Ways (A Review Article)." *Jewish Observer*, June 1977, 24–25.

Nissenbaum, Stephen. *The Battle for Christmas.* New York: Knopf, 1996.

O'Dea, Thomas F., and Janet O'Dea Aviad. *The Sociology of Religion.* Englewood Cliffs, N.J.: Prentice-Hall, 1983.

O'Malley, Michael. *Keeping Watch: A History of American Time.* New York: Viking, 1990.

Oppenheim, Esriel Magnus. "Orthodoxy on the Campus." *Jewish Life* 26 (December 1958): 46–51.

Palen, J. John. *The Suburbs.* New York: McGraw-Hill, 1995.

Park, Chris C. *Sacred Worlds: An Introduction to Geography and Religion.* London: Routledge, 1994.

Pelcovitz, Ralph. "The Challenge of College." *Jewish Life* 30 (July–August 1963): 18–23.

Perlow, Yaakov. "The Clash between Modernity and Eternity." *Jewish Observer* 26 (January 1994): 9–15.

Plotinsky, Anita Heppner. "The Hebrew Academy of Indianapolis, 1971–1986." *Indiana Jewish History* 21 (August 1986): 23–35.

Powell, Bruce J. "Jews at a Glance (Kipahology)." *Sh'ma Magazine*, n.d., 69.

"Progress in the Mid-West." *Young Israel Viewpoint*, September–October 1958, 29–31.

Putnam, Robert. "Bowling Alone: America's Declining Social Capital." *Journal of Democracy* 6 (January 1995): 65–78.

Rakeffet-Rothkoff, Aaron. *The Silver Era in American Jewish Orthodoxy: Rabbi Eliezer Silver and His Generation.* New York: Yeshiva University Press, 1981.

Raphael, Marc Lee. *Profiles in American Judaism: The Reform, Conservative, Orthodox, and Reconstructionist Traditions in Historical Perspective.* San Francisco: Harper & Row, 1984.

Reitman, H. J. A. "North York: The Development of a Suburb." Master's thesis, University of Toronto, 1962.

Ribalow, Harold U. "My Child Goes to Jewish Parochial School: A Parent's Report Card." *Commentary* 17 (January 1954): 64–67.

Richmond, Anthony. *Ethnic Residential Segregation in Metropolitan Toronto.* Downsview, Ont.: York University Institute for Behavioural Research, Ethnic Research Programme, 1972.

Riesman, David. *The Lonely Crowd: A Study of the Changing American Character.* New Haven: Yale University Press, 1950.

Roof, Wade Clark. *Spiritual Marketplace: Baby Boomers and the Remaking of American Religion.* Princeton: Princeton University Press, 1999.

Roof, Wade Clark, and William McKinney. *A Generation of Seekers: The Spiritual Journey of the Baby Boom Generation.* San Francisco: Harper & Row, 1993.

Rose, Albert. *Governing Metropolitan Toronto: A Social and Political Analysis, 1953–1971.* Berkeley: University of California Press, 1972.

Rosenberg, Louis. *Canada's Jews: A Social and Economic Study of Jews in Canada in the 1930s.* 1939. Reprint. Montreal: McGill-Queen's University Press, 1993.

Rosenblum, Yonason. "'*Torah Umadda*': A Critique of Rabbi Dr. Norman Lamm's Book and Its Approach to Torah Study and the Pursuit of Secular Knowledge." *Jewish Observer* 25 (March 1992): 27–40.

Rosenthal, Gilbert S., ed. *The Jewish Family in a Changing World.* New York: Thomas Yoseloff, 1970.

Rubinstein, Samuel W. "The Jew in the Present-Day South." *Jewish Life* 15 (April 1948): 60–64.

Rudavsky, Oren, and Menachem Daum (producers). *A Life Apart: Hasidism in America.* New York: PBS Films, 1997.

Ryan, Mary P. *Cradle of the Middle Class: The Family in Oneida County, New York, 1790–1865.* Cambridge: Cambridge University Press, 1981.

Rybczynski, Witold. *Waiting for the Weekend.* New York: Viking, 1991.

Sack, Daniel. "Food and Eating in American Religious Cultures." In *Perspectives on American Religion and Culture,* edited by Peter W. Williams, 203–15. Oxford: Blackwell, 1999.

Sacks, Maurie. "Computing Community at Purim." *Journal of American Folklore* 102 (1989): 275–91.

Sanua, Marianne. "Stages in the Development of Jewish Life at Princeton University." *American Jewish History* 76 (1987): 391–415.

Sarna, Jonathan. "The Debate over Mixed Seating in the American Synagogue." In *The American Synagogue: A Sanctuary Transformed,* edited by Jack Wertheimer, 363–94. Cambridge: Cambridge University Press, 1987.

———. "The Evolution of the American Synagogue." In *The Americanization of the Jews,* edited by Robert Seltzer and Norman J. Cohen, 215–29. New York: New York University Press, 1995.

Schack, William. "Zoning Boards, Synagogues, and Bias: Religious Tolerance in the Suburbs." *Commentary* 23 (May 1957): 430–38.

Schick, Marvin. "The New Style of American Orthodoxy." *Jewish Life* 34 (January–February 1967): 29–36.

Schiff, Alvin I. *The Jewish Day School in America.* New York: Jewish Education Committee Press, 1966.

Schiller, Mayer. "*Torah Umadda* and *The Jewish Observer* Critique: Towards a Clarification of the Issues." *Torah U-Madda Journal* 6 (1995–96): 58–90.

Schloff, Linda Mack. "Overcoming Geography: Jewish Religious Life in Four Market Towns." *Minnesota History* 51 (Spring 1988): 2–14.

Schmidt, Leigh Eric. *Consumer Rites: The Buying and Selling of American Holidays.* Princeton: Princeton University Press, 1995.

Schoenfeld, Stuart. "Jewish Education and Jewish Continuity in the United States and Canada: A Political Culture Perspective." Paper presented at the annual meeting of the American Sociological Association, Toronto, August 1998.

———. "Re-reading an American Classic: Crestwood Heights as a Study of the Invisible Religion." *Canadian Review of Sociology and Anthropology* 25 (1988): 456–63.

Schremp, Gerry. *Kitchen Culture: Fifty Years of Food Fads*. New York: Pharos Books, 1991.

Scott, Jamie, and Paul Simpson-Housley, eds. *Sacred Places and Profane Spaces: Essays in the Geographics of Judaism, Christianity, and Islam*. New York: Greenwood Press, 1991.

Seeley, John R., R. Alexander Sim, and E. W. Loosley. *Crestwood Heights: A Study of the Culture of Suburban Life*. New York: Basic Books, 1956.

Seidman, Aaron B. "On Choosing a College Away from Home." *Jewish Life* 35 (November–December 1967): 22–28.

Seltzer, Robert M., and Norman J. Cohen, eds. *The Americanization of the Jews*. New York: New York University Press, 1995.

Shapiro, Edward S. *A Time for Healing: American Jewry since World War II*. Baltimore: Johns Hopkins University Press, 1992.

Sharpe, William, and Leonard Wallock. "Bold New City or Built-Up 'Burb? Redefining Contemporary Suburbia." *American Quarterly* 46 (March 1994): 1–30.

———. "Response: Contextualizing Suburbia." *American Quarterly* 46 (March 1994): 55–61.

Sheshkin, Ira M. "Jewish Metropolitan Homelands." *Journal of Cultural Geography* 13 (Spring–Summer 1993): 119–32.

Shipps, Jan. *Mormonism: The Story of a New Religious Tradition*. Urbana: University of Illinois Press, 1985.

Shoulson, Charles. "Let Us Look to Our Own." *Jewish Life* 15 (June 1948): 48–50.

———. "Synagogues and Centers." *Jewish Life* 15 (October 1947): 61–63.

Sigal, John, David August, and Joseph Beltempo. "Impact of Jewish Education on Jewish Identification in a Group of Adolescents." *Jewish Social Studies* 43 (Summer–Fall 1981): 229–36.

Sigelschiffer, Saul. "Torahtown Is on Its Way." *Jewish Life* 26 (December 1958): 29–35.

Silk, Mark. *Spiritual Politics: Religion and America since World War II*. New York: Touchstone, 1988.

Singer, David. "Is Club Med Kosher?" *Tradition* 21 (Fall 1985): 27–36.

Sklare, Marshall. *Conservative Judaism: An American Religious Movement*. Glencoe, Ill.: Free Press, 1955.

Soloveitchik, Haym. "Migration, Acculturation, and the New Role of Texts in the Ḥaredi World." In *Accounting for Fundamentalisms: The Dynamic Character of Movements*, ed. Martin E. Marty and R. Scott Appleby, 197–235. Chicago: University of Chicago Press, 1994.

———. "Rupture and Reconstruction: The Transformation of Contemporary Orthodoxy." *Tradition* 28 (1994): 64–130.

Somerville, Patricia, and Catherine Macfarlane. *A History of Vaughan Township Churches*. Maple, Ont.: Vaughan Township Historical Society, 1984.

Speisman, Stephen A. *The Jews of Toronto: A History to 1937*. Toronto: McClelland and Stewart, 1979.

Stansell, Christine. *Sex and Class in New York, 1789–1860*. Urbana: University of Illinois Press, 1987.

Stern, Marc A. "Kosher Food and the Law." *Judaism* 39 (Fall 1990): 389–401.

Stilgoe, John. *Borderland: Origins of the American Suburb, 1820–1939*. New Haven: Yale University Press, 1988.

Stolper, Pinchas. "What Does Jewish Youth Really Want?" *Jewish Life* 30 (January–February 1963): 49–54.

Strong-Boag, Veronica. "Home Dreams: Women and the Suburban Experiment in Canada, 1945–60." *Canadian Historical Review* 72 (December 1991): 471–504.

Sussman, Lance J. "The Suburbanization of American Judaism as Reflected in Synagogue Building and Architecture, 1945–1975." *American Jewish History* 75 (September 1985): 31–47.

Tabak, Israel. "The National Torah Tour." *Jewish Life* 16 (April 1949): 5–9.

Tannenbaum, Marc H. "Religion," *American Jewish Year Book* 60 (1959): 53–67.

Teixiera, Carlos. "Ethnicity, Housing Search, and the Role of the Real Estate Agent: A Study of Portuguese and Non-Portuguese Real Estate Agents in Toronto." *Professional Geographer* 47 (May 1995): 176–83.

Teixiera, Carlos, and Robert Murdie. "The Role of Ethnic Real Estate Agents in the Residential Relocation Process: A Case Study of Portuguese Homebuyers in Suburban Toronto." *Urban Geography* 18 (1997): 497–520.

Thomas, June Manning. "The Forces of Urban Heterogeneity Can Triumph." *American Quarterly* 46 (March 1994): 49–54.

Trillin, Calvin. "Drawing the Line." *New Yorker* 70 (12 December 1994): 50–62.

Tuchman, Gaye, and Harry Gene Levine. "New York Jews and Chinese Food: The Social Construction of an Ethnic Pattern." *Journal of Contemporary Ethnography* 22 (October 1993): 382–407.

Tuchman, Louis M. "Chanukah—or Jewish Christmas?" *Jewish Life* 29 (October 1961): 47–51.

Tulchinsky, Gerald. *Taking Root: The Origins of the Canadian Jewish Community*. Hanover, N.H.: University Press of New England [for] Brandeis University Press, 1993.

Ueda, Reed. *Avenues to Adulthood: The Origins of the High School and Social Mobility in an American Suburb*. Cambridge: Cambridge University Press, 1987.

Vance, James E. Jr. *The Continuing City: Urban Morphology in Western Civilization*. Baltimore: Johns Hopkins University Press, 1990.

Van Esterik, Penny. "Celebrating Ethnicty: Ethnic Falvor in an Urban Festival." *Ethnic Groups* 4 (1982): 207–28.

Warner, Steven. *New Wine in Old Wineskins*. Berkeley: University of California Press, 1988.

Waugh, Earle H. "Reducing the Distance: A Muslim Congregation in the Canadian

North." In *American Congregations*, Vol. 1: *Portraits of Twelve Religious Communities*, edited by James P. Wind and James L. Lewis, 572–611. Chicago: University of Chicago Press, 1994.

Waxman, Chaim. "The Sabbath as Dialectic: The Meaning and Role." *Judaism* 31 (Winter 1982): 37–44.

Waxman, Mordecai, ed. *Tradition and Change: The Development of Conservative Judaism*. New York: Burning Bush Press, 1958.

Webber, Melvin. "Order in Diversity: Community without Propinquity." In *Cities and Space: The Future Use of Urban Land*, edited by Lowdon Wingo, 23–54. Baltimore: Johns Hopkins University Press, 1963.

Weightman, Barbara. "Changing Religious Landscapes in Los Angeles." *Journal of Cultural Geography* 14 (Fall–Winter 1993): 1–20.

Weinfeld, Morton. "Canadian Jews and Canadian Pluralism." In *American Pluralism and the Jewish Community*, edited by Seymour Martin Lipset, 87–106. New Brunswick, N.J.: Transaction Books, 1990.

Weisfeld, Israel H. "Jewry in the Southwest." *Jewish Life* 16 (June 1949): 54–60.

Weiss, Avraham. "The Eruv: A Microcosm of the Shabbat Spirit." *Tradition* 23 (Summer 1987): 40–46.

———. *Women at Prayer: A Halakhic Analysis of Women's Prayer Groups*. Northvale, N.J.: Jason Aronson, 1997.

Weiss, Joseph. "Why Wear a Yarmulka?" *Jewish Life* 20 (March 1953): 20–26.

Weiss, Samson. "Youth, Change, and the Eternal Torah." *Jewish Life* 30 (January–February 1963): 17–20.

Weissman, Deborah. "Bais Yaakov: A Historical Model for Jewish Feminists." In *The Jewish Woman: New Perspectives*, edited by Elizabeth Koltun, 139–48. New York: Schocken Books, 1977.

Wellman, Barry. "The Community Question: The Intimate Network of East Yorkers." *American Journal of Sociology* 84 (1979): 1201–31.

Wellman, Barry, and Barry Leighton. "Networks, Neighborhoods, and Communities." *Urban Affairs Quarterly* 14 (1979): 363–90.

Werb, Morris R. "Jewish Suburbia: An Historical and Comparative Study of Jewish Communities in Three New Jersey Suburbs." Ph.D. diss., New York University, 1959.

Wertheimer, Jack. "The Orthodox Moment." *Commentary* 107 (February 1999): 18–24.

———. *A People Divided: Judaism in Contemporary America*. New York: Basic Books, 1993.

———. *The Uses of Tradition: Jewish Continuity in the Modern Era*. New York: Jewish Theological Seminary of America, 1992.

———. ed. *The American Synagogue: A Sanctuary Transformed*. Cambridge: Cambridge University Press, 1987.

Westfall, William. *Two Worlds: The Protestant Culture of Nineteenth-Century Ontario*. Montreal: McGill-Queen's University Press, 1989.

Whyte, William H. Jr. *The Organization Man*. New York: Touchstone, 1956.

Wind, James P., and James L. Lewis, eds. *American Congregations*, Vol. 1: *Portraits of Twelve Religious Communities*. Chicago: University of Chicago Press, 1994.

———., eds. *American Congregations*, Vol. 2: *New Perspectives in the Study of Congregations*. Chicago: University of Chicago Press, 1994.

Winston, Diane. "Babylon by the Hudson; Jerusalem on the Charles: Religion and the American City." *Journal of Urban History* 25 (November 1998): 122–29.

Winter, Gibson. *The New Creation as Metropolis*. New York: Macmillan, 1963.

———. *The Suburban Captivity of the Churches: An Analysis of Protestant Responsibility in the Expanding Metropolis*. Garden City, N.Y.: Doubleday, 1961.

Wirth, Louis. "The City." *American Journal of Sociology* 44 (1938): 1–24.

———. *The Ghetto*. Chicago: University of Chicago Press, 1928.

Wunsch, James S. "The Suburban Cliche." *Journal of Social History* 28 (Spring 1995): 643–58.

Wuthnow, Robert. *The Restructuring of American Religion: Society and Faith since World War II*. Princeton: Princeton University Press, 1988.

———. *Sharing the Journey: Support Groups and America's New Quest for Community*. New York: Free Press, 1994.

———., ed. *"I Come Away Stronger": How Small Groups Are Shaping American Religion*. Grand Rapids, Mich.: W. B. Eerdmans, 1994.

Wyschogrod, Michael. "The Problem of the Intellectual." *Jewish Life* 30 (January–February 1963): 11–14.

Zelinsky, Wilbur. "An Approach to the Religious Geography of the United States." *Annals of the Association of American Geographers* 51 (June 1961): 139–93.

Zerubavel, Eviatar. *Hidden Rhythms: Schedules and Calendars in Social Life*. Chicago: University of Chicago Press, 1981.

## INDEX

Agudath Israel, 98, 99

*Agunoth*, 69

Aish Hatorah, 16, 85

Amish, 9

Angel, Marc, 16

Anglicans, 61

Anti-Semitism, 45

Art Scroll, 126–27

Asbury and West United Church, 44

Associated Hebrew Day School, 41, 49, 85, 94, 98, 103, 108; founding of, 92; relocation to Bathurst Street of, 92, 102; growth of, 102

Bais Ya'acov, 95

Barton's Chocolates, 111–12, 121

Bathurst Manor, 35, 75, 177 (n. 73)

Bathurst Street, 74, 75, 119, 120; postwar development of, 35–37; traffic and parking problems on, 36–37; zoning of, 37; Jewish population along, 40–41; pedestrian activity on, 41–42; as sacred space, 41–42, 44, 53–54; clustering of stores on, 42; avoidance of by suburban Jews, 43–44; perceptions of, 44; as "path," 50; continuity of, 85

Bathurst Village, 75–76

Baycrest Center, 41

Belsky, Meir, 141

Ben-David, Mordecai, 126

Berman, Saul, 15

Beth Avraham Yosef of Toronto (BAYT): as new style of suburban synagogue, 84–85; *mehitsah* design of, 85

Beth Jacob High School for Girls, 103–4

Beth Jacob schools, 100

Bialik Day School, 101, 107

Bienenfeld, Jeffrey, 74

B'nai Torah Congregation, 77–80, 85, 86; founding of, 77–78; as religious center, 78–79; decorum in, 79; *mehitsah* design in, 79; traditionalist styles in, 79; construction of, 177 (n. 79)

B'nei Akiva, 98, 99

Books, Orthodox Jewish, 126

Brookline, Mass., 27

Brown, Tom, 117

Campbell, Colin, 125

Camp Moshava, 99, 137

Camps, Orthodox Jewish, 138

Canadian Housing and Mortgage Corporation, 20, 35

Canadian Jewish Congress, 104

"Caring communities," 6, 154–55

Carlebach, Shlomo, 126

Catholics, 16, 61

Centrist Orthodox Jews. *See* Modern Orthodox Jews

Chai Lifeline, 156

Christianity: lifestyle regulations in, 8; fundamentalism in, 16, 82, 150; and material culture, 113; continentalization of, 145

Church extension, 60–61
Church of Jesus Christ of Latter-day
    Saints, 8
Chyet, Stanley, 147
Clanton Park, 40
Clanton Park Synagogue, 78, 79, 81, 85,
    86, 98, 135; ethnic composition of, 39;
    occupations of members of, 40, 62–
    64; founding of, 58–60; construction
    of, 60; mobility of members of, 61; as
    social center, 67; committees in, 68;
    women in, 68; youth in, 69; decorum
    in, 70
Cleveland, Ohio, 44
Cohen, Steven, 12, 72, 110
Community Hebrew Academy of
    Toronto (CHAT): founding of, 103;
    as Orthodox school, 107
Congregation Beth Jacob, 177 (n. 73)
Congregation Beth Meyer, 45
Congregation Shomrai Emunah
    (Washington, D.C.), 65, 69–70
Consumerism, Orthodox Jewish, 112–
    13; criticism of, 128–29
Continentalization, Orthodox Jewish:
    and synagogues, 133–36; and day
    schools, 136–37; and camps, 137–38;
    and *kashruth*, 138–39; and Internet,
    142

Don Mills, 35

Edah, 15–16
Edell, Sol, 3–4, 60
Education
—Jewish: *melamed* in, 88; mimetic
    learning in, 88, 89; of girls, 89, 95;
    public funding for, 100. See also
    *Ḥeder*; Schools—Orthodox Jewish;
    Talmud Torah
—public: attitudes of American Jews
    toward, 89–90
Eitz Chaim Day School, 41, 94, 96, 97,
    98, 103, 107, 137; and B'nai Torah,

77–78; founding of, 92; relocation
    to Bathurst Street of, 92, 102; growth
    of, 102
*Eruv*: construction of, 51; opposition
    to, 51–52; and community build-
    ing, 52
—in Toronto: expansion of, 52–53, 57;
    opposition to, 53
Excommunication, 82

Far Rockaway, N.Y., 139–40
Federations, Jewish, 100
Felder, Gedalia, 117
Feldman, Eliot, 51
Feldman, Emanuel, 141
Feuerstein, Moses, 73
Feuerstein family, 157
Finke, Roger, 56
Fishman, Robert, 6, 152
Forest Hill, Ont., 30, 32, 38, 87
Forest Hills Golf Club, 75
Freedman, Morris, 111, 112
Fried, Avraham, 126

Gans, Herbert, 112
Gasner, Cynthia, 65
Glatt Yacht, 129
Golan Heights Winery, 121
Golder's Green (London), 51
Gordon, Albert, 149
Gorelick, Morris, 59
Gospel of wealth, 113
Greenberg, Yitzchak, 15
Gruenwald, Myer, 117

*Ḥaredi* Orthodox Jews: and centrist
    Orthodox Jews, 11–12; history of, 13,
    and secular culture, 13–14; and non-
    Orthodox Jews, 14; Toronto commu-
    nity of, 53, 148–49; "authenticity"
    of, 147
Hebrew Academy of Indianapolis, 101
*Ḥeder*, 89, 90
Herberg, Will, 150

Hertzberg, Arthur, 101
H. F. Epstein Hebrew Academy
  (St. Louis), 91–92
*Hiddur mitzvah*, 10, 113
Hildesheimer, Esriel, 12
Hillel houses, 106
Hirsch, Samson Raphael, 12
Hofstedter, Sandy, 60
Holy Blossom Temple, 28

Independent High School, 107, 108
Indianapolis, Ind., 152
Internet, 131, 142, 151–52
Islam, 8

Jackson, Kenneth, 20
Jewish community, in Toronto: his-
  tory of, 28; population of, 28, 29;
  early suburbanization of, 30; eth-
  nicity of, 43; and non-Jews, 44; and
  anti-Semitism, 45; in northeast
  North York, 49–50; and Bathurst
  Street, 75, 84–85; in Thornhill, 83
Jewish continuity, 101, 110
Jewish Orthodox Feminist Alliance
  (JOFA), 69
Jewish Welfare Federation of India-
  napolis, 100

*Kashruth*: laws of, 114–15; organiza-
  tions supervising, 115; personal su-
  pervision of, 115; in urban settings,
  115–16; deception in, 116; profession-
  alization of, 117–18; women's role
  in, 118; and continentalization, 138.
  *See also* Kosher food; Kosher hotels;
  Kosher lifestyle; Kosher restaurants;
  Kosher travel; Kosher wine
Kashruth Council (Toronto), 117, 118,
  123
Kaufman, David, 66
Kehillat Shaarei Torah, 49–50, 51
Kelman, Wolfe, 126
Kensington, 50, 133; Jewish infrastruc-

ture in, 28–29; Jewish abandonment
  of, 42–43
Kensington Market, 28
Kesser Winery, 122
Kideckel, Sam, 58–59
Kideckel, Sarah, 58–59
Kiryas Joel, N.Y., 14
Klaff, Vivian, 46
Klein, Stephen, 111
Kof-K, 129
Kong, Lily, 22
Kosher food: packaging of, 118, 122; and
  nonkosher food, 119; variety of, 119;
  stores selling, 119–20; as "healthy"
  food, 129–30; and non-Jews, 129–30
Kosher hotels, 124
Kosher lifestyle, 121–24
Kosher Restaurant Database, 142
Kosher restaurants: in immigrant
  neighborhoods, 122; in suburban
  Toronto, 122–23; criticism of, 123;
  variety of, 123–24
Kosher travel, 124, 139
Kosher wine, 121–22
Kotler, Aaron, 13

Lane, Ruth, 78
Lastman, Mel, 45
Lawrence Manor, 35, 38
Leiner Affair, 45
Leo Baeck School, 101
Liebman, Charles, 11, 18
Litvin, Baruch, 73
Lubavitch, 85
Lutherans, 61
Lynch, Kevin, 50

Magazines, Orthodox Jewish, 140
Maimonides, Moses, 88
Maimonides Day School (Boston), 92,
  95, 179 (n. 22)
Mather, Cotton, 56
*Meḥitsah* debates, 72–74; UOJCA in,
  73; and continentalization, 134

Methodists, 55
Miami Boys Choir, 126
*Mikveh*: modernization of, 127–28; in suburban Toronto, 128
Mimetic culture, 14
Modern Orthodox Jews: and *haredi* Orthodox Jews, 11–12; history of, 12; movement to right by, 14–15
Monsey, N.Y., 139
Mozelsio, Yves, 187 (n. 22)
Murray House, 79
Music, Jewish, 126

National Conference of Synagogue Youth (NCSY), 104, 110, 156
National Jewish Center for Learning and Leadership (CLAL), 15
National Jewish Outreach Program, 16
Ner Israel Yeshiva, 77, 85, 103, 137
Netivot Hatorah Day School, 108
Neuberger, Max, 57
New Square, N.Y., 14
North York, Ont.: early history of, 32; geography of, 32; religious landscape of, 32; postwar development of, 33–35; Jewish population in, 38; hardships of suburbanization into, 57
North York Synagogue Council, 81

Ochs, David, 117
Organized Kashruth Laboratories (OK), 115
Or Haemet Sephardic Day School, 85
Or Sameyach, 85
Orthodox Jewish community: maturation of, 79–80, 82; and universities, 105, 106; geography of, 133, 151; continental perceptions of, 140–41, 185 (n. 39); tensions within, 168 (n. 36)
—suburban: as "caring community," 8, 153–55; new traditionalism in, 108–9; socioeconomic status of, 124–25, 126–27; criticism of, 148; invisibility of, 148; neighborhood structures of, 153, homogeneity in, 155–56, 185 (n. 19); secular values in, 156; economics of, 157–58, 187 (n. 23)
—in Toronto: and American Orthodox Jews, 19–20; in Kensington, 29; suburbanization into North York, 38; socioeconomic status of, 39; ethnicity in, 39, 133; mobility of, 61–62; shift from pioneering of, 77–83; in communal affairs, 80–81; and integration of CHAT, 107–8; conflicts within, 148; materialism in, 148–49
Orthodox Jewish Community Council, 81
Orthodox Jews: stereotypes of, 10; numbers of, 11, 167 (n. 17); and *haredi* Orthodox Jews, 14–15; and non-Orthodox Jews, 14–16, 81–82; occupations of, 64, 157, 174 (n. 28), 187 (n. 22); materialism and, 112–13; as consumers, 117, 123, 138; and space, 153. See also *Haredi* Orthodox Jews; Modern Orthodox Jews
Orthodox Judaism: restrictiveness of, 5; time in, 7; and suburban society, 7–10; space in, 8; family in, 9; materialism in, 9–10, 113; variations within, 11; scholarship on, 18; and education, 88
Orthodox Union (OU), 111, 115, 127; founding of, 116; number of products supervised by, 118–19, 138; Passover directory of, 141; website of, 142
Our Way (NCSY), 156

Park Forest, Ill., 150
Presbyterians, 60–61
Price, Abraham, 52–53, 102, 117
Price, Frederick, 112
Puritans, 55

Rabbinical Alliance of America, 82

Rabbinical Council of America (RCA), 69, 82, 129; membership in, 132; and National Torah Tours, 135–36

Rabbinical Council of Ontario, 81

Reichmann family, 13, 24, 157

Religion: as community builder, 6; frontier, 55–56; and suburban youth, 103; and materialism, 113; and food, 113–14; and continentalization, 145; and growth of conservative denominations, 150; and spirituality, 150; in suburbia, 150, 175 (n. 38)

Riesman, David, 154

Riskin, Shlomo, 15

Rockland County, N.Y., 14, 149; zoning in, 44; Jewish spaces in, 46

Rubinstein, Bill, 57

Rubinstein, Samuel, 140

Sabbath: prohibitions on, 7, 40; as community builder, 8, 153–55; and employment, 64; driving on, 166 (n. 13)

Sacks, Maurie, 164

Sacred space, 27, 170 (n. 5)

Sarna, Jonathan, 72

Schenirer, Sarah, 95

Schools

— Conservative and Reform Jewish, 101–2. *See also* Bialik Day School; Independent High School; United Synagogue Day School

— Orthodox Jewish: and public schools, 90–91; numbers of, 91, 136; in suburbs, 91–92; education of girls in, 95, 179 (n. 22); modernizations in, 95–97; professionalization of, 96; and middle class, 96, 103–4; secular studies in, 96–97; and community, 97–98; and synagogues, 98; and youth culture, 98; economics of, 99–100, 158; public funding for, 100; Jewish communal funding for, 100, 104; and Jewish continuity, 101; and high schools, 102–3; and continentalization, 136–37; and special-needs children, 155

— Orthodox Jewish, in Toronto: and sacred space, 92–94; and religious pioneering, 94. *See also* Associated Hebrew Day School; Beth Jacob High School for Girls; Community Hebrew Academy of Toronto; Eitz Chaim Day School; Ner Israel Yeshiva; Netivot Hatorah Day School; Or Haemet Sephardic Day School; Yeshivat B'nei Akiva Or Chaim

Schottenstein family, 157

Second Vatican Council, 142

Sephardic Jews, 167 (n. 20)

Shaarei Shomayim Synagogue, 85; relocation to Bathurst Street of, 46–48; *meḥitsah* design in, 79

Shaarei Tefillah Synagogue, 78, 79, 81, 85, 86, 94, 134, 135; founding of, 38; as social center, 67; committees in, 68; *meḥitsah* design in, 71–72; dedicates sanctuary, 74

Shaare Zion Congregation, 49

Shapiro, Edward, 109, 124

Shemen, Nachman, 117

Shma Yisroel, 126

Silverberg, Joe, 4

Silverberg, Lillian, 4, 57

Sklare, Marshall, 149

*Smart Shopper's Guide* (Toronto), 125

Social capital, 154

Sofer, Jacob, 53

Soloveitchik, Haym, 14, 18, 88, 89

Soloveitchik, Joseph B., 15, 74, 95, 179 (n. 22)

Spring Farm, 41, 84–85

Stark, Rodney, 56

Stern College for Women, 106, 138

Stone family, 157

Suburbia: community in, 6, 151–52; lifestyle choices in, 6, 166 (n. 7); time in, 7; family in, 9; materialism in, 9; and Orthodox Judaism, 9–10; continentalization of, 142; homogeneity of, 142, 156; space and place in, 152

Synagogue centers, 66–67

Synagogue Council of America, 15, 82

Synagogues, urban, 66; Orthodox Jewish: new suburban styles of, 66–72; as social centers, 67, 133; bureaucraticization of, 68; junior congregations in, 69–70; decorum in, 70, 176 (n. 4); design of, 70–71; pioneering in, 72, 74, 83; and continentalization, 133–36; prayer *nusaḥ* in, 134; national organizations of, 135; exclusiveness of, 155; financial support of, 158. *See also* Beth Avraham Yosef of Toronto; B'nai Torah Congregation; Clanton Park Synagogue; Congregation Beth Jacob; Kehillat Shaarei Torah; Shaarei Shomayim Synagogue; Shaarei Tefillah Synagogue; Shaare Zion Congregation; Torath Emeth Jewish Centre

Talmud Torah, 89, 90

Tannenbaum, Joseph, 41, 83–84

Taylor, E. P., 35

Teaneck, N.J., 27

Temple Sinai, 44

Tendler, Moshe, 16

Thornhill, Ont., 41, 148; religious composition of, 83

Torah Education Network, 137

Torah Leadership Seminar, 137

Torah tapes, 127

Torah Tours (RCA), 135–36

Torah Umesorah: founding of, 91; mission of, 95–96; and continentalization, 136

Torath Emeth Jewish Centre, 92, 98; as

social center, 67; *meḥitsah* design in, 71, 79

Toronto, Ont., suburban: ethnic groups in, 20, 152; similarities of to American suburbs, 20–21. *See also* Forest Hill, Ont.; North York, Ont.; Thornhill, Ont.; York Township, Ont.

*Toronto Community Directory*, 125

Torrance, J. C., 60

Twin Rivers, N.J., 51

Ultra-Orthodox Jews. See *Ḥaredi* Orthodox Jews

Union of Orthodox Jewish Congregations of America (UOJCA), 12, 82, 111; Women's Branch of, 68; and *meḥitsah* debates, 73; membership in, 132; and new suburban synagogues, 134; and continentalization, 134–35

Union of Orthodox Rabbis, 82, 132–33

United Church of Canada, 61

United Jewish Welfare Fund, 107

United Synagogue Day School (USDS), 101; and Independent High School, 107

Va'ad Hoeir (St. Louis), 116

Vaughan Township, Ont., 83

Washington, D.C., suburban, 64–65

Waxman, Chaim, 8

Weber, Max, 158

Weisblatt, Aaron, 4, 98

Weiss, Samson, 73

Wenner, Marvin, 78

Wertheimer, Jack, 5

Whyte, William, 150

Wilson Heights United Church, 45

Wirth, Louis, 6

Women, Orthodox Jewish: clothing of, 12; occupations of, 65; and congregational sisterhoods, 68; in suburban synagogues, 68–69, 175 (n. 44); and *tefillah* groups, 69; as kosher consumers, 117–18; as homemakers, 118; hair covering of, 125; and *mikveh* ritual, 127–28

Women's Branch of the Union of Orthodox Jewish Congregations of America, 68

Wurzburger, Walter, 16

Wuthnow, Robert, 16

Yachad (NCSY), 156

Yarmulke, 108–9; commercialization of, 125

Yavneh, 106

Yeshivat B'nei Akiva Or Chaim, 107–8

Yeshiva University, 12, 13, 105, 106, 137; geographic distribution of students at, 133, 138, 141; and continentalization, 137, 138

Yeshurun Society, 106

Yonge Street, 32–33

York Township, Ont., 30, 32, 38

Young Israel of Cleveland, 134

Youth

— Orthodox Jewish: in suburban synagogues, 69–70; in youth groups, 70; public protests of, 81, 104; social activities of, 98–99; and counterculture, 104–5; and drugs, 104–5; socialization of, 106; traditionalism of, 108–9 and continentalization, 136–38. *See also* National Conference of Synagogue Youth

—suburban, 87, 103